The Church We Believe In

One, Holy, Catholic and Apostolic

Francis A. Sullivan, S. J.

PAULIST PRESS
NEW YORK/MAHWAH, N.J.

Acknowledgments

The articles reprinted in *The Church We Believe In* first appeared in the following publications and are reprinted with permission: Quotations from *The Documents of Vatican II*, copyrighted 1966 by the American Press, Inc., N.Y., N.Y.; Emile Mersch, *The Theology of the Mystical Body*, tr. C. Volert, St. Louis, American Press, Inc., 1951, pp. 479–480; Excerpts from Secretariat for Promoting Christian Unity Information Service, 1985, by the United States Catholic Conference; "Justice in the World" from Synod of Bishops, 1971 by the United States Catholic Conference; Declaration from the Fourth Synod of Bishops, 1974 by the United States Catholic Conference; Excerpts from Congregation for the Doctrine of Faith, "Instruction on Christian Freedom and Liberation," 1986 published in *Origins* 15, 1985–1986.; the Scripture quotations are from the *Revised Standard Version of the Bible*, copyrighted 1946, 1952, and 1971 by the Division of Christian Education of the National Council of the Churches of Christ in the U.S.A.

Library of Congress Cataloging-in-Publication Data

Sullivan, Francis Aloysius.
    The church we believe in.

    Bibliography: p.
    1. Church.   2. Catholic Church—Doctrines.   I. Title.
BX1746.S797   1988   262   88-23184
ISBN 0-8091-3039-4 (pbk.)

Published by Paulist Press
997 Macarthur Boulevard
Mahwah, N.J. 07430

Printed and bound in the United States of America

Contents

Abbreviations   v

Foreword   1

1. The Church We Believe In   3

2. The One Church of Christ "Subsists"
   in the Catholic Church   23

3. The One Church: A Communion of Churches   34

4. "Marked with a Genuine though Imperfect Holiness"   66

5. "The Catholic Unity of the People of God"   84

6. "Universal Sacrament of Salvation"   109

7. Sacrament of "Integral Salvation"   132

8. The Church Is Apostolic   152

9. Apostolicity in Ecumenical Dialogue   185

10. One, Holy, Catholic and Apostolic   210

    Notes   225

    Indexes   236

Abbreviations

1. DOCUMENTS OF THE SECOND VATICAN COUNCIL

AG   *Ad Gentes:* Decree on the Church's Missionary Activity

CD   *Christus Dominus:* Decree on the Bishops' Pastoral Office in the Church

DV   *Dei Verbum:* Dogmatic Constitution on Divine Revelation

GS   *Gaudium et Spes:* Pastoral Constitution on the Church in the Modern World

LG   *Lumen Gentium:* Dogmatic Constitution on the Church

NA   *Nostra Aetate:* Declaration on the Relationship of the Church to Non-Christian Religions

OE   *Orientalium Ecclesiarum:* Decree on Eastern Catholic Churches

SC   *Sacrosanctum Concilium:* Constitution on the Sacred Liturgy

UR   *Unitatis Redintegratio:* Decree on Ecumenism

2. OTHER SOURCES

AAS   *Acta Apostolicae Sedis*

A-NF   *Ante-Nicene Fathers*, American Reprint Edition, Grand Rapids, 1977

AS   *Acta Synodalia Concilii Vaticani II*, Vatican City, 1970 ff.

CCL   *Corpus Christianorum, series Latina*, Turnholt, 1953 ff.

CDF   Congregation for the Doctrine of the Faith

CSEL   *Corpus Scriptorum Ecclesiasticorum Latinorum*, Vienna, 1866
          ff.

D-S   Denzinger-Schönmetzer, *Enchiridion Symbolorum, Defini-
          tionism, Declarationum*, 34th edn. Herder, 1967

ETL   *Ephemerides Theologicae Lovanienses*

GiA   *Growth in Agreement*, ed. Harding Meyer and Lukas
          Vischer, Ramsey/Geneva, 1984

Mansi   *Sacrorum Conciliorum nova collectio*, ed. J.D. Mansi, Flor-
          ence, 1759 ff., continued by L. Petit and J. Martin, Paris
          and Leipzig, 1901–27

NRT   *Nouvelle Revue Théologique*

PG   *Patrologiae cursus completus, series graeca*, ed. J.P. Migne,
          Paris, 1857 ff.

PL   *Patrologiae cursus completus, series latina*, ed. P.J. Migne,
          Paris, 1844 ff.

Th Inv Karl Rahner, *Theological Investigations*, 1961 ff.

TS   *Theological Studies*

SPCU   Secretariat for Promoting Christian Unity

WCC   World Council of Churches

Foreword

This book, like my previous one called *Magisterium: Teaching Authority in the Catholic Church* (Paulist, and Gill and Macmillan, 1983), is the fruit of a good many years of teaching this matter to the young men and women who are my students at the Gregorian University in Rome. However, it is not intended as a theology textbook. I have written it with all those people in mind who belong to the "We" of the title.

In the first place, this means my fellow-Catholics, since I write from what I take to be a distinctively Catholic point of view. However, I sincerely hope that many other Christians will be able to recognize their own faith in much of what I have to say about the church, even though I expect there will be some things they will have difficulty with. In any case, they should know that I mean to include them among the "We" who "believe in the church."

I take this opportunity to express my thanks to Christopher O'Donnell, O.Carm., to Gerald O'Collins, S.J., and to Teresa Clements, D.M.J., who have read this book in manuscript, and have given me many helpful suggestions for its improvement.

Francis A. Sullivan, S.J.
Easter 1988.

1

1 ‖ The Church We Believe In

Practically all Christians, however divided in other respects, are united in professing their faith in "one, holy, catholic and apostolic church." This fourfold description of the church is part of the solemn profession of faith which was promulgated by the First Council of Constantinople (A.D. 381),[1] and which subsequently became the common creed of the Christian churches of both East and West. It is this creed, commonly known as "Nicene,"[2] which Catholics, Orthodox, and a great many other Christians use when they profess their faith together in the course of their Sunday worship.

While it is generally recognized that differences in ecclesiology are the ones that constitute the most stubborn obstacles to Christian reunion, there are good grounds for hope in the fact that most Christians do agree in professing their faith in "one, holy, catholic and apostolic church." Indeed, honest facing up to the contradiction between our common faith in the "one church," and the divided state of Christianity, is a prime motive for the ecumenical movement.

It is true, of course, that the mere fact that Christians use the same words in professing their faith about the church does not eliminate their deep differences in ecclesiology. Profoundly divergent answers will be given when one asks: What do you mean when you say "the church"? and How do you understand it to be one, holy, catholic and apostolic? Ecumenical progress, then, calls for the effort to reach a common understanding of the faith we profess. Theology has an important role to play here, because theology is defined as "faith seeking understanding." Ecumenical dialogue is most fruitful when it is a concerted effort, on the part of people coming from

3

different theological traditions, to seek a deeper understanding of the creed in which they already profess a common faith, in the hopes that such a deeper understanding will get beneath their differences to the common ground where they are at one.

An essential step in this process is for Christians to seek to deepen and clarify their understanding of their faith in the light of their own respective traditions. Such is the purpose of this book. What we are seeking here is an understanding of our profession of faith concerning the church, in the light of the Roman Catholic tradition. In doing this, we shall be paying special attention to the teaching of the Second Vatican Council, especially in its Dogmatic Constitution on the Church *Lumen gentium*, and in its Decree on Ecumenism *Unitatis redintegratio*. We shall be seeking a deeper understanding of our Catholic faith concerning the church, and its oneness, holiness, catholicity and apostolicity.

It is not our purpose to develop the apologetic argument by which, in the past, the effort was made to prove that only the Catholic Church satisfied the requirements of these four "notes of the church," so that it alone had the right to consider itself the one true church of Christ. One of the many drawbacks of that approach was that it restricted consideration of these "notes" of the church to their visible or empirical aspects. The supposition of such an apologetic (and often polemical) approach was that the four "notes" were more visible and easily verified than the church itself, and hence could serve to identify the true church.[3] But there is much more to the oneness, holiness, catholicity and apostolicity of the church than what we can see of them. We shall be looking at them not merely as visible "marks" or "notes," but in their full reality as attributes or properties of the church, in all their aspects, whether empirically verifiable, or knowable only by faith. Indeed, as we shall see, just as the church itself must be recognized to be a "mystery of faith," so each of these four properties shares in its nature as "mystery." That is why a truly theological approach is needed: starting with what we believe, and seeking a deeper understanding of our faith.

Leaving the consideration of the oneness, holiness, catholicity and apostolicity of the church to following chapters, we shall begin with some reflections on the significance of the fact that in the creed, after professing our faith in God the Father, in our Lord Jesus Christ, and in the Holy Spirit, we go on to profess faith in the church. Can we believe in the church in the same way that we believe in God? What right does the church have to be included in the creed as an object of our faith? What does it mean to say that the church, along with such mysteries as the incarnation and the redemption, is also a "mystery of faith"? These are some of the questions to which we shall now turn our attention.

In What Sense Do We "Believe In" the Church?

In the English translation of the creed with which Catholics profess their faith during Sunday Mass, after saying: "We believe in one God the Father" . . . "We believe in one Lord Jesus Christ" . . . "We believe in the Holy Spirit" . . . we also say: "We believe in one holy catholic and apostolic church." This translation does not bring out the difference between "believing in" God and "believing in" the church: a difference which the official Latin version of the creed expresses by using the term: "believe in" only with reference to the Divine Persons. The Latin text does not say, as the English does: "We believe *in* the church."[4]

Since we do not follow the Latin in its restriction of the term "believe in" to refer to belief in God, it is all the more important for us to understand the difference between "believing in" God and "believing in" something other than God. When we say we believe in God, what we mean is that we *put our faith* in God: we commit ourselves to God as the ground of our very being, as the ultimate motive of our faith, as the one in whom we place our trust, in whom we put our hope for salvation and eternal life. It is not a question of merely believing that God exists, or believing certain things about him. It is a question of a commitment that we make of ourselves to him, in faith, hope and trust. We cannot make such an act of faith in any creature; we cannot "believe in" any created reality in the same unique way in which we believe in God.[5]

In what sense, then, do we "believe in" the church? To answer this question, let us look at the creed again. When we have said "We believe in God the Father," we go on to profess our belief in what he has revealed to us about his work of creation; when we have said "We believe in one Lord Jesus Christ" we go on to express our belief in his incarnation, death, resurrection and future coming in glory; when we have said "We believe in the Holy Spirit" we go on to express our belief in the church, baptism, resurrection of the dead, life everlasting. The difference, with regard to our faith, is between God himself and the created works that God has accomplished and revealed to us. It is the very nature of these works of God on our behalf, that even after they have been revealed, they still far surpass our capacity fully to grasp or understand them. In that sense they are rightly called "mysteries" of our faith. While they are not identical with God, they are so associated with him who is the ultimate mystery that, even when revealed to us, they must remain, at least in this life, objects of faith rather than of complete understanding. As we have said above, theology is defined as "faith that seeks understanding"; but since the object of faith is "mystery," the understanding that theology can reach will always fall short of a total grasp of the reality.

What that means, then, is that when in the creed we say "We believe in the church," we are acknowledging the fact that the church, like the incarnation of the Son of God and his death and resurrection for our redemption, is a "mystery of our faith": an element in the whole "economy of salvation" which God has accomplished and revealed to us. We are accepting the church as part of the total object of our Christian faith. We are professing our faith that the church is not a purely human institution, but is a work of God, a part of God's plan for the salvation of the world.

This follows, in the first place, from the very fact of the inclusion of the church among those things about which Christians profess their faith in the creed. It is surely significant that we find mention of the church in the baptismal creed that was in use in Rome around the end of the second century. It would be useful to recall here what we know about the development of the early Christian creeds.

The formulation of "creeds" had its origin in the practice of requiring that converts should make a profession of Christian faith as they were being baptized. In the early church, baptism was a real bath, in which the candidate was totally immersed three times in the baptismal pool. Prior to each immersion, the candidate was asked to profess his faith: the first time in God the Father, the second time in the Lord Jesus Christ, and the third time in the Holy Spirit. The earliest baptismal creeds that have come down to us are in the form of three questions, to which the candidate would reply: "I do be-

lieve." (We still use this form of profession of faith when we renew
our baptismal vows at the Easter vigil.) It seems almost certain that
in the most primitive form, the third question would have been simply: "Do you believe in the Holy Spirit?" But we know, from the
Apostolic Tradition of Hippolytus, written about the year 215, that
by the end of the second century, the third question asked of the
one being baptized in the church of Rome was: "Do you believe in
the Holy Spirit in the holy church?"[6]

From the third century on, every baptismal creed that has come
down to us, whether in the earlier question-and-answer form, or in
the later declaratory form (such as we have in the so-called Apostles'
Creed, which is still our baptismal creed), mentions the "holy
church" after the Holy Spirit.[7] Actually, the church never appears
in a baptismal creed without the adjective "holy"; the Apostles'
Creed adds "catholic," and, as we have already seen, it was the creed
of the Council of Constantinople in 381 that definitively settled on
the four attributes that were already being mentioned in the baptismal creeds of some Eastern Christian churches.

If one asks what prompted the second century church to begin
to require that candidates for baptism profess their faith in the "holy
church," the most likely answer is the one suggested by J.N.D.
Kelly, a foremost authority on the history of the creeds.[8] He suggests that it was because about this time, as we know from the writings of St. Irenaeus, the gnostic heretics, who posed the most
serious threat to the true faith, despised the people who belonged to
the churches over which the bishops presided. The gnostics prided
themselves on having a higher, more perfect knowledge of revelation
than was being taught by the bishops, so they gathered in their own
private meetings, despising the Christian churches and their leaders. Against the gnostics, St. Irenaeus insisted that it was only in
the holy church that the Holy Spirit could be found and his gifts
received.[9] In this atmosphere it is understandable why those seeking
baptism should be asked to profess their faith "in the Holy Spirit in
the holy church."

The Church As a Mystery of Faith

We have said that in seeking a deeper understanding of what
Catholics believe about the church we shall be paying special atten-

tion to the teaching of the Second Vatican Council. It is appropriate, then, that in considering the reasons that justify the description of the church as a mystery of faith, we should begin by examining the first chapter of *Lumen gentium*, which is entitled "The Mystery of the Church." When the theological commission presented this text to the council, they explained their use of the term "mystery" here in the following way: "The word 'mystery' does not mean merely something unknowable or obscure, but, as is now generally recognized, it signifies a reality which is divine, transcendent and salvific, and which is also revealed and manifested in some visible way. Hence this term, which is thoroughly biblical, seems altogether appropriate for designating the church."[10]

This last phrase makes it clear that it is the church itself that is being described as a "mystery." As a reality which is "divine," the church is no merely human institution; as "transcendent," it will always surpass our efforts fully to grasp it; as "salvific," it forms part of God's plan of salvation for humanity. At the same time, it is not something invisible; it has been revealed and manifested to us in a visible way.

The commission also noted that "mystery" is a thoroughly biblical term. It is true that the Bible does not explicitly describe the church as a mystery; the closest approach to this is the text in Ephesians (5:31f) where the "becoming one flesh" of man and wife is described as a "great mystery" in its application to Christ and the church. But the "mystery" which is one of the major themes of Colossians and Ephesians is intimately associated with the church: it is God's design to include the Gentiles in his plan of salvation, and thus to bring the whole world under Christ as its head (cf. Col 1:26f; 2:2; Eph 1:9f; 3:1–6).

Chapter One of *Lumen gentium* proceeds to offer a number of considerations that justify seeing the church as a mystery. The first of these is the suggestion that the church can be looked on as a "kind of sacrament."

The Church As a "Kind of Sacrament"

The opening words of the Constitution on the Church *Lumen gentium*, "the light of the nations," refer not to the church but to Christ. But the next sentence introduces the church as "in Christ a kind of sacrament: that is, a sign and instrument of intimate union with God and the unity of all humanity." It is striking that the very first description of the church in this document involves applying to the church itself the notion of "sacrament"—an idea that most Catholics had been accustomed to think of only with reference to one or another of the seven sacraments. In fact it was only quite recently that theologians had begun to speak of Christ as the "primordial sacrament," and of the church as "sacrament of salvation." What does such use of the idea of "sacrament" contribute to our understanding of Christ and his church?

First of all, it is important to note that to speak of the church as "a kind of sacrament" is already to suggest that it belongs to the category of "mystery," because *sacramentum* was one of the words that the early Latin Christians used to translate the Greek word *musterion:* mystery. Just above we have referred to the passages in Colossians and Ephesians which speak of "the great mystery" of God's plan of universal redemption in Christ. In each of these key passages, the Latin New Testament translated *musterion* as *sacramentum*. Hence, we can be sure that when the Latin Fathers described something as *sacramentum*, they had very much in mind its nature as "mystery."

A good example of this is St. Augustine's description of the origin of the church: "It was from the side of Christ as he slept on the cross that there came forth the wondrous sacrament which is the whole church."[11] This one sentence suggests some of the reasons that prompted St. Augustine to describe the church as *sacramentum*, where the word clearly means "mystery." First of all, he sees the church as the fruit of Christ's passion and death, thus having its origin not in a mere act of institution, but in the redemptive work accomplished by Christ on the cross. He sees the church as symbolized by the blood and water that flowed out from the side of Christ: no doubt because this blood and water were identified with the sacraments of baptism and eucharist, the most fundamental elements in the life of the church. Finally, the reference to Christ "sleeping the sleep of death" presents Christ as the "new Adam" from whose side the church came forth as the "new Eve," thus suggesting that as the first Eve was drawn from Adam's side to be his bride and "helper" (Gen 2:18), so the church is the bride of Christ who has a helping role to play in Christ's ongoing work for the salvation of humanity. The richness and depth of the ideas about the origin, nature and function of the church suggested in this one sentence of St. Augustine offer a striking illustration of the fact that when the Latin Fathers used the term *sacramentum* of the church, they had in mind its nature as a mystery of Christian faith. No merely human institution could be described in terms such as these. It is to be noted, too, that the nature of the church as "mystery" is rooted in its intimate association with Christ and the mystery of our redemption.

Association with Christ is also seen as the basis of the description of the church as "sacrament" when the council speaks of the church as being "in Christ a kind of sacrament: that is, a sign and instrument of intimate union with God and of the unity of all humanity" (LG 1). Here the term "sacrament" is being used not only with its original meaning as "mystery," but with a further, specific meaning which the term acquired in the course of its Christian usage through its application to such "mysteries" as baptism and the eucharist. For the council explains that it is applying the term "sacrament" to the church insofar as the church, like the seven sacraments, is a "sign and instrument" of divine grace. Over the centuries, the term "sacrament" had become identified with those acts of liturgical worship which are understood both to signify and instrumentally to effect the sanctifying of the person who receives them. While these are rather simple acts, performed with ordinary things like water, bread and wine, by quite human ministers, they are accepted in Christian faith to be genuine "mysteries," since they not only signify but really contain and effect the divine realities of grace which they symbolize.

It is in this sense that the Council describes the church as "in Christ a kind of sacrament," explaining that this is because the church is "a sign and instrument of intimate union with God and the unity of all humanity." What this means is that the church, like the seven sacraments, is an "efficacious sign of grace": a visible, historical institution which contains and effects a hidden, divine reality. The council specifies a twofold grace of which the church is "sign and instrument": namely, "intimate union with God" (the vertical dimension) and the "unity of all humanity" (the horizontal dimension). Intimate union with God involves the reconciliation of sinners with God, the enjoyment of friendship with him in this life, and the intimacy of the beatific vision in the life to come. The "unity of all humanity" describes the universal peace and harmony that would prevail from the recognition of God as the one Father of all peoples and nations, and the practical living out of the love which all owe to one another as children of God and members of his family. The role of the church: to be a sign and instrumental cause of such realities as these, is surely grounds for recognizing the church as a "mystery," containing and effecting results that go far beyond what any merely human institution could accomplish. Of course it is only "in Christ," that is, as his instrument, that the church can have such a role. As the council says in a later passage, it is Jesus who is the "author of salvation and the source of unity and peace," while God has established the church to be "a visible sacrament of this saving unity" (LG 9).

We shall return in a later chapter to the notion of the church as "universal sacrament of salvation"; for now it is enough to have seen how this idea contributes to our understanding of the reasons why the church is recognized as a "mystery of faith."

The Church As the Work of the Trinity

As the triune God: Father, Son and Holy Spirit, is the ultimate mystery of Christian faith, so the nature of the church as mystery is rooted in its relationship with the mystery of the Trinity. After the initial article which presents the church as a "kind of sacrament," the following three articles of *Lumen gentium* explain how the church is related to each of the Divine Persons. Here again our purpose is simply to point out the basis for including the church among the mysteries of faith to be confessed in the creed.

In LG 2 the church is seen as part of the Father's plan to share divine life with mankind. The church is thus seen to have a history that extends far beyond merely human calculations, being foreshadowed from the beginning of the world, prepared through the old covenant with the people of Israel, and directed toward the gathering of all the just in the universal church of the world to come.

Article 3 of the text goes on to explain how the church is the fruit of Christ's redemptive work on earth. Carrying out the Father's plan, Christ inaugurated a new phase of God's reign on earth, and the church is seen as the presence of God's kingdom "in mystery."

Here again the church is seen as the fruit of Christ's passion and death, stressing its origin in the mystery of redemption and its role in the ongoing work of redemption by the celebration of the eucharistic sacrifice. Thus the focus is on the church as an integral element in the mystery of our salvation.

In the creed the mention of the church always comes in the third article, in association with the Holy Spirit. *Lumen gentium*, 4 suggests some of the many reasons why this is so fitting. It is the role of the Spirit to sanctify the church, to dwell in her as in a temple, to guide her into all truth, to maintain her unity, to furnish her with gifts for ministry, to renew her and lead her to final union with Christ. The article concludes with a quotation from St. Cyprian, describing the church as "a people made one with the unity of the Father, the Son and the Holy Spirit."[12] One can also conclude that the church is truly a mystery, by reason of its unique relationship with each of these Divine Persons.

The Church and the Kingdom of God

In LG 5 the council develops the idea of the church as mystery in virtue of its role with regard to the present reign of Christ and the future kingdom of God. As Christ came to inaugurate a new phase of God's reign over the world, and manifested the presence of this reign by his works of power over the forces of evil, so the church has the mission to proclaim and promote the reign of Christ as Lord, and to be on earth "the initial budding forth of his kingdom," while ever looking forward to the final coming of the kingdom of God. While the church on earth cannot be identified with the present reign of Christ (which surely extends beyond the limits of the church), still it is the function of the church both to manifest the presence of his gracious reign and to promote it among men, so that, while the text does not use the term in this way, the church can be seen as the sacrament: that is, the sign and instrument of Christ's reign in this age, pointing to and preparing people for entry into God's future kingdom. Here again we see solid reasons for recognizing the church as a mystery, deeply engaged as it is in the working out of God's plan for the coming of his kingdom.

Biblical Images of the Church

One consequence of the nature of the church as "mystery" is that it cannot be adequately defined or even described by any one simple concept. This is brought out by the variety of images which the scriptures have used with reference to the church, suggesting that one can approach a description of this mystery only by trying to see it in the light which each of these many images can cast on it. This is the approach which is suggested in LG 6, which mentions a number of biblical images, such as those associated with shepherding, with agriculture, and with building. For our present purpose it will suffice to dwell briefly on just the last one mentioned, namely, that of the church as bride of Christ. This image was developed most fully by St. Paul in Ephesians 5:21–33, where he presents the love of Christ for the church as the model for the love which husbands should have for their wives. In this passage, St. Paul explicitly terms the union between Christ and his bride the church a "great mystery." It was out of love for the church that Christ gave up his life, so as to purify her and prepare her for marriage with himself; and now that she is united with him he nourishes and cherishes her as his own body. It hardly needs to be said that such a relationship as this surely justifies the description of the church as a "mystery."

The Church As the Body of Christ

After presenting a variety of biblical images of the church in article 6, the constitution devotes the whole of the following article to the distinctively Pauline notion of the church as the body of Christ, thus emphasizing the particular importance of this idea for the theme of this chapter: the mystery of the church. Because of this importance, it will also be appropriate for us to analyze this section at somewhat greater length.

After a brief introductory paragraph, article 7 consists of two parts: the first based on the teaching of St. Paul in his major epistles: 1 Corinthians and Romans, and the second on the later epistles, especially Colossians and Ephesians.

In the introductory paragraph, the key sentence reads: "By communicating his Spirit to his brothers, called together from all peoples, Christ made them mystically into his own body." Equally important is the beginning of the second paragraph: "In that body the life of Christ is poured into the believers. . . . " Here we see the reason why the idea of the church as "body of Christ" is not a mere image: it is a way of expressing the fact that the members of the church are living a supernatural life by virtue of the same divine life, the same Holy Spirit, of which the sacred humanity of Christ enjoys the fullness. Christ in glory shares his own life with his disciples by communicating his "life-giving Spirit" to them. As the text says, he thus makes them "mystically" into his own body. It is important to understand the force of the word "mystically"; its root is the same as that of the word "mystery." The word "mystically" here, and "mystical" in the expression "mystical body," really mean that there is a mystery involved in the sharing of the same divine life between Christ and his church. This sharing of the same life is the reason why the church is Christ's "body" in a way that is much more than a mere figure of speech.

The following paragraph shows how St. Paul's idea of the church as Christ's body is firmly based on his insight into the effects of the sacraments of baptism and the Eucharist. It is through baptism that believers receive the fruits of Christ's death and resurrection, namely, his life-giving Spirit; and when they eat the eucharistic body of Christ, their life in one body with him and with one another receives a new dimension of reality.

The second part of article 7 develops further aspects of this doctrine, found mainly in Colossians and Ephesians. In these letters St. Paul introduced an idea he had not used in the earlier letters, namely, that of Christ as head of his body the church. Paul developed this idea along two lines: first, applying to Christ the attributes associated with the notion of "head" as the one having priority over the members of his body, and, second, seeing the "head" as the model for all the other members to follow and imitate.

There follows a paragraph on the role of the Holy Spirit, the gift by which Christ shares his life with the members of his body. Here the text introduces a new insight from the writings of the Fathers of the church: namely, that the Holy Spirit is like the soul of the church, since it is the source of the body's life, unity and vital activities.

The final paragraph invokes the passage of Eph 5:22–28 where

St. Paul applies to Christ and his church the idea from Gen 2:24 that a man and his wife become "one flesh." So also, the church is both Christ's bride and his body, which he loves, nourishes and cherishes, and fills with divine gifts.

While St. Paul did not use the term "mystical" body, it is certainly appropriate, provided one keeps in mind that what this word tells us is that we are dealing with a mystery. On the other hand it would be a grave mistake to give to the adjective "mystical" a meaning that would practically eliminate the concreteness which the noun "body" had for St. Paul.

The Church As "One Complex Reality"

With article 8 we arrive at what is generally recognized to be the most profoundly theological article of the whole constitution on the church. As we know from the commentary given by the theological commission when it presented this text to the council, the primary intention of this article was to dispel any impression that the "mystery" which had been described in the preceding seven articles was something of the ideal order: something which could be the object of an act of faith, but which was not the same thing as the "institutional church" of everyday experience.

The concern of the commission to counteract such an impression was certainly not without foundation. The idea that the "mystical body" was a purely spiritual reality, an invisible "sphere of divine grace," quite different from the visible church, was not only a popular error, it was a point of view that had been advocated by not a few Catholic theologians. In fact, the first draft of the constitution on the church at the First Vatican Council in 1870, which began with the presentation of the church as the mystical body, was strongly criticized on the grounds that the church was not something mystical, but was rather a visible, hierarchical society.[13] This reflected the fact that in the theological schools, the notion of the mystical body was generally treated as an aspect of the theology of grace, whereas ecclesiology had to do with the church as a "perfect society." The treatment of the mystical body in the treatise on grace easily led to the conclusion that "being in the state of grace" was the criterion of membership in this body. This involved a very real difference between the mystical body and the church, since on the one hand many non-Christians might be in the state of grace, whereas membership in the church did not necessarily require this. In any case, a mystical body composed only of people in the state of grace would be visible only to God, since only God would know who belonged to it. It would clearly be something other than the visible church.

Twenty years before the Second Vatican Council Pope Pius XII issued his encyclical *Mystici corporis* in which one of his main purposes was precisely to show that authentic Catholic tradition did not support such a separation between "mystical body" and "visible church." Indeed, the Pope insisted that the mystical body and the visible church are one and the same reality.[14]

Unfortunately, what made his teaching difficult for many to accept was that he not only identified the mystical body with the church, but he identified it in an exclusive way with the Roman Catholic Church, with the consequence that other Christians, even in the state of grace, could not be considered to be really (*reapse*) members of Christ's mystical body.[15] Since quite a few Catholic theologians did not see how such people could be excluded from the mystical body, they continued to maintain a real difference between the mystical body and the church, with the result that Pope Pius returned to this question is his encyclical *Humani generis* in 1950, and again insisted that Catholics must hold that the mystical body of Christ and the Roman Catholic Church are one and the same thing.[16] However, even this second statement of Pius XII did not really eliminate the impression that, at least in popular thinking, the mystical body was a purely spiritual reality, something that could hardly be identified with the visible, hierarchical church.

This was one aspect of the problem which the theological commission at Vatican II intended to confront. Another aspect was the fact that, on the one hand, practically all Christians accepted the "one, holy, catholic and apostolic church" in their profession of faith, but many could not recognize any existing church as corresponding to the one described in the creed. This led to the idea that the church of the creed must be seen as an object not only of faith but also of hope: an ideal church which will be realized only when the presently divided churches are again reunited, or when the future kingdom of God has come. The result, again, is a dichotomy between the church of faith and the church of experience: between the mystical body and the institutional church.

It was this dichotomy that the theological commission wished to confront in the final article of their chapter on the "mystery of the church." Their approach was to recognize that some aspects of the church can only be grasped by faith, while others are a matter of experience; that the factors that constitute the church as a "spiritual communion" are different from the factors that constitute it as a "hierarchical society"—and nonetheless, the spiritual community and the hierarchical society are not two different realities. On the contrary, there is but one church: a *complex reality*, which is, under different aspects, *both* a "community of faith, hope and charity" and a "visible society"; both mystical body and hierarchically structured church; both visible assembly and spiritual community. While these terms bring out very different facets of the church, it is one and the same church that all of them describe.

The complex nature of the church is even more strikingly brought out when the text goes on to describe it as composed of both human and divine elements. While it does not give specific examples of such elements, it is useful to suggest some examples here. Under the heading of human elements, one would no doubt include, besides the men and women who make up the people of God, all those factors in the life of the church that make it an appropriate subject for research by such human sciences as history, sociology, social psychology, and the like. While these sciences cannot reach the depths of the mystery of the church, there is still a great deal in the make-up of the church as a human institution which these sciences can analyze, and concerning which they can make pertinent observations.

What did the theological commission have in mind when it spoke of "divine elements" in the church? We have already mentioned the idea, familiar to St. Augustine and other Fathers of the church, that the Holy Spirit is like the soul of the church. Does this justify speaking of the Holy Spirit as the divine element in the composition of the church? There are problems with such a proposal. If one sees the church as a complex reality, made up of divine and human elements, then whatever the divine elements are, they would seem to be really a part of the whole. But one cannot really think of the Holy Spirit, a Divine Person, as being really a part of something. For this reason, the Constitution is careful not to describe the Holy Spirit in a way that would suggest that the Spirit is literally the soul of the mystical body. It said, rather, that "his work could be compared by the holy Fathers with the functions which the soul fulfills in the human body" (LG 7).

If not the Holy Spirit, then, what are the "divine elements" that enter into the composite reality which is the church? I suggest that the term "divine" here is best understood in the sense in which we are accustomed to speak of created grace as "divine grace," referring to its source in God, and to its effect of raising those who receive it into union with God. In this hypothesis, the divine elements in the make-up of the church would consist of all those gifts of divine grace with which the Holy Spirit endows the church. These include not only the various gifts by which individual members of the church are made holy, but even more importantly those grace-gifts which enter into the very structure of the church. *Lumen gentium* speaks of such gifts in n. 4: "The Spirit furnishes and directs her with various gifts, both hierarchical and charismatic, and adorns her with the fruits of his grace." In another context it speaks of "the charism of infallibility of the church herself" (LG 25). What this means is that the hierarchical structure of the church is also composed of human and divine elements, since the "various hierarchical and charismatic gifts" of the Holy Spirit are essential to that very structure. One cannot therefore think of the "institutional church" as a purely human organization. Even precisely as "institutional," it is a complex reality, composed of both human and divine elements. Without the Spirit's "hierarchical and charismatic gifts," it would perhaps be an institution, but it would no longer be the institutional *church*.

If we identify the "divine element" in the church not with the Holy Spirit but with his created gifts of grace, how then should we understand the relationship between the Holy Spirit and the church? The conciliar text answers this question by proposing that this relationship is something like the relationship between the humanity of Christ and the Divine Word. It might help to identify the several elements in this analogy. The individual humanity of Jesus is compared with the social humanity of the church. The humanity of Jesus is inseparably united with the Divine Word; the church is vivified by the Holy Spirit. The humanity of Jesus serves the Divine

Word as a living instrument of our salvation; the church serves the Holy Spirit as his instrument for the building up of the body of Christ (and thus for the ongoing work of salvation).

Of course we have to remember that we are dealing here with an analogy, which means that two things are somewhat, but not perfectly, alike. The union between Jesus as man and the Divine Word is such that there is really only one person there. Jesus is not added as a fourth person to the Trinity: he is truly the Second Person incarnate. The church, on the other hand, as the people of God, is made up of a great number of persons who do not lose their individual personhood by being members of the church. If one speaks of Christ and his church as being "one mystical person," this is for the same reason that we speak of the church as Christ's "mystical body"—namely, because he shares his divine life with his church. And this divine life is the fruit of the Holy Spirit's indwelling in the church. But there is not the kind of "hypostatic union" between the Holy Spirit and the church that would mean that the Holy Spirit is the "divine personality" of the church, in the way that the Divine Word is the one Person in Christ. Because of the hypostatic union, everything that Jesus did was really attributable to the Divine Person; it is certainly not the case that everything the church does can be attributed to the Holy Spirit. We cannot blame the Holy Spirit for the many mistakes and failures that have marred the church's history. On the other hand, everything the church has accomplished for the salvation of men and women and for the promotion of Christ's reign on earth, it has been able to do only through the power of the Holy Spirit working through it as his instrument. While the union between the church and the Holy Spirit is not "hypostatic," it is an inseparable dynamic union, and is an essential aspect of the mystery of the church. Any notion of the church that would overlook the role of the Holy Spirit in it would be sadly deficient.

There is another corollary to the analogy between the church and the mystery of the Incarnate Word that can help us to understand how the church can be both a visible institution and a mystery of faith at the same time. The fact that Jesus walked among his disciples as a man whom they could see and touch did not make him any the less a mystery to be grasped only by faith. When Peter confessed Jesus as "the Christ, the Son of the living God" (Mt 16:16), Jesus reminded him that it was his Father in heaven who had revealed this to him. When Thomas cried out: "My Lord and my God," he was acknowledging that the Jesus who stood before him in tangible form was a mystery far beyond his capacity to understand. Likewise, the opening sentence of the first letter of John declares that what the disciples of Jesus had heard, had seen with their eyes, and touched with their hands, was in reality "the Word of life which had been from the beginning with the Father" (1 Jn 1:1–2).

In other words, for his own disciples, Jesus was both a man like themselves and a mystery for their faith. In fact, the deepest aspect of the mystery was precisely the union of human and divine in the same person. God as pure spirit is indeed a mystery; but God incarnate in the man of Nazareth is the mystery of mysteries. In the light of the analogy between the church and the Incarnate Word, we can see that there is no contradiction involved when we say that the visible, institutional church is also a mystery for our faith. There is no reason to imagine that there are two churches: one that we can believe in as the "mystical body," the "bride of Christ," the "temple of the Holy Spirit," and the other the empirical institution that confronts us in our daily life. The mystery is that there is really but one church which is both object of our (sometimes painful) experience and object of our confession of faith, just as for the disciples there was but one Jesus, whom they could see to be a man like themselves, but whom they also came to believe in as their Lord and their God.

Where Is the Church to Be Found Today?

We arrive now at the paragraph which has received more comment than probably any other in the documents of Vatican II. It begins: "This is the unique church of Christ which in the creed we avow as one, holy, catholic and apostolic." The initial word "This" clearly refers back to the "complex reality" described in the previous paragraph: that church which is both "mystical body" and "hierarchically structured society." To describe this as "the unique church of Christ" is to insist that there is and can be only one church of Christ, just as it would be absurd to think of Christ having more than one mystical body or more than one mystical bride. This unique church, then, is the "one, holy, catholic and apostolic church" in which practically all Christians profess their faith in the creed.

But can this mystery of faith be concretely identified with any historical Christian church? The first answer to this question is: yes, it is none other than the church of the New Testament, the church which Christ, after his resurrection, entrusted to Peter (Jn 21:17), commissioning him and the other apostles to be its pastors and teachers (Mt 28:18f). It is noteworthy that this answer focuses on the risen Christ as founder of the church. In a later passage, *Lumen gentium* points to the sending of the Holy Spirit by the glorified Christ as the act by which he "has established his body, the church, as the universal sacrament of salvation" (LG 48). In this context of faith, the theological commission is not dealing with questions that can be raised about the intention of Jesus, during his public ministry, to lay the foundation for his future church. It is sufficient to recognize the New Testament church, the church of Acts and the letters of St. Paul, as the one which Christians acknowledge to be the church of Jesus Christ, the church of their profession of faith.

But now comes the crucial question, the one on which believing Christians are so deeply divided: is the church of the New Testament, the church of their faith, to be found concretely existing in any Christian church today?

The answer of the *final text* of *Lumen gentium* is as follows: "This church, constituted and organized in the world as a society, subsists in the Catholic Church, which is governed by the successor of Peter and by the bishops in union with that successor, although many elements of sanctification and of truth can be found outside of her visible structure. These elements, however, as gifts properly belonging to the Church of Christ, possess an inner dynamism toward Catholic unity" (LG 8).

The words "final text" have been emphasized, because there is a very significant difference between what the council finally said at this point and previous drafts of the Constitution (and, indeed, previous official statements of Roman Pontiffs). Our next chapter will be devoted to the examination of the many questions which this text raises. We shall conclude the present chapter on "the church as a mystery of faith" by simply quoting the explanation which the theological commission gave of the passage of *Lumen gentium* we have just cited. "The intention is to show that the church, whose inner, hidden nature has been described . . . is to be found concretely existing in this world, in the Catholic Church."[17] "The mystery of the church is not something imaginary, ideal or unreal: it exists in the concrete Catholic society which is governed by the successor of Peter and the bishops in communion with him."[18] The burden of this first chapter has been to insist that while the church is a "mystery," it is not something of the ideal order; something altogether different and distinct from the "institutional church". The next chapter will analyze the claim that the "one, holy catholic and apostolic church" of Christian faith is to be found "subsisting" in the Roman Catholic Church.

2 ‖ The One Church of Christ "Subsists" in the Catholic Church

In the first chapter we have had occasion to mention the fact that Pope Pius XII, in his encyclical *Mystici corporis* (1943), and again in his encyclical *Humani generis* (1950), had insisted that the Mystical Body of Christ and the Roman Catholic Church are one and the same thing, with the consequence that only Roman Catholics are really members of Christ's Body. This of course was not a new idea in official Catholic teaching. Pope Pius XI, in the encyclical *Mortalium animos* (1928), excluding the participation of the Catholic Church in the then incipient ecumenical movement, had similarly declared that no one could be in the one church of Christ who was not in obedience to the authority of the Pope.[19]

After Pope John XXIII had announced the convocation of the Second Vatican Council, a preparatory theological commission was formed in 1960, with Cardinal Ottaviani, Prefect of the Holy Office, as its head, and Fr. Sebastian Tromp, chief collaborator with Pius XII in the writing of *Mystici corporis*, as its secretary. From the texts produced by this commission, one can safely judge that its expectation was that the council would in no case depart from what was already official teaching of the Popes. Hence it is no surprise when we find the following statement in the draft of the constitution on the church that was presented by this commission to the council in the fall of 1962: "The Roman Catholic Church is the Mystical Body of Christ . . . and only the one that is Roman Catholic has the right to be called church."[20]

Among the criticisms that were made of this draft during the week that it was discussed by the council (Dec. 1–7, 1962), one that

23

was heard a number of times concerned this exclusive identification between the Mystical Body and the Catholic Church.[21] As is well known, the frosty reception given to the whole draft was enough to convince the leadership of the council that it should be quietly withdrawn without even being put to a vote. So during the spring and summer of 1963 a new draft of the constitution on the church was prepared, which, it must be said, did incorporate quite a lot of material from the previous one, while differing a great deal from it in tone and general approach.

On the question we are dealing with, the new draft followed the previous one in asserting that the one and only church of Christ is the Roman Catholic Church, but it added the significant admission that "many elements of sanctification can be found outside its total structure" and that these are "things properly belonging to the church of Christ."[22] The last phrase at least implied that such "elements of sanctification" as are to be found outside the Catholic Church are ecclesial in nature, and that suggests that there is at least something of church beyond the limits of the Catholic Church.

This is the draft that was discussed for the whole month of November 1963, and on which the bishops submitted their proposals for emendation. In the interval between the conciliar periods of 1963 and 1964, a considerable revision was made of the draft document on the church, and it was while the theological commission was preparing the revised text that the question was raised about the consistency of maintaining on the one hand that the church of Christ was simply identical with the Catholic Church, and then admitting that there were "ecclesial elements" outside of it. The solution arrived at was to change the text from saying that the church of Christ *is* the Catholic Church, to saying that it *subsists in it*. The official explanation given to justify this change, when the revised text was presented to the bishops, was: "so that the expression might better agree with the affirmation about the ecclesial elements which are found elsewhere."[23] Unfortunately for the commentators, no further elucidation was offered as to the precise sense in which the word "subsists" was intended to be taken.

The one fact that is absolutely certain is that the decision no longer to say "is"—a decision ratified by the vote of the council—is a decision no longer to assert such absolute and exclusive identity between the church of Christ and the Catholic Church as had been claimed by the previous drafts. There would have been no point in making this change if the new term "subsists in" were to be understood in the same exclusive sense that had been affirmed by the simple copulative "is." The explanation given by the commission includes the explicit recognition that the "elements of sanctification and of truth" found outside the Catholic Church are ecclesial in nature; it is to be noted that the words "and of truth" were added by the commission at the same time.

Practically all commentators have seen in this change of wording a significant opening toward the recognition of ecclesial reality in the non-Catholic world.[24] But much remained to be clarified. One can distinguish at least three questions that need to be answered:

1. What is the significance of this change from "is" to "subsists in" for our thinking about the Catholic Church?

2. What is its significance for our thinking about other Christian churches?

3. What is its significance for our thinking about the universal church of Christ?

The first point to be noted is that none of these questions can be given a satisfactory answer on the basis of this one text of *Lumen gentium* alone. What we are seeking is the "mind of the council" about some of the most basic questions relating to what the Decree on Ecumenism calls the "Catholic principles of ecumenism." The people working on the draft document on the church were very much aware of the fact that at the same time a document on ecumenism was being prepared, and they intended to leave the ecumenical aspects of ecclesiology to be handled in that decree.[25] Actually these two documents were promulgated on the very same day: November 21, 1964. In the allocution which he gave on that occasion, Pope Paul VI, in addressing himself especially to the non-Catholic observers, made the explicit point that the doctrine on the church in *Lumen gentium* was to be interpreted in the light of the further explanations given in the Decree on Ecumenism.[26] So we shall seek the answers to our questions in both of these documents, and in the official reports given by the respective commissions to the council fathers.

The Meaning of the Term "Subsists In"

The official explanation given for the change from "is" to "subsists in" sheds no further light on the way the commission intended the word "subsists" to be taken. However, the commission also provided a report that briefly summarized the contents of each paragraph of Chapter 1. The second paragraph of article 8, in which our phrase occurs, was summarized as follows: "There is but one church, and on this earth it is present in the Catholic Church, although ecclesial elements are found outside of it."[27] Here the Latin word that corresponds to *subsistit* is the very simple *adest*. This is a good reason for not following those commentators who have interpreted the word "subsists" in the light of a philosophical notion of "subsistence."[28] One went so far in this direction as to suggest that the Catholic Church is to other Christian communities what *esse subsistens* (divine being) is to created beings.[29] Another philosophical approach is to imagine that the church of Christ is being thought of here as a kind of "platonic idea" which has its "concrete form of existence" in the Catholic Church. Some German translations of the text actually lend themselves to such an interpretation.[30]

However, most commentators rightly reject the idea that the word "subsists" is being used here in any such technical philosophical sense.[31] It is a good working rule that, in the absence of clear indications to the contrary, terms used in conciliar documents are meant to be taken in the ordinary sense that the word has in common usage. If one looks up the word *subsistere* in a Latin lexicon, one finds that the primary meaning is "to stand still, to stay, to continue, to remain," etc. That such is actually the correct meaning of the word in our passage is confirmed both by the context and by other places in the conciliar documents where the same word occurs.

If one reads the whole paragraph, one sees that the church of Christ which is said to subsist in the Catholic Church is not an ideal church, needing to be concretely realized in this world, but is the historical church of the New Testament: the church that Jesus entrusted to Peter and the other apostles to be propagated and governed. It makes excellent sense to say that this church continues to exist, and that it is still to be found in the Catholic Church, the one, namely, that is governed by the successors of Peter.

Other passages confirm this interpretation of the word "subsist," especially two that occur in the Decree on Ecumenism. In n. 4 we are told that "the unity which Christ gave to his church can never be lost, and it *subsists* in the Catholic Church." Later on, in n. 13, the decree speaks of the Anglican Communion as one of the separated Christian communities in which Catholic traditions and institutions at least in part continue to subsist.

But the all-important question, on which we are seeking the mind of the council, is still to be answered: namely, in exactly what way does the church of Christ subsist in the Catholic Church? The key to the answer to this question is found in the Decree on Ecumenism, n. 2, which gives us the best description to be found in the documents of Vatican II of the kind of unity that Christ gave to his church. There we see that while it is essentially a communion of faith, hope and love, whose principal cause is the Holy Spirit, the church is also intended to be visibly united in the profession of the same faith, the celebration of the sacraments, in the fraternal concord of one people of God. In order to bring about and maintain such unity, Christ endowed his church with a threefold ministry of word, sacraments and leadership, first entrusted to the apostles with Peter at their head, and then continued in the college of bishops under the Pope.

If we keep in mind this description of the unity which Christ gave to his church, we can see how significant is the statement in the same decree, n. 4: "We believe that the unity with which Christ from the beginning endowed his church is something it cannot lose; it subsists in the Catholic Church, and we hope that it will continue to increase until the end of time." On the other hand, the decree goes on to say, with complete frankness, that our separated brethren and their churches do not enjoy that kind of unity which Christ intended his church to have (UR 3).

Another statement of the Decree on Ecumenism that suggests the mind of the council on our question is the assertion: "It is through the Catholic Church alone that the whole fullness of the means of salvation can be obtained" (UR 3). This does not mean that there are not many such means of salvation present and effectively used in other Christian churches and communities; this fact is explicitly recognized in the same context. But at the same time it is said, in general, of the separated communities, that "we believe they suffer from defects" in this regard. One can only conclude that it is in the Catholic Church *alone* that the church of Christ subsists with that fullness of the means of salvation which Christ entrusted to the apostolic college.

To sum up: the Decree on Ecumenism provides us with a clear answer to the question as to how the council intends us to understand the statement that the church of Christ subsists in the Catholic Church. It means that the church of Christ still exists in the Catholic Church with that particular kind of unity, and with all the means of salvation, with which Christ endowed it: and it is only in the Catholic Church that it continues so to exist.

Of course it must be kept in mind that this is a question of *institutional* integrity: of fullness of the *means* of salvation. There is no question of denying that a non-Catholic community, perhaps lacking much in the order of means, can achieve a higher degree of communion in the life of Christ in faith, hope and love than many a Catholic community. The means of grace have to be used well to achieve their full effect, and the possession of a fullness of means is no guarantee of how well they will be used.

At this point it should be noted that the interpretation proposed here of the mind of the council would not certainly follow from the mere use of the word "subsists" in LG 8. The Latin word *subsistere* by itself does not necessarily connote such structural integrity as is claimed for the Catholic Church. In fact, the council used the same word, with the qualifier *ex parte*, "partially," or "incompletely," when it said that certain Catholic traditions and institutions continue to subsist in the Anglican Communion (UR 13). This has to be kept in mind if the question is raised whether the church of Christ can be said to "subsist" in other Christian churches. It would seem that if one is going to use such language, and still be consistent with the mind of Vatican II, one must be careful to qualify one's statement in some such way as the council itself qualified its statement about the Catholic traditions that "subsist" in the Anglican Communion.

This bring us to our second question: what is the significance of the change from "is" to "subsists in" for our thinking about the rest of the Christian world? It will be recalled that in the immediate context, in LG 8, the council speaks only of the presence of elements of sanctification and truth outside the Catholic Church: elements which it describes as gifts properly belonging to the church of

Christ. How important are such elements, in the mind of the council? And does the council go beyond the acknowledgement of the presence of such elements, to recognize the ecclesial nature of non-Catholic communities as such? These are the questions to which we must now address ourselves.

Are There Only "Elements of Church" Outside the Catholic Church?

We shall begin by considering the interpretation which the Congregation for the Doctrine of the Faith has given of the mind of Vatican II on this point, in the critique which it published in 1985, concerning Leonardo Boff's book *Church, Charism and Power*.[32] In criticizing Boff's statement to the effect that the church of Christ can be said to subsist also in other Christian churches, the Congregation offered its own interpretation of the mind of the Second Vatican Council, with the following statement:[33]

> The council, rather, had chosen the word *subsistit* precisely to make it clear that there exists only one subsistence of the true Church, whereas outside of its visible structure there exist only elements of Church which, being elements of the church itself, tend and lead toward the Catholic Church (LG 8). The Decree on Ecumenism expresses the same doctrine (UR 3–4), which was again clarified in the Declaration *Mysterium Ecclesiae* n. 1 (AAS 65, 1973, 396–398).

While the phrase "there exists only one subsistence" is somewhat obscure, there can be no doubt about the interpretation that the Congregation for the Doctrine of the Faith is giving to the use of "subsists in" in LG 8: it means: (1) it is only in the Catholic Church that the church of Christ can be said to "subsist," and (2) it subsists in the Catholic Church in so exclusive a way that outside of her limits there can be found *only elements* of church. While this is an authoritative interpretation, it is certainly not so authoritative as the documents of the council themselves, and is open to verification as to whether it really corresponds to the mind of the council. We have already quoted Pope Paul VI to the effect that the doctrine about the church in *Lumen gentium* is to be understood in the light of further explanations given in the Decree on Ecumenism. The Congregation claims that its interpretation is confirmed by that decree. We shall have to examine the basis on which this claim is made.

But, before looking at the Decree on Ecumenism, there is an important text of *Lumen gentium* itself that sheds light on this question. In article 15, LG describes the many ways in which the Catholic Church is linked or joined with other Christians. It declares that these Christians, consecrated to Christ by their baptism, also recognize and receive other sacraments *in their own churches and ecclesiastical communities*. It is particularly noteworthy that this phrase which we have emphasized was added, as the theological commission's report explained, in response to many requests of the bishops. The same report goes on to say: "The elements which are mentioned concern not only individuals but their communities as well; in this fact precisely is located the foundation of the ecumenical movement. Papal documents regularly speak of separated eastern churches. For Protestants recent Pontiffs have used the term 'Christian communities.' "[34]

Lumen gentium n. 8 recognized that there are elements of sanctification and truth to be found outside the limits of the Catholic Church. The Congregation for the Doctrine of the Faith interpreted this to mean that there are *only elements* of church outside the Catholic Church, even though the text itself did not say *"only* elements"; it used the adjective *plura:* "several" or "many." But the explicit reference, in n. 15, to the reception of such "elements" as sacraments, by other Christians, *in their own churches and ecclesiastical communities*, and the explanation of this phrase, given by the same theological commission that introduced the phrase "subsists in" in n. 8, makes it obvious that this commission did not share the view that outside the Catholic Church there exist *only elements* of church. Their commentary on n. 15 shows beyond doubt that such "elements" as sacraments cannot be understood as existing in isolation, independently of the churches and communities in which Christians receive them. The commission further observes that the recognition of this fact is fundamental for the whole ecumenical movement.

What is to be said of the claim that the interpretation of the Congregation is confirmed by the Decree on Ecumenism? The following is the most pertinent section of UR 3, to which the CDF referred in support of its claim.

Moreover some, even very many, of the most significant elements or endowments which together go to build up and give life to the Church herself can exist outside the visible boundaries of the Catholic Church: the written word of God; the life of grace; faith, hope and charity, along with other interior gifts of the Holy Spirit and visible elements. All of these, which come from Christ and lead back to him, belong by right to the one Church of Christ.

The brethren divided from us also carry out many of the sacred actions of the Christian religion. Undoubtedly, in ways that vary according to the condition of each Church or Community, these actions can truly engender a life of grace, and can be rightly described as capable of providing access to the community of salvation.

It follows that these separated Churches and Communities, though we believe they suffer from defects already mentioned, have by no means been deprived of significance and importance in the mystery of salvation. For the Spirit of Christ has not refrained from using them as means of salvation which derive their efficacy from the very fullness of grace and truth entrusted to the Catholic Church.

It is truly difficult to see how the interpretation of the CDF, to the effect that outside the Catholic Church one can find nothing but *elements* of church, can stand up against the explicit recognition by the Decree on Ecumenism of the significance of the separated churches and communities *as such* in the mystery of salvation. (The words "as such," while not in the Abbott translation, are justified by the word *ipsae* in the Latin text, which has "ipsae Ecclesiae et Communitates.")

It did not escape the notice of some less ecumenically minded bishops that this text was clearly attributing a salvific role not just to the sacraments that might be found in non-Catholic communities, but to these churches and communities as such. This occasioned a proposal to emend the text, so as to say rather: "In these communities means of salvation are preserved which the Holy Spirit has not refrained from using. . . . " The response of the commission was as follows: "Wherever valid means of salvation are being used, which, as social actions, characterize those communities as such, it is certain that the Holy Spirit is using those communities as means of salvation."[35]

Finally, the whole of chapter 3 of the Decree on Ecumenism would have to be drastically revised if the council had meant to say that outside the Catholic Church there exist *only elements* of the church. The very title of this chapter reads: "Churches and Ecclesial Communities Separated from the Roman Apostolic See." In the first part of this chapter, entitled "The Special Position of the Eastern Churches," these churches, while not in full communion with Rome, are certainly recognized as "particular churches," in something more than a merely conventional sense of the term.[36] It is obviously not a merely polite use of the term "church" when the decree speaks as follows of the separated eastern churches: "This most sacred Synod gladly reminds all of one highly significant fact among others: in the East there flourish many particular or local Churches; among them the Patriarchal Churches hold first place; and of these, many glory in taking their origins from the apostles themselves" (UR 14).

What about the others that are called "ecclesial communities"? The distinction is based on what may be called a principle of "eucharistic ecclesiology": i.e., there is not the full reality of church where there is not the full reality of the Eucharist.[37] However, the very term "ecclesial" suggests a recognition that these communities have an ecclesial, that is, churchly character. The official report of the commission explains the use of this term in the following way: "It must not be overlooked that the communities that have their origin in the separation that took place in the West are not merely a sum or collection of individual Christians, but they are constituted by social ecclesiastical elements which they have preserved from our common patrimony, and which confer on them a truly ecclesial character. In these communities the one sole Church of Christ is present, albeit imperfectly, in a way that is somewhat like its presence in particular churches, and by means of their ecclesiastical elements the Church of Christ is in some way operative in them."[38]

In other words, while the Decree on Ecumenism did not hesitate to speak of the separated eastern churches as "particular churches" without qualification, it was the mind of the commission responsible for this text that the western communities that lack the full reality of the Eucharist—without attempting to decide which ones these were—still have an ecclesial character, and are at least analogous to particular churches of the Catholic Church.

Early on in this chapter, we suggested that the decision of Vatican II to say of the church of Christ not that it "is" but that it "subsists in" the Catholic Church would have consequences for our thinking about the Catholic Church, the other Christian churches, and the universal church of Christ. With regard to the Catholic Church, we have proposed that what the council meant by saying that the church of Christ subsists in it is that it is there alone that the church which Christ founded continues to exist with the fullness of the means of grace which Christ gave to his church and wants it always to have. With regard to other Christian churches, we have shown that the council recognized the presence of more than just "elements" of church in them; it explicitly recognized the separated eastern churches as particular churches, and acknowledged the ecclesial character of the separated "ecclesial communities" of the west, seeing "significance and importance in the mystery of salvation," not only in the sacraments and other "elements of sanctification and truth" present in them, but in these Christian communities as such.

There remains the third question: in the light of Vatican II, how should we understand the universal church of Christ? If the church of Christ is no longer to be identified exclusively with the Roman Catholic Church, what are its limits? And if, as we profess in the creed, the church of Christ is one, how are we to understand its unity? These are some of the questions to be taken up in our next chapter.

3 ‖ The One Church: A Communion of Churches

As the title of this chapter indicates, there is but one church, even though there are many churches. The title also suggests that in the case of the church, the key to the problem of "the one and the many" lies in the concept of "communion." We shall begin our study of this problem by looking at the way the New Testament speaks of the church, of churches, and of the communion by which the many churches are one church.

First of all we should recall what the word "church" meant for those who wrote the New Testament. Writing in Greek, their word was *ekklesia:* a word that we find in one place in the New Testament with the meaning it had in the common language of the day, where it referred to a public assembly for political purposes (Acts 19:39–40). Etymologically, *ekklesia* reflects the fact that the people were "called out" for such an assembly by a herald. Besides the fact that Christians saw themselves as "called out" by God for membership in the church, the choice of the word *ekklesia* for the Christian church was also prompted by the fact that this word had been used by the translators of the Bible into Greek to render the Hebrew word *qahal*, in passages where this word referred to the assembly of the Israelites, the people of God of the old covenant. Seeing themselves as the new Israel, the people of God of the new covenant, the early Christians also spoke of themselves as the *ekklesia tou theou*, the assembly, or church, of God.

The fact that the word *ekklesia* meant "assembly" or "congregation" explains its use in the plural, since, after the spread of the Christian message from Jerusalem, there were as many such "assemblics" as there were places where Christians gathered for worship. Since, in those early days, Christians had no public churches, but met in private homes, one finds references to the *ekklesia* in such and such a house (e.g. 1 Cor 16:19; Rom 16:5; Col 4:15). There are also a number of places where one finds the word in the plural; thus St. Paul speaks of "the churches of God" (1 Cor 11:16; 2 Thess 1:4), of "all the churches of the Gentiles" (Rom 16:4), and of "all the churches of Christ" (Rom 16:16).

How could all those churches really constitute one church? Two hypotheses are possible. One could imagine that the many churches, previously independent of one another, had at some point decided to form a federation, and thus became one church. Or one could think of a single church, conscious of its oneness and universality from the beginning, which spread by multiplying local congregations in different localities, without losing its original sense of identity.

Perhaps one might be inclined to prefer the first hypothesis, on the grounds that in the earlier letters of Paul, the term "church," both in the singular and the plural, regularly refers to the local churches, while it is only in the later letters of the Pauline corpus, especially Colossians and Ephesians, that "the church" means the one universal church of Christ.

However, the second hypothesis is the one that best corresponds to the evidence of the New Testament. First of all, there is no indication at all of any such process of federation among previously independent churches. Secondly, the earlier letters of St. Paul also bear strong witness to his sense that it is truly one and the same church that is present in Thessalonica, Corinth and Rome.

Thus, when Paul wrote his letter to the church at Rome—a church he had not founded and had not yet even visited—he could speak of himself along with the Roman Christians, saying: "As in one body we have many members, and all the members do not have the same function, so we, though many, are one body in Christ, and individually members one of another" (Rom 12:4–5).

Even earlier than the letter to the Romans is Paul's first letter to the Corinthians, one of whose main purposes was to restore unity to this local church that was threatened by factions. In this context, we find striking evidence of Paul's sense of the oneness of the whole church of Christ when we examine the reasons he gave to the Corinthians to back up his exhortation to unity within that local church. For instance, to show how wrong they were when some said: "I belong to Paul," and others "I belong to Apollos," and others "I belong to Cephas," Paul cried out: "Is Christ divided? Was Paul crucified for you? Or were you baptized in the name of Paul?" (1 Cor 1:13). The reasons why the Corinthians ought to behave as one church are the same reasons that make all Christians everywhere one church: Christ has been crucified for all, and all have been baptized equally into him. A little later on, Paul reminds them that he and Apollos are God's fellow workers, but the church is God's field, God's building. And this is a building of which no one can lay any other foundation than that which is laid, which is Jesus Christ (1 Cor 3:9–11). Paul's argument applies not just to the local church of Corinth, but to the whole church of Christ.

One of the causes of dissension among the Corinthians was ambition to possess the more spectacular charismatic gifts. While this seems to have been a problem unique to Corinth, Paul again proposed arguments for unity that went beyond the immediate local church. First, he insisted on the one divine source of all the various gifts: "All these are inspired by one and the same Spirit, who apportions to each one individually as he wills" (1 Cor 12:11). Then he introduced the analogy of the body, where the variety of members does not hinder, but rather enhances, the unity of the body (12:12–26). His conclusion is: "Now you are the body of Christ, and individually members of it. And God has appointed in the church first apostles, second prophets, third teachers . . . " (12:27–28). The body of Christ to which the Corinthians belong is identified with the church which God himself has organized, appointing its apostles, prophets and teachers. He does not seem to have had just the local church of Corinth in mind here.

Finally, in the same letter to the Corinthians, Paul says of himself: "I am the least of the apostles, unfit to be called an apostle, because I persecuted the church of God" (1 Cor 15:9). Paul had begun this letter with his salutation to "the church of God which is at Corinth." In both cases, it seems certain that when Paul said "the church of God," he had in mind not just the local church of Jerusalem (which he had persecuted) or the local church of Corinth (to which he was writing), but the one and only church of God: present now in Corinth as it had already been in Jerusalem.

Addressing the same Corinthians in his second letter to that church, Paul declares: "We are the temple of the living God; as God said: 'I will live in them and move among them, and I will be their God and they shall be my people' " (2 Cor 6:16). Obviously it is not just the local church of Corinth, but the whole Christian church that is God's temple and his new people.

Paul's letter to the Galatians is another of his earlier letters where he speaks in the plural of "the churches of Galatia" (1:2) and of "the churches of Christ in Judea" (1:22). But this letter also contains striking proof of his sense of the oneness of the church, when he declares: "As many of you as were baptized into Christ have put on Christ. There is neither Jew nor Greek, there is neither slave nor free, there is neither male nor female; for you are all one in Christ Jesus" (3:27–28). The reasons that made all the individual Christians, despite their differences of race, social standing or sex, into "one person in Christ Jesus" applied equally well to the many local churches. Some consisted mostly of Jewish Christians, and others mostly of Gentiles, but they were all one church in Christ Jesus.

This oneness of the church, despite the tensions arising from the fact that it was made up of converts from both Judaism and the Gentile world, is one of the major themes of the letter to the Ephesians. Addressing himself to Gentile Christians, Paul says: "You are no longer strangers and sojourners, but you are fellow citizens with the saints and members of the household of God, built upon the foundation of the apostles and prophets, Christ Jesus himself being the cornerstone, in whom the whole structure is joined together and grows into a holy temple in the Lord, in whom you also are built into it for a dwelling place of God in the Spirit" (Eph 2:19–22). The "saints" with whom the Gentile Christians are now "fellow-citizens" are the Jewish Christians of the mother-church of Judea. A little later on in the same letter, Paul declares it to be a "mystery of Christ" that the Gentile Christians are "fellow-heirs" with their Jewish brethren, being "members of the same body and partakers of the promise in Christ Jesus through the gospel" (3:4–6). Then he sums up all the reasons why there is and can be only one church in the whole world: "There is one body and one Spirit, just as you were called to the one hope that belongs to your call, one Lord, one faith, one baptism, one God and Father of us all" (4:4–6).

The Communion By Which Many Churches Are One Church

The sentence we have just quoted affirms the oneness of the church as "one body" on the basis of what Christians have in common—the same triune God: Spirit, Lord and Father; the same hope, same calling, same faith, same baptism. This "having the same things in common," which forms a bond of unity among those who share them, is the foundation of the concept of *koinonia*, or "communion." (The root of the Greek word is the adjective *koinon*, meaning common.) It is because Christians and their churches share such essential things in common that they are "in communion" with one another, and thus constitute one body, one church. For the kind of communion that justifies speaking of many churches as one church, it is not necessary that they have absolutely everything in common. As we have mentioned, some New Testament churches consisted mostly of Jewish Christians, others mostly of Gentiles. Hence there was much that they did not have in common, because the Christians of Judea continued for some time to observe many prescriptions of the Mosaic law which the Gentile Christians did not observe. So it was a question of discerning which things it was essential for Christians to have in common for them to constitute one church. The list St. Paul gave in Eph 4:4–6 enumerates some of these essentials: "one Spirit, one hope, one calling, one Lord, one faith, one baptism, one God and Father." But it is not likely that Paul intended to give a complete list here of the things he considered essential for Christian unity. In another context he mentioned something that certainly must be added to this list: sharing the same Eucharist. "The cup of blessing that we bless, is it not a participation (*koinonia*) in the blood of Christ? The bread which we break, is it not a participation (*koinonia*) in the body of Christ? Because there is one bread, we who are many are one body, for we all partake of the one bread" (1 Cor 10:16–17). It is not hard to see why the term "communion" became especially associated with the Eucharist, in which Christians share the same body and blood of Christ, thus forming and strengthening their bond of unity with the Lord and with one another.

One of the constant preoccupations of St. Paul was to maintain the bond of communion not only among the churches he had founded, but even more between his churches and the older

Christian churches of Judea. The reason for his preoccupation was the danger that the Jewish Christian communities might not recognize his Gentile churches as true churches, because Paul's converts did not accept circumcision and observe the ritual prescriptions of the Mosaic law. Paul insisted that this difference of observance was non-essential as far as ecclesial communion was concerned. It is instructive, then, to see which elements of communion he did insist on, as the ones that were essential for the unity of the church.

Communion As Sharing the Same Faith in the Same Gospel Message

The strong language with which St. Paul opened his letter to the Galatians shows that in his eyes, Christian communion stands or falls on the issue of holding the same faith on the basis of the same gospel message. Here are his words:

> I am astonished that you are so quickly deserting him who called you in the grace of Christ and turning to a different gospel—not that there is another gospel, but there are some who trouble you and want to pervert the gospel of Christ. But even if we, or an angel from heaven, should preach to you a gospel contrary to that which we preached to you, let him be accursed. As we have said before, so now I say again, if any one is preaching to you a gospel contrary to that which you received, let him be accursed (Gal 1:6–9).

Those whom Paul refers to as "wanting to pervert the gospel of Christ" had been telling the Galatians, who were Gentile converts, that they had to accept circumcision and observe the ritual prescriptions of the Mosaic law in order to be saved. Paul, on the contrary, taught that salvation depended entirely on faith in Christ and the redemption he accomplished by dying on the cross. In Paul's view, to insist on the observance of circumcision and other such ritual prescriptions as necessary for salvation was equivalent to denying that Christ's sacrifice was sufficient for our redemption. As far as Paul was concerned, Jewish Christians could continue to observe the Mosaic law if they wished, but what he vehemently objected to was that some of them went around telling his Gentile converts that they had to observe it as well. For Paul that went against the very heart of the gospel truth that salvation had been won for all by Christ, and was received by believing in him and living in the Spirit which he poured out on believers when they were baptized.

Paul's opponents claimed that his teaching about freedom from circumcision was in contradiction to the gospel as taught by the great apostles who had been Jesus' disciples, Peter and John, and by Jesus' relative James, who was now the leader of the Jewish Christian community at Jerusalem. Paul, of course, had not been a disciple of Jesus as they had been, so it was easy for his opponents to label him an outsider who really didn't know the authentic Christian message, and was preaching a different gospel from that preached by the original apostles.

For Paul this charge was so serious that if it were proved true, he would admit that all his years of preaching had been in vain. As he told the Galatians, he went up to Jerusalem to get a clear decision on this question once and for all. As a test case he took along with him his fellow missionary Titus who, like other Gentile converts, had not been circumcised when he became a Christian. Evidently, Paul's thinking was that if the apostles at Jerusalem thought circumcision was necessary, they would certainly require its observance by a man who was engaged in missionary work along with Paul. It is worth quoting Paul's own account of this visit to Jerusalem here in full:

> Then after fourteen years I went up again to Jerusalem with Barnabas, taking Titus along with me. I went up by revelation; and I laid before them (but privately before those who were of repute) the gospel which I preach among the Gentiles, lest somehow I should be running or had run in vain. But even Titus, who was with me, was not compelled to be circumcised, though he was a Greek. But because of false brethren secretly brought in, who slipped in to spy out our freedom which we have in Christ Jesus, that they might bring us into bondage—to them we did not yield submission even for a moment, that the truth of the gospel might be preserved for you. And from those who were reputed to be something (what they were makes no difference to me; God shows no partiality) those, I say, who were of repute added nothing to me; but on the contrary, when they saw that I had been entrusted with the gospel to the uncircumcised, just as Peter had

been entrusted with the gospel to the circumcised (for he who worked through Peter for the mission to the circumcised worked through me also for the Gentiles), and when they perceived the grace that was given to me, James and Cephas and John, who were reputed to be pillars, gave to me and Barnabas the right hand of fellowship, that we should go to the Gentiles and they to the circumcised; only they would have us remember the poor, which very thing I was eager to do (Gal 2:1–10).

This eloquent account speaks for itself. One point that the English translation does not bring out is that the Greek word translated "fellowship" in verse 9 is *koinonia*. The "right hand of *koinonia*" is a sign that James, Peter and John, on the one hand, and Paul and Barnabas on the other, have the same gospel in common; they are "in communion" concerning the gospel message, including the message of freedom from circumcision for Gentile converts. The reason Paul was so concerned to show that he was in communion with the original apostles in preaching the same gospel, is that it was only if they shared the same faith on the basis of the same gospel that his Gentile churches would be in communion with the churches that had been founded by the older apostles. It is obvious that in Paul's eyes, the many local churches could not be one church, one body of Christ, if they did not have the same faith in common. This was the very essence of the communion that made them the one church of Christ.

Communion in Fraternal Love: Sharing Between Churches

The last verse of the passage we have quoted from Galatians mentions what seems in Paul's eyes to have been the second most important element of communion binding the churches together: namely, the bond of love that showed itself concretely in care for the poor. When Paul says: "They would have us remember the poor, which very thing I was eager to do," what he had in mind was not just the charity that individual Christians would show to their poorer neighbors, but rather the help that his relatively well-off Gentile churches could give to the poor churches of Judea. We do not know why these churches suffered so much from poverty; possibly it was the result of persecution and the confiscation of goods;

possibly it was a consequence of their earlier practice of selling their property and giving it in to be distributed to the poor (cf. Acts 4:32–37). We have the first instance of financial help being sent to the churches of Judea when the disciples at Antioch "determined, everyone according to his ability, to send relief to the brethren who lived in Judea" on the occasion of the famine predicted by the prophet Agabus (Acts 11:27–30). From the context, it seems likely that St. Paul was engaged in ministry in the church of Antioch at that very time.

It was many years later, after Paul had founded a number of Gentile churches in Asia Minor and Greece, that the apostles at Jerusalem urged him to remember the poor, "which very thing," Paul says, "I was eager to do."

If we observe that, in this context, "remembering the poor" meant encouraging his Gentile churches to share their goods with the poor churches of Judea, we will understand why Paul was so eager to do this very thing. It was the most effective way he could think of to show that his Gentile converts, even though they did not observe the Mosaic law as the Jewish Christians did, were truly in communion with them. As the very word *koinonia* means "sharing," "having things in common," this sharing of material goods would be an effective symbol of the deeper sharing of the same faith and the same life in Christ that the Gentiles now had with their Jewish Christian brothers and sisters.

It was for this reason that Paul organized the great collection to be taken up in all the churches he had founded, on behalf of the poor churches of Judea. He devoted two whole chapters of his second letter to the Corinthians to this collection (chap. 8–9), and spoke of it also in his letter to the Romans. We shall quote this shorter passage, which brings out the deep significance which this collection had for Paul.

> At present I am going to Jerusalem with aid for the saints. For Macedonia and Achaia have been pleased to make some contribution for the poor among the saints at Jerusalem; they were pleased to do it, and indeed they are in debt to them, for if the Gentiles have come to share in their spiritual blessings, they ought also to be of service to them in material blessings (Rom 15:25–27)

The original Greek shows, more clearly than the translation, that the underlying motive behind this collection is the *koinonia*, the communion, that binds Paul's Gentile churches together with the Jewish Christian churches of Judea. In verse 26, the word "contribution" is used to translate the Greek *koinonia;* then in verse 27, the phrase "have come to share in" is a verbal form of the same noun. This mutual sharing—of spiritual goods coming from the older Jerusalem church, and of material goods, coming from the richer Gentile churches—would symbolize and strengthen the bond of communion that made them one church. And this explains why Paul was so eager to do this very thing.

In fact he was so eager to accomplish this task that he insisted on going up personally to Jerusalem with the money that had been collected, even though he knew by revelation that imprisonment and afflictions awaited him there (cf. Acts. 20:22–23). On the way he told the elders of the church at Ephesus that this was the last time they would see him in this life (Acts 20:25). But he felt that it was so essential to make this tangible proof of communion between his churches and the churches of Judea that he was ready for suffering and even death in order to accomplish it. In his letter to the Ephesians, Paul said of Christ: "He loved the church and gave himself up for her" (Eph 5:25). One could also say of Paul: "He loved the church, and was ready to die in the cause of her communion."

Ecclesial Communion in the Acts of the Apostles

Needless to say, St. Paul is not the only witness to the sense of communion that bound the early Christians and their local congregations into one church. This is also one of the themes stressed by Luke in the Acts of the Apostles.

The first reference to *koinonia* in Acts is found in the description of the Jerusalem community, after Peter's discourse at Pentecost: "Those who received his word were baptized, and there were added that day about three thousand souls. And they devoted themselves to the apostles' teaching and fellowship, to the breaking of bread and the prayers" (Acts 2:41–42). Here we find the essential elements of ecclesial communion: one baptism, one faith (based on the apostles' teaching), one fellowship (*koinonia*), one Eucharist (the breaking of bread and prayer).

As we have had occasion to mention earlier, the primitive Christian community of Jerusalem expressed this fellowship by the sharing of their possessions. Luke tells us: "All who were baptized were together, and had all things in common, and they sold their possessions and goods and distributed them to all as had any need" (Acts 2:44–45).

Throughout the New Testament period, the Jerusalem church was made up of Jewish Christians who were still observing the Mosaic law (cf. Acts 21:20). It is most significant, therefore, to see how this community reacted to the formation of Christian churches made up of people who were not Jews and did not observe the law. The first such local church was made up of Samaritans who were converted and baptized by Philip, one of the seven leaders of the Greek-speaking Christians at Jerusalem. Luke tells us: "Now when the apostles at Jerusalem heard that Samaria had received the word of God, they sent to them Peter and John, who came down and prayed for them that they might receive the Holy Spirit; for it had not yet fallen on any of them, but they had only been baptized in the name of the Lord Jesus. Then they laid their hands on them and they received the Holy Spirit" (Acts 8:14–16). While Luke does not say this in so many words, it is without doubt his intention, in recounting how the Samaritans received the Holy Spirit through the ministry of the apostles from Jerusalem, to highlight the fact that whereas Jews and Samaritans had long been hostile to one another, now that they shared faith, baptism and the Holy Spirit, they were in communion as members of the one church of the apostles.

The first Christian church made up of converted Gentiles was formed at Antioch, the principal city of Syria, through the preaching of Greek-speaking Christians who had left Jerusalem during the persecution that followed the martyrdom of St. Stephen. Luke tells us: "News of this came to the ears of the church in Jerusalem, and they sent Barnabas to Antioch. When he came and saw the grace of God, he was glad; and he exhorted them all to remain faithful to the Lord with steadfast purpose; for he was a good man, full of the Holy Spirit and of faith. And a large company was added to the Lord" (Acts 11:22–24). Luke had previously introduced Barnabas as a converted Levite, a native of Cyprus, and a prominent member of the

Jerusalem community. Here again we see the sense of oneness linking the Christian churches together, despite the difference of culture and religious observance between them. This oneness was soon to be expressed in a practical way, when the church at Antioch sent relief to the poorer brethren in Judea (Acts 11:27–30). Even the use of the word "brethren" here testifies to the sense of communion binding Jews and Gentiles together in one Christian family.

We have already seen Paul's account of his visit to Jerusalem to settle the question of the freedom of the Gentile converts from the obligation to accept circumcision and observe the ritual prescriptions of the law. Luke's account, while differing in details, agrees with Paul's on the basic fact that the leaders of the Jewish Christian community recognized that the freedom of the Gentile Christians from the law of circumcision was not an obstacle to ecclesial communion. However, there were some pagan practices that were so offensive to Jews that, in the interests of sharing a common life together, it was decided to require of the Gentile Christians that they refrain from such things as eating meat that had been offered in sacrifice to idols, or that still had the animal's blood in it. Such things were so repugnant to Jews that they would have made table-fellowship between Jewish and Gentile Christians impossible. Thus it is clear that the purpose of these regulations was to remove a barrier to a very practical expression of ecclesial communion. The fact that the Jerusalem church would require the observance of such regulations of the Gentile churches of Syria and Cilicia, and that the Christians of these churches "rejoiced at the exhortation" given them by the emissaries who brought them the decision from Jerusalem, gives eloquent witness to their sense of being in communion as one church.

Ecclesial Communion in the Fourth Gospel

While the word "church" does not occur in the fourth gospel, it is certainly the church that is meant when Jesus declares: "I have other sheep that are not of this fold; I must bring them also, and they will heed my voice. So there shall be one flock, one shepherd" (Jn 10:16). It is generally agreed that the "other sheep" who are not of the fold are the Gentiles. Hence this saying is to be understood as a reference to the future Christian church that will be made up of Jews and Gentiles. Here the essential bond of communion, making them "one flock," is the fact that all belong to the one shepherd, having heard his voice, that is, having responded to his call to faith. Here it is Jesus himself whose voice the future believers in him will hear.

Of course they will actually hear his voice through the preaching of his disciples. This is brought out in Jesus' prayer for the unity of his future church: "I do not pray for these only, but also for those who believe in me through their word, that they may all be one; even as thou, Father, art in me, and I in thee, that they also may be in us, so that the world may believe that thou hast sent me. The glory which thou hast given me I have given to them, that they may be one even as we are one, I in them and thou in me, that they may become perfectly one, so that the world may know that thou hast sent me and hast loved them even as thou hast loved me" (Jn 17:20–23). Here the bond of unity is the fact that all will believe in Jesus through the word of his disciples, for whose unity Jesus has already prayed (17:11). Hence the future church will be a community marked by apostolic faith (based on the witness of the apostles), and by visible unity (since its unity will be a sign bringing others to believe in Jesus).

The first letter of John describes this witness of the apostles in the following terms: "That which we have seen and heard we proclaim also to you, so that you may have fellowship with us; and our fellowship is with the Father and with his Son Jesus Christ" (1 Jn 1:3). Here the word translated "fellowship" is the Greek *koinonia;* it is through communion with the original disciples of Jesus that all who accept their witness in faith will have communion with God the Father and with his Son Jesus Christ. Here again the essential bond of unity is a common faith based on the witness of the apostles. Without the word "church" being used, we have another testimony to the communion by which the many Christians and their many churches are one church of Christ.

Ecclesial Communion During the Patristic Period

The church historian Ludwig Hertling has treated this topic in very readable fashion in a little book, translated with an introduction by Jared Wicks under the title: *Communio: Church and Papacy in Early*

Christianity.[39] Since space does not permit our going into detail here, we shall mention some of the highlights of this book, recommending its reading to those desirous of a more complete picture.

By the middle of the second century, the church in each locality was under the leadership of a single bishop. Hertling describes ecclesial communion as "the bond that united the bishops and the faithful, the bishops among themselves, and the faithful among themselves, a bond that was both effected and at the same time made manifest by eucharistic communion."[40] The word "communion" was not the only term the early Christians used of this bond of unity; such terms as "peace," "love," "harmony" and "concord" were also used as synonyms of *communio* or *koinonia.* Thus, for instance, the words *in pace* (in peace), found so frequently on Christian tombs, refer to the fact that the person had lived and died "in the peace of the church," that is, in Christian communion.

The essential condition for being in the communion of the church was to be in communion with one's local bishop, which meant professing the faith as it was taught by the bishop. Profession of this faith was required when a person entered the Christian community by baptism, and persevering in the same faith was a condition for sharing the Eucharist which the bishop celebrated for his church. Communion in the Eucharist was the visible expression of the bond that united the Christians of a local church with their bishop and with one another. Christians guilty of grave offenses against the faith (heresy) or against church unity (schism), or who were living scandalous lives, were excluded from sharing in the Eucharist until they repented and were reconciled with the church by their bishop.

Christian faith and the Eucharist were likewise the essential bonds of communion linking the bishops, and, through them, the many local churches, in the communion of the one universal church. Various practices helped to express and strengthen these bonds of communion. One such practice was for bishops to furnish Christians about to take a journey with letters recommending them to the bishops of the various churches along their way. This would insure the Christian traveler not only of being admitted to the Eucharist in each church, but also of being given hospitality by its bishop. This practice also made it necessary for bishops to keep up-to-date lists of the bishops of other cities, and facilitated their correspondence with each other, since traveling Christians would carry such letters for them.

Unfortunately it sometimes happened that a bishop would lead his church into heresy, and then it was important for orthodox bishops aware of this to inform the others of this fact, so as to warn them against communicating with a heretical bishop. Since sharing the same Eucharist was the tangible sign of being in communion, it was taken for granted that to receive the Eucharist from a heretical bishop meant being in communion with him, and hence forfeiting communion with the orthodox bishops and their churches.

In the second part of his book, Fr. Hertling shows how communion with the bishop of Rome came to be recognized as a sure criterion of being in the rightful Christian communion. We shall not dwell on this point here. It is sufficient for our purpose to have seen some indications of how conscious the early Christians were of the fact that through their communion of faith and Eucharist with their local bishop, they were in communion with the whole Christian church throughout the world.

"Church" and "Churches" in the Documents of Vatican II

We have seen that the writers of the New Testament and the early church saw no conflict in speaking of one church and of many churches, because they understood the one church to be the communion of the many churches, each of which was simply the church as it was effectively present in a particular place.

It is time now to see what light the documents of Vatican II shed on our topic: "the one church: a communion of churches." We shall take these terms in reverse order: first "churches," then "communion," and finally "the one church," in each case looking for the meaning they have in the documents of the council.

The Catholic Churches

As we have seen, the council used the term "churches" in speaking of the separated eastern churches as well as of the churches in communion with Rome. We shall first look at the places where it speaks of the Roman Catholic churches, beginning with the most local of these: the parochial congregations. These are described in LG 28, where the council, speaking of the ministry of parish priests, says: "As they sanctify and govern under the bishop's authority that part of the Lord's flock entrusted to them, they make the universal church visible in their own locality." And a bit further on: "Having become from the heart a pattern to the flock (1 Pet 5:3), let them so lead and serve their local church that it may worthily be called by that name by which the one and entire people of God is distinguished: namely, the church of God (cf. 1 Cor 1:2; 2 Cor 1:1 and passim)." The scriptural references here suggest that as St. Paul could speak of the church at Corinth as "the church of God," as the "body of Christ" (1 Cor 12), as the "bride of Christ" (2 Cor 11:2) and as the "temple of the Holy Spirit" (1 Cor 3:16–17), so one can apply all these terms also to each parochial congregation. Each is *the* church as it is made present and visible in its particular place. The one church is above all made effectively present when the local church is an actual "congregation," that is, when it is gathered for the liturgy of word and sacrament at the Eucharist. It is the very nature of the Eucharist that it can only be celebrated locally: in a particular place with a particular congregation. This fact gives a unique importance to the local church as "the church of God in this place."

However, the parochial congregation lacks something essential for the ongoing life of the church: namely, the capacity to provide for its future ministry by ordination. For this, each parish depends on its being in communion with a bishop, and thus being a particular church within the larger church under the care of a bishop: the diocese. *Lumen gentium* speaks of the diocesan churches when it describes the pastoral role of bishops: "The individual bishops are the visible principle and foundation of unity in their particular churches, which are fashioned on the model of the universal church. It is in and from such individual churches that the one unique Catholic Church has its existence" (LG 23).

The Decree on the Bishops' Pastoral Office in the Church (*Christus Dominus*) also speaks of the particular churches under the pastoral care of bishops, when it describes the diocese.

> A diocese is that portion of God's people which is entrusted to a bishop to be shepherded by him with the cooperation of the pres-

bytery. Adhering thus to its pastor and gathered together by him in the Holy Spirit through the gospel and the Eucharist, this portion constitutes a particular church in which the one, holy, catholic and apostolic church of Christ is truly present and operative (CD 11).

In the last paragraph of *Lumen gentium* 23, the council moves from the diocesan churches to speak of particular churches, each of which comprises a number of dioceses. What justifies speaking of such a group of dioceses as one particular church is the fact that they share a common discipline, liturgical usage, and theological and spiritual heritage. In some cases they are also united in the fact that all the bishops recognize the authority of a patriarch over their church.

Within the Catholic Church, the most obvious examples of such particular churches are the eastern Catholic churches, which are the subject of a special decree of the Second Vatican Council: *Orientalium ecclesiarum*. These are also referred to as the "eastern rites," but the council clearly prefers to call them "churches." What is distinctive of these churches is that, while they are in communion with Rome, their canonical, liturgical, theological and spiritual traditions are rather of eastern than of western Christianity. In most cases, each of these eastern Catholic churches is united under the authority of a patriarch (cf. OE 7–11).

As distinct from these churches of the eastern rites, all the churches of the Latin rite together make up the western church, which must also be recognized as a particular church. This is the "Latin Catholic Church," a term which must not be taken as synonymous with "Roman Catholic," since the latter embraces all the churches in communion with Rome, including the eastern Catholic churches.

The Eastern Churches Separated from Rome

The third chapter of the Decree on Ecumenism, entitled "Churches and Ecclesial Communities Separated from the Roman Apostolic See," is divided into two parts, the first of which is entitled: "The Special Position of the Eastern Churches." It is important to observe that whenever the Decree on Ecumenism speaks of eastern churches, it refers to those that are separated from Rome. These include the churches that use the title "Orthodox" (those that accept the decisions of the seven ecumenical councils of the first millennium), as well as others, such as the Nestorian and Coptic churches, which rejected one or another of these councils.

As we have already seen in the preceding chapter, there can be no doubt about the fact that, despite their separation from Rome, these eastern Christian communities are recognized as particular churches, comparable, if not equal in every respect, to the particular churches of the Catholic Church. The language the council uses in describing them is unequivocal in this respect. Here are some of the more pertinent passages of this section of the Decree on Ecumenism.

> This most sacred Synod gladly reminds all of one highly significant fact among others: in the East there flourish many particular or local Churches; among them the Patriarchal Churches hold first place; and of these, many glory in taking their origins from the apostles themselves. As a result, there prevailed and still prevails among Orientals an eager desire to perpetuate in a communion of faith and charity those family ties which ought to thrive between local Churches, as between sisters (14b).

> Therefore, this sacred Synod urges all, but especially those who plan to devote themselves to the work of restoring the full communion that is desired between the Eastern Churches and the Catholic Church, to give due consideration to these special aspects of the origin and growth of the Churches of the East, and to the character of the relations which obtained between them and the Roman See before the separation, and to form for themselves a correct evaluation of these facts (14c).

> Everybody knows with what love the Eastern Christians enact the sacred liturgy, especially the celebration of the Eucharist, which is the source of the Church's life and the pledge of future glory. Hence, through the celebration of the Eucharist of the Lord in each of these Churches, the Church of God is built up and grows in stature, while through the rite of concelebration their bond with one another is made manifest (15a).

> Although these Churches are separated from us, they possess true sacraments, above all—by apostolic succession—the priest-

hood and the Eucharist, whereby they are still joined to us in a very close relationship. Therefore, given suitable circumstances and the approval of Church authority, some worship in common is not merely possible but is recommended (15c).

After reading the very positive description of the separated eastern churches in UR 14–18, one might ask whether the council intends to say that, as far as their qualification to be recognized as "particular churches" is concerned, the separated eastern churches are just as fully "churches" as are the particular Catholic churches. While there is no clear answer to this question in the section of the Decree on Ecumenism from which we have been quoting, a negative reply seems to be necessary, in the light of a statement made earlier in the Decree, n. 3, which says: "It is through the Catholic Church alone, which is the universal help toward salvation, that the fullness of the means of salvation can be obtained. It was to the apostolic college alone, of which Peter is the head, that we believe our Lord entrusted all the blessings of the new covenant, in order to establish on earth the one Body of Christ into which all those should be fully incorporated who already belong in any way to God's people." Now if it is through the Catholic Church alone that the fullness of the means of salvation can be had, it follows that the separated churches must lack some such means of salvation. But this in turn would mean that they lack something that pertains to the very nature of a church. If one asks what this lack would be in the case of the Orthodox Churches, the answer could be indicated by the reference to Peter as the head of the apostolic college. It would seem that the "Petrine ministry" itself is to be understood as a "means of salvation," in the sense that it is a ministry for the unity of the church and its perseverance in the true faith.

While the decree does not spell this out, it would seem to be a logical conclusion from what it does say. At the same time, however, it is clear that the council did not hesitate to recognize the separated eastern communities as particular churches, and that, in doing so, it was using the term "churches" in a strictly theological, and not a merely conventional way. An authoritative confirmation of this assertion can be seen in the fact that Pope Paul VI repeatedly referred to the separated eastern churches as "sister churches."[41]

The Separated "Ecclesial Communities"

In the preceding chapter we have suggested that the council's distinction between "churches" and "ecclesial communities" is based on the principle that there is not the full reality of church where there is not the full reality of the Eucharist. That this is the reason for the distinction is implied by the fact that in UR 22c it is only about "the ecclesial communities separated from us" that the council states: "We believe that especially because of the lack of the sacrament of orders they have not preserved the genuine and total reality of the Eucharistic mystery." Confirmation of this interpretation of the text is had in a report given to the bishops by the commission responsible for this text. Explaining the title of the second part of chapter three, which reads: "The Separated Churches and Ecclesial Communities in the West," the commission observed: "It is to be noted that among the separated communities there are some, namely the Old Catholics, which, like the Orthodox communities, should be called churches, according to sound theological doctrine admitted by all Catholics, in view of the valid sacrament of orders and valid Eucharist which they possess."[42]

This statement makes it perfectly clear that the council considered the presence of valid orders and Eucharist so essential to the nature of a church that they preferred not to use this term of those communities lacking them. It is to be noted, however, that while this report singled out the Old Catholic Church as a western church having valid orders and Eucharist, it was not the intention of the council to specify in its decree which of the western communities it recognized as churches (implying the recognition of their orders and Eucharist as valid). Thus, for instance, the council certainly did not intend to make any statement concerning the validity of Anglican orders.

In this connection one might ask whether Pope Paul VI's use of the term "church" when speaking of the Anglican communion can be taken to imply his recognition of the validity of Anglican orders.[43] Since it is most unlikely that he would have chosen so indirect a way to reverse the decision taken by Pope Leo XIII in this matter, one must conclude that his use of the term "church" did not always have the same significance that it had in the documents of the council. It is also evident that in ecumenical discussions since the council, most Catholics will call "churches" all those separated communities that prefer to be called by that title, noting that there are some that prefer not to be so called.

What remains to be considered is the important question: what did the council intend to say about these communities when it described them with the adjective "ecclesial"? The use of this word itself surely signifies a recognition of their "churchly" character. In the preceding chapter we have already quoted a section of the official report of the conciliar commission, explaining the use of this term. It is important enough to warrant quoting again here.

> It must not be overlooked that the communities that have their origin in the separation that took place in the West are not merely a sum or collection of individual Christians, but they are constituted by social ecclesiastical elements which they have preserved from our common patrimony, and which confer on them a truly ecclesial character. In these communities the one sole Church of Christ is present, albeit imperfectly, in a way that is somewhat like its presence in particular churches, and by means of their ecclesiastical elements the Church of Christ is in some way operative in them.[44]

This report shows that in the judgment of the commission, these communities are rightly called "ecclesial" because they are analogous to particular churches of the Catholic Church. In the decree *Christus Dominus*, n. 11, the council describes a Catholic diocese as "a particular church in which the one holy catholic and apostolic Church of Christ is truly present and operative." What the commission says about the "ecclesial communities" is that the one church of Christ is present and operative in them, too—but in a way that is imperfect, is "somewhat like" its presence in those that are particular churches in the full sense.

While carefully qualified, the fundamental assertion remains: the one sole church of Christ is present and operative in these ecclesial communities. And that has to mean that, conversely, each of them, in some real though imperfect way, makes the church of Christ effectively present as an instrument of salvation in a particular place for a particular group of people. This is coherent with the recognition by the council that these ecclesial communities "have by no means been deprived of significance and importance in the mystery of salvation. For the Holy Spirit has not refrained from using them as means of salvation" (UR 3). In a real but imperfect way, the ecclesial communities participate in the nature and function of the one church of Christ as "sacrament of salvation."

It must be remembered, of course, that any judgments about "imperfection" or "defects" regarding these communities refers to the lack of some element which Catholics believe to be necessary for the institutional integrity of a church. There is no claim that a church having the fullness of the means of grace will necessarily be a holier Christian community than one lacking something of such fullness.

Ecclesial Communion in the Documents of Vatican II

We have already seen that the concept of communion involves the bond of unity that is formed among those who have something in common. The adjective "ecclesial" means that the things that are held in common pertain to the nature of the church: such as sharing faith, baptism and other sacraments, and belonging to a Christian community. Limiting our attention here to the kind of communion that is specifically ecclesial, we are transmitting to another chapter the consideration of a spiritual communion which can be shared by people who do not have Christian faith, and yet are living in the state of grace. Their communion with Christians who are in the state of grace is a real communion, but it is not strictly ecclesial, and we are not considering it here.

Ecclesial Communion within the Catholic Church

We begin by seeing how Vatican II describes the communion that binds Catholics and their particular churches together in the one Catholic Church.

Lumen gentium describes the links by which Catholics are incorporated into the church in the following way:

> They are fully incorporated into the society of the Church who, possessing the Spirit of Christ, accept her entire system and all

the means of salvation given to her, and through union with her visible structure are joined to Christ, who rules her through the Supreme Pontiff and the bishops. This joining is effected by the bonds of professed faith, of the sacraments, of ecclesiastical government, and of communion. He is not saved, however, who, though he is part of the body of the Church, does not persevere in charity. He remains indeed in the bosom of the Church, but, as it were, only in a "bodily" manner and not "in his heart." (LG 14)

It is certain that the expression "possessing the Spirit of Christ" used here is equivalent to the more common expression: "being in the state of grace." A distinction is drawn between Catholics who are fully incorporated in the church, and others who remain incorporated, but not fully. Full incorporation, which is the same as full communion, requires the spiritual bond of the state of grace, but it requires other bonds as well: "of professed Catholic faith, of sacraments, of ecclesiastical government, and of communion." Catholics who retain these latter bonds, but are not in the state of grace, are in a situation of imperfect communion with the Church.

This is an extremely significant development in Catholic doctrine about ecclesial communion. It follows logically from the nature of the church as a complex reality: as both a spiritual community and a sacramental, hierarchical society. Since the church is both of these, full incorporation in it must involve participating in it spiritually as well as sacramentally and juridically. This means that full ecclesial communion involves a complex of different kinds of bonds linking people to the church and to one another. "Having the Spirit of Christ" is by far the most important, but, being a purely spiritual bond, it is fully knowable only to God. The profession of the same faith and the reception of the same sacraments constitute communion in the distinctively ecclesial means of grace. The church, as St. Thomas Aquinas declared, is formed by the faith and the sacraments.[45] So up to here we are dealing with a communion that results from our sharing in grace and the ecclesial means of grace. I suggest that this can be called "theological communion," because it is based on a sharing in things that affect our relationship with God.

There follow the bonds of ecclesiastical government and of communion. Here we are dealing with bonds that consist in the kind of relationships that bind people to one another. For Catholics to be linked to the church by the "bond of ecclesiastical government" means that they recognize their parish priest, their diocesan bishop and the Pope, as their lawful pastors, and in turn they are recognized by their pastors as members of their flock. This relationship is of the juridical order: that is, it involves the mutual recognition of rights and duties between human persons. The Catholic acknowledges certain obligations regarding his parish priest, bishop and the Pope, and they in turn recognize his right to their pastoral care and ministry. We call this "juridical communion."

At this point the question arises: what did the council have in mind by the last term in the list of bonds linking Catholics to the church: "and of communion"? Surely those already mentioned in the list involve communion, both theological (faith and sacraments) and juridical (ecclesiastical government). It would seem likely that in this context, the distinct bond of "communion" refers to the relationships which bind Catholics together in the life of the church as a community. It would embrace all those ways in which Catholics express their solidarity with one another as members of the same church. Perhaps "fellowship" is the best word to express this aspect of ecclesial communion.

An important difference must be noted between theological communion and juridical communion. Since the former means sharing in grace and the means of grace, and since these are realities of which people can have more or less, it is the nature of theological communion that it admits of degrees of fullness. A Catholic in the state of grace has a fullness of communion which the Catholic in the state of unrepented grave sin does not have. This is also a difference of communion in sacramental life, since the Catholic who is not in the state of grace must refrain from receiving the Eucharist.

On the other hand, a Catholic who renounces his allegiance to his bishop or to the Pope has broken off his juridical communion with the church entirely. Such a relationship does not admit of degrees; either one recognizes the local Catholic bishop and the Pope as one's legitimate pastors or one does not. Besides, renouncing allegiance to the pastors of the Catholic Church would normally mean a break with the Catholic church community as well.

To sum up: full ecclesial communion in the Catholic Church is a complex reality, involving the fullness of theological communion in grace, faith and sacramental life, juridical communion with the pastors of the Catholic Church, and fellowship with the Catholic community.

Another important treatment of Catholic ecclesial communion is found in the Decree on Ecumenism, n. 2. Here the council first stresses the role of the Holy Spirit, who, it says, "brings about that marvelous communion of the faithful and joins them together so intimately that he is the principle of the Church's unity." But the Holy Spirit does not accomplish this purpose without human cooperation. Rather, "it is through the faithful preaching of the gospel by the apostles and their successors—the bishops with Peter's successor at their head—through their administration of the sacraments, and through their loving exercise of authority that Jesus Christ wishes his people to increase under the influence of the Holy Spirit. Thereby, too, he perfects his people's communion in unity: in the confession of one faith, in the common celebration of divine worship, and in the fraternal harmony of the family of God."

Here we see that full Catholic communion, while ultimately attributed to the Holy Spirit as its "principle," calls for the exercise of the threefold ministry of word, sacraments and pastoral leadership. The immediate fruit of this ministry is the visible unity of the church in the profession of faith, sacramental life and fellowship, but the ultimate purpose is the interior, spiritual communion of the church in faith, charity, and the life of grace in the Holy Spirit.

The One Catholic Church: A Communion of Churches

Up to this point, we have been speaking of the bonds of communion that link Catholics to their church. Now we turn to the communion by which the many particular Catholic churches are one Catholic Church.

The visible sign that all the Catholic parishes in a given area form one particular Catholic Church is the fact that all their parish priests are in full communion with the bishop of the diocese. Similarly, all the Catholic dioceses in the world are manifestly one Catholic Church because all their bishops are in full communion with each other and with the Pope, whom they all recognize as their supreme pastor.

The juridical communion which binds the Catholic bishops to

each other and to the Pope is called "hierarchical communion."[46] It consists in the mutual recognition of their rights and duties with respect to one another and with respect to the Pope, as lawfully constituted pastors of the Catholic Church. All the bishops who are linked by this bond of hierarchical communion are members of the episcopal college, of which the bishop of Rome is the head.

The communion binding all the particular Catholic churches together in the one Catholic Church is "full communion," both theological and juridical. It is important to note, however, that such full communion does not require a uniformity of canonical, liturgical, theological and spiritual traditions. This is most clearly seen in the fact that the eastern Catholic churches are in the full communion of the Catholic Church, while maintaining their own eastern traditions. It must be admitted that the important distinction between "full communion" and "total uniformity" has not always been understood or put into practice in the history of the Catholic Church, especially in regard to the eastern churches. However, the Second Vatican Council insisted strongly on this distinction, especially in its decree on the eastern Catholic churches, and in the following passage of *Lumen gentium* n. 23:

> Moreover, within the Church particular Churches hold a rightful place. These Churches retain their own traditions without in any way lessening the primacy of the Chair of Peter. This Chair presides over the whole assembly of charity and protects legitimate differences, while at the same time it sees that such differences do not hinder unity but rather contribute toward it.

Communion between the Catholic Church and the Separated Churches

Since the full communion of the Catholic Church includes the "hierarchical communion" by which all its bishops recognize the supreme pastoral authority of the Pope and are recognized by him as the lawful pastors of their particular churches, it is obvious that the separated eastern churches are not in full communion with the Catholic Church. However, as we have seen, ecclesial communion is a complex reality, consisting of both theological and juridical aspects. The Second Vatican Council, especially in its Decree on Ecumen-

ism, nos. 14–18, has made it clear that there is indeed a very great
degree of theological communion between the Catholic Church and
the juridically separated Churches of the eastern tradition. The various elements of such communion are described in the passage of
that decree which we have quoted above.[47] It suffices to say here
that the Council has recognized the existing bonds of communion in
faith and sacramental life to be such as to justify a considerable degree of mutual sharing of the Eucharist and other sacraments between Catholics and the Orthodox, even before juridical
communion is restored.[48] This change of church discipline is striking proof of the depth of theological communion which the Catholic
Church recognizes has actually persisted between itself and the eastern churches despite almost a thousand years of juridical separation.

Communion with the Ecclesial Communities of the West

It is clear that these communities are not in juridical communion with the Catholic Church. Furthermore, as we have seen, the
use of the term "ecclesial community" rather than "church" indicates that we are speaking of those communities which "because of
the lack of the sacrament of orders have not preserved the genuine
and total reality of the eucharistic mystery" (UR 22). This involves
a defect of theological communion as far as sacramental life is concerned, and severely limits the possibility of the kind of eucharistic
sharing that the council recommended with the separated bodies it
called "churches." Furthermore, as far as theological communion in
faith is concerned, the degree to which Catholics and other Christians can be said to share a common faith will depend on the beliefs
of each particular community. Hence it is very difficult to make general statements in this regard.

However, in the section of the Decree on Ecumenism entitled
"The Separated Churches and Ecclesial Communities of the West,"
the council does speak of a number of elements of faith and sacramental life which constitute bonds of existing theological communion between the Catholic Church and the various ecclesial
communities (UR 20–23). There is communion in basic Christian
faith among all those "who openly confess Jesus Christ as God and
Lord and as the sole mediator between God and man unto the glory

of the one God, Father Son and Holy Spirit" (UR 20). There is "a love, veneration and near cult of the sacred Scriptures" in which these Christians seek to hear the voice of God and contemplate the life and teachings of Christ (UR 21) There is the sacrament of baptism, by which the Christian "becomes truly incorporated into the crucified and glorified Christ and is reborn to a sharing of the divine life. . . . Baptism, therefore, constitutes a sacramental bond of unity linking all who have been reborn by means of it" (UR 22). Furthermore, while these communities do not have "the genuine and total reality of the eucharistic mystery," still, "when they commemorate the Lord's death and resurrection in the Holy Supper, they profess that it signifies life in communion with Christ and they await his coming in glory" (UR 22). Indeed, their worship "sometimes displays notable features of an ancient common liturgy" (UR 23).

Speaking of individual Christians who belong to these communities, the council declares: "All who believe in Christ and have been properly baptized are brought into a certain, though imperfect, communion with the Catholic Church" (UR 3). What we wish to point out here is that we can rightly speak of a certain though imperfect communion which links these ecclesial communities as such with the Catholic Church. For, as the conciliar commission insisted, they are not a mere sum of individual Christians. If their members are in communion with us by reason of their Christian faith and baptism, it is because their communities have preserved and handed on this faith to them and have initiated them into Christian life by baptism. Everything that justifies speaking of these communities as "ecclesial" actually constitutes a bond of ecclesial communion linking them to the Catholic Church.

The One Church of Christ:
A Communion of Christian Churches

One of the "Catholic principles of ecumenism" enunciated by the council is that the unity which Christ bestowed on his church is something she can never lose; indeed, it "subsists" in the Catholic Church (UR 4). It is clear that the unity intended by this statement is the full communion: theological, juridical, hierarchical, which links all the particular Catholic churches in the one Catholic

Church. If one were to insist that the church of Christ can be found only where there is such full communion linking all its particular churches, then one would have to identify the church of Christ in an exclusive way with the Roman Catholic Church. Undoubtedly, this was the common teaching in the Catholic Church prior to Vatican II.

However, as we have seen, in the opening to ecumenism which the Second Vatican Council espoused, a new understanding of the dimensions of Christ's church became possible. The key elements in this new understanding are: (1) the recognition of the nature of the church as a communion of particular churches; (2) the recognition that outside the limits of the Roman Catholic Church there are not merely "elements of church," but there are "churches and ecclesial communities"; (3) the recognition that there exists a real, though imperfect, ecclesial communion linking these churches and ecclesial communities with the Catholic Church.

Drawing these elements together, we propose that, in the presently divided state of Christianity, one can and must recognize that the one church of Christ exists not only where there is full ecclesial communion, but also where there are particular Christian churches that are linked together in the sharing of the same sacramental and eucharistic life and the sharing of substantially the same faith, even though there is not the fullness of juridical communion between them. Admittedly, this is not the full unity which Christ wishes his church to have. But it is a genuine and high degree of theological communion among bodies all of which the council has recognized as particular churches.

Did the council ever speak of the Catholic Church and the separated eastern churches together as one church? It seems that it did, when it said: "Through the celebration of the Eucharist of the Lord in each of these [separated eastern] churches, the Church of God is built up and grows in stature" (UR 15). It does not seem possible that the council meant exclusively the Roman Catholic Church when it spoke of the "Church of God" which is built up by the celebration of the Eucharist in the separated eastern churches. It is equally unlikely that it meant only the church of the east. We conclude that the "Church of God" has to be understood here as the communion of all the particular churches in which the Eucharist is validly celebrated, even though they are not all in full juridical communion with one another.

Among Catholic theologians who have discussed this question since the council, Louis Bouyer is one who has been particularly forthright in upholding the position we are advocating here. To the question whether the long-standing separation between east and west has meant the loss of the church's unity, he has replied: "To this question only one response can be made, namely, that the Orthodox Church and the Catholic Church, although both have been terribly tempted by the spirit of division, continue nevertheless to be one sole church, in spite of all appearances to the contrary."[49]

Yves Congar has expressed his agreement with the position taken by Bouyer, and has seen confirmation of it in an expression that Pope Paul VI used in his letter of July 25, 1967 to Patriarch Athenagoras. In this very cordial letter, in which he described himself as "the bishop of the Church of Rome and the head of the Catholic Church," and spoke of the "eastern church" and the "western church" as "sister-churches," Paul VI declared it to be his determination to do everything within his power that would be of benefit to "the universal holy Church."[50] Congar, I believe rightly, takes this last expression as an indication that Paul VI believed that, despite the imperfect communion between them, the "sister-churches" of east and west were still together in the "universal holy Church."[51]

The One Church: A Communion of Churches and Ecclesial Communities?

Can one extend the limits of the church of Christ so as to include the "ecclesial communities," taking this term to mean those which do not have "the genuine and total reality of the eucharistic mystery"? Obviously, this is more problematic, because we are no longer dealing with "churches" in the sense in which Vatican II was willing to use this term. However, the council recognized the ecclesial character of these communities, and the theological commission explained that this must mean that the church of Christ is somehow present and operative in them. We believe this justifies our saying that, in a qualified sense, the ecclesial communities are within the limits of the one church of Christ.

This proposal is based, first of all, on the unicity of the church. Since this means that there is and can be only one church, it follows that there can be "churches" only insofar as in some real way they all participate in the reality of the one church. The universal church has to be understood as a communion of churches; otherwise every use of the term "church" in the plural would contradict the unicity of the church.

Secondly, Vatican II recognized that both terms, "communion" and "churches," admit of greater or lesser degrees of fullness or perfection. The council recognized the existence of real though imperfect communion where there is not full theological or juridical communion. It acknowledged the ecclesial character of bodies that it was not prepared to call "churches" in the full sense of the term.

We propose that the nature of the one church as a communion of churches is still verified, in an analogous and imperfect way, when one extends it to include the ecclesial communities.

In this hypothesis, what would be the outer limits of the church? The presence of the church can be recognized only where there is an ecclesial community of Christian faith and sacramental life (the latter consisting at least in the use of the sacrament of baptism and some form of the celebration of the Lord's supper). Beyond these limits there is certainly the presence of Christ's grace and the possibility of salvation, but there is not the ecclesial reality that we mean by church.

At this point the question may be raised whether the view proposed here is one that Catholics are free to hold, in view of the statement made by the Congregation for the Doctrine of the Faith in its Declaration *Mysterium Ecclesiae*, to the effect that "Catholics are not to imagine that Christ's Church is nothing more than a collection (divided but still possessing a certain unity) of churches and ecclesial communities."[52]

I am convinced that there are significant differences between the proposal made above and the opinion censured by the Congregation. First of all, the idea that "Christ's Church is nothing more than a collection of churches and ecclesial communities" would seem to reduce the Catholic Church to the status of being merely one among the many churches of such a "collection," ignoring the crucial fact that it is in the Catholic Church alone that the church of

Christ subsists with the unity and integrity of doctrine and structure that Christ intends it to have.

Secondly, to describe Christ's church as "nothing more than a collection (divided, but still possessing a certain unity)" suggests a mere juxtaposition of bodies that have nothing but a very superficial relationship to one another. Such a mere "collection" (the Latin text has *summa*) would be something essentially different from what has been proposed here, which is based on the theological concept, endorsed by the council, of a real though imperfect ecclesial communion linking bodies all of which have ecclesial character, even though some are less fully churches than others. What we are proposing is that where there are ecclesial communities linked by ecclesial communion, there is some real, however imperfect, presence of Christ's church. This by no means contradicts Catholic belief that the fullness of church and the fullness of ecclesial communion are found only in the Catholic Church.

Nor does it prevent our saying (if we still wish to use the expression) that the Catholic Church is the "one true church of Christ," provided that by "true church of Christ" we mean the church that has preserved the unity and institutional integrity that Christ wants his church to have. But, in the light of the Decree on Ecumenism, we can hardly still intend to make the exclusive claim made in the preparatory *schema de Ecclesia* to the effect that "only the one that is Roman Catholic has the right to be called Church."[53]

If the church of Christ is still to be found even where ecclesial communion is not as full as it ought to be, we have to admit that the church, as it exists today, does not have the unity that Christ wants it to have. However, if we have to admit that the church is not as holy as it ought to be, can we not also admit that it is not as one as it ought to be? Indeed, is not this admission the basic reason for the ecumenical movement?

But is it true that the church is not as holy as it ought to be? This is the question to which we must now turn our attention.

4 || "Marked with a Genuine Though Imperfect Holiness"

The phrase we are using as the title of this chapter is found in *Lumen gentium* 48, where the council is describing what it calls "the eschatological nature of the pilgrim church." The fact that the church in this world is "marked with a genuine holiness" is seen as a consequence of its "eschatological nature"; the fact that its holiness is "imperfect" is a consequence of its being a "pilgrim church." These are ideas that we must spell out in this chapter.

Another key statement of Vatican II about the holiness of the church is found in the opening paragraph of *Lumen gentium* chapter 5, on "The Call of the Whole Church to Holiness," which begins: "Faith teaches us that the church, whose mystery is being set forth by this sacred Synod, is indefectibly holy" (LG 39).[54] We shall have to ask what it means to claim that the church is "indefectibly holy," what grounds there are for this claim, and how the church can be both "indefectibly holy" and "imperfectly holy" at the same time. This statement also reminds us that the church that is believed to be indefectibly holy is the church "whose mystery is being set forth" by the council. At the beginning of our consideration of the holiness of the church, then, we recall what we said in our first chapter to the effect that what makes the church a "mystery" is its nature as one "complex reality" composed of divine and human elements: being both a spiritual communion of faith, hope and charity, and a hierarchically structured society. From the start, then, we have to keep in mind this complex nature of the church, so as not to fall into the trap of imagining two churches: one a holy "mystical body" and "bride of Christ" and the other a corrupt and sinful hierarchical society. The mystery of the church, which is also the mystery of her holiness, consists precisely in the fact that there is only one church which is both "mystical body" and sinful people. Or, to put it more acutely, the mystery is that the church is the people of God which, as consisting of real *people*, is inevitably marked by sin, but, as people *of God*, cannot fail to be holy.

Taking in order the key ideas suggested in the two sentences we have quoted from *Lumen gentium*, we shall consider, first, what is meant by "genuine holiness"; second, in what sense and for what reasons the church is believed to be "indefectibly holy"; and third, how the church can be both "indefectibly" and "imperfectly" holy at the same time.

What Is "Genuine Holiness"?

The Christian notion of holiness is derived from the Bible, where God alone is recognized as the truly Holy One, where the essential affirmation about God is the cry of the seraphim in Isaiah's vision: "Holy, holy, holy is the Lord of hosts" (Is 6:3), and God's description of himself is seen in the command: "You shall be holy, for I the Lord your God am holy" (Lev 19:2). To ask of the biblical writers in what the holiness of God consists is to ask what makes God to be God and makes him different from everything else that exists.

It follows that for any creature to be holy can only mean that in some way it derives its holiness from God. A person or thing can be holy only insofar as it is made holy by God and for God. It is God who makes creatures holy, by separating them from all that is profane, or not associated with God, and in some way bringing them into a relationship with himself that gives them a share in holiness. The biblical notion of holiness, then, involves a "being set apart" from what is not of God, so as to belong in a special way to God.

Hence, while the Bible knows God alone to be the "Holy One," it does not hesitate to speak of a holy people, holy temple, holy assembly, holy land, holy commandments. All of these are holy, but only because and insofar as God has made them holy. Thus, the holiness of the people is due to God's initiative: "For you are a people holy to the Lord your God; the Lord your God has chosen you to be a people for his own possession, out of all the peoples that are on the face of the earth" (Dt 7:6). The temple and its priests are holy because they have been set apart and consecrated to the service and worship of God; so also God has set apart his chosen people to be "a kingdom of priests and a holy nation" (Ex 19:6).

The initiative always comes from God, but a response is called for from the people: "And the Lord said to Moses: 'Say to all the congregation of the people of Israel, You shall be holy, for I the Lord your God am holy. Every one of you shall revere his mother and his father, and you shall keep my sabbaths: I am the Lord your God. Do not turn to idols or make for yourselves molten gods; I am the Lord your God" (Lev 19:1–4).

Biblical holiness, then, is a gift given by God, but it is also a commandment to be obeyed; it is an indicative: "You are holy," but also an imperative: "Be holy."

The New Testament derives its notion of holiness from the Old, and likewise sees it both as a gift given and a command to be fulfilled. Thus, Paul addresses the Corinthians as "those sanctified in Christ Jesus" who are at the same time "called to be saints" (1 Cor 1:2), showing that while their holiness as the "church of God" is due to God's initiative, they are also called to practice a holiness of life that demands their own effort as well. Similarly, later in this same letter, Paul assures the Corinthians that despite their former sinfulness, they have been "washed, sanctified, justified in the name of the Lord Jesus Christ and in the Spirit of our God." This is obviously God's doing. But because of this, they are to "shun immorality" and "glorify God in their bodies" (1 Cor 6:11,18,20).

The first letter of Peter describes the Christians to whom it is addressed as "chosen and destined by God the Father and sanctified by the Spirit for obedience to Jesus Christ" (1 Pet 1:2). The initiative is the Father's, sanctification is the work of the Spirit, but this calls for obedience to Jesus on the part of those chosen and made holy. This obedience is spelled out a bit later on in the same letter: "As obedient children do not be conformed to the passions of your former ignorance, but as he who called you is holy, be holy yourselves in all your conduct, since it is written: 'You shall be holy, for I am holy' " (1 Pet 1:14–16). The letter goes on to attribute to the Christian community all the terms that described the holiness of the people of the Old Covenant: "But you are a chosen race, a royal priesthood, a holy nation, God's own people, that you may declare the wonderful deeds of him who called you out of darkness into his marvelous light. Once you were no people but now you are God's people; once you had not received mercy but now you have received mercy" (1 Pet 2:9–10). Not surprisingly, there follows immediately the exhortation to live up to such a calling: "Beloved, I beseech you as aliens and exiles to abstain from the passions of the flesh that make war against your soul. Maintain good conduct among the Gentiles, so that in case they speak against you as wrongdoers, they may see your good deeds and glorify God on the day of visitation" (1 Pet 2:11–12).

In What Sense Is the Church Indefectibly Holy?

Following Vatican II, we have insisted that the church is a "complex reality." It is no surprise, then, when we find that its holiness, too, is complex, and that in order to give an adequate account of it, we have to distinguish various aspects of its holiness, corresponding to various aspects of the church itself. We propose to distinguish three ways in which the church is holy: first, with the objective, effective holiness of its formal elements; second, with a holiness of consecration as a priestly people; and third, with a holiness of grace and virtue. We shall consider each of these in turn.

The Church Is Holy By Reason of the Holiness of Its Formal Elements

The church is rightly described as the people of God, and that means that it is made up of a number of men, women and children. But the church is not a mere multitude of people; what makes a number of people to be a Christian church is the fact that they share Christian faith, are baptized, gather to celebrate the Eucharist, and recognize certain persons as their pastors. A Christian church is a *structured* people: structured by such formal, constitutive elements as Christian faith, sacraments, and the charismatic and hierarchical gifts that equip people for ministry. When we say that the church owes its institution to Christ, we mean that these formal elements are not mere products of human ingenuity; rather, they are the fruit of Christ's ministry, passion, death and resurrection and the sending of the Holy Spirit. They are gifts which Christ has bestowed on his church to make it an effective instrument of grace and salvation.

St. Paul speaks of such gifts in the passage of his letter to the Ephesians where he says: "Christ ascended far above all the heavens that he might fill all things. And his gifts were that some should be apostles, some prophets, some evangelists, some pastors and teachers, to equip the saints for the work of ministry, for building up the body of Christ" (Eph 4:10–12). When we speak of the "formal elements" of the church we mean all the gifts mentioned here by Paul, and all the other gifts by which Christ has equipped his church for ministry.

What we are saying now is that the church is holy by reason of the objective, effective holiness of these formal elements. Such things as the word of God on which Christian faith is based, the sacraments, the gifts that equip people for ministry, are holy in themselves because they are Christ's gifts, and derive their holiness from him. They are objectively holy, because their holiness does not depend on the subjective holiness of the person who preaches the word or administers the sacraments. They are effectively holy in that they are the gifts by which the church is enabled to cooperate with the Holy Spirit in building up a holy people for the Lord.

The word of God remains holy whether the preacher or hearer is holy or not. The sacraments are holy even though a person may administer or receive them unworthily. In that sense they have an indefectible holiness which human sinfulness cannot diminish or destroy. And insofar as these formal elements are constitutive of the church, the church itself is indefectibly holy. Such indefectible holiness is proper to the church precisely as it is the divinely constituted sacrament of salvation, because it is these formal elements that enable the church to be an effective instrument of grace and holiness in the world.

But of course the church does not consist only of its formal elements. While one can say with St. Thomas Aquinas that the church is constituted by faith and sacraments,[55] it does not consist of just these; rather it consists of people who are formed and structured into a church by faith and sacraments. For the church to be holy it is not enough that its formal elements are holy; it must be a holy people, made up of holy men, women and children.

We shall now consider two ways in which the church is such a holy people.

Holiness of Consecration

As we have seen above, the biblical notion of holiness involves a being set apart in some way so as to be the more closely associated with God. Such holiness is attributed to persons and things that are set apart and dedicated to divine worship, such as the temple, its altar and vessels, and, above all, the priests who offer prayer and sacrifice to God on behalf of the people. This is a holiness of consecration: a holiness that marks a person by reason of being called and set apart for priestly ministry. It calls for the personal holiness of a virtuous life on the part of one so intimately involved in the worship of the holy God. But the holiness of consecration does not depend on or consist in personal virtue; it is the effect of having been set apart and anointed, and thus consecrated ("made sacred") for the worship and service of God.

The Bible attributes such priestly holiness not only to individuals like Aaron, but to the whole people of Israel. Thus, through Moses, God says to his people: "Now therefore, if you will obey my voice and keep my covenant, you shall be my own possession among all peoples; for all the earth is mine, and you shall be to me a kingdom of priests and a holy nation" (Ex 19:5–6). So also, in the book of the prophet Isaiah: "You shall be called the priests of the Lord, men shall speak of you as the ministers of our God" (Is 61:6).

As we have already seen, New Testament writers predicate of the church all the terms that had described the holiness of the people of God of the old law. This includes its holiness of consecration to the priestly service of God. Thus, the writer of the first letter of Peter exhorts his readers: "Like living stones be yourselves built into a spiritual house, to be a holy priesthood, to offer spiritual sacrifices acceptable to God through Jesus Christ." A little later he describes them as "a chosen race, a royal priesthood, a holy nation, God's own people" (1 Pet 2:5,9). Similarly, in the book of Revelation, Christ is described as the one "who loves us and has freed us from our sins by his blood and made us a kingdom, priests to his God and Father" (Rev 1:5–6). Later on, we hear the heavenly song: "Worthy art thou to take the scroll and to open its seals, for thou wast slain and by thy blood didst ransom men for God from every tribe and tongue and people and nation, and hast made them a kingdom and priests to our God, and they shall reign on earth" (Rev 5:9–10).

As one would expect, the New Testament teaching about the church as a priestly people is further developed in the second chapter of *Lumen gentium* entitled "The People of God." The first reference to the priestly character of the new people of God is found in article 9: "For those who believe in Christ, who are reborn not from a perishable but from an imperishable seed through the Word of the living God (cf. 1 Pet 1:23), not from the flesh but from water and the Holy Spirit (cf. Jn 3:5–6), are finally established as 'a chosen race, a royal priesthood, a holy nation, a purchased people' . . . you who in times past were not a people, but are now the people of God" (1 Pet 2:9–10). This is further developed in article 10: "Christ the Lord, High Priest taken from among men 'made a kingdom and priests to God his Father' (Rev 1:6; cf. 5:9–10), out of this new people. The baptized, by regeneration and the anointing of the Holy Spirit, are consecrated into a spiritual house and a holy priesthood. Thus through all those works befitting Christian men they can offer spiritual sacrifices and proclaim the power of him who has called them out of darkness into his marvelous light."

In these texts of Vatican II we see that Christians are consecrated to this royal priesthood through their sacramental initiation, by being "reborn of water and the Holy Spirit." The priesthood of all the faithful which is conferred through baptism and confirmation is further described as being, "in its own special way, a participation in the priesthood of Christ" (LG 10). This association with Christ's priesthood is a further aspect of the holiness of consecration which is conferred by the sacraments of Christian initiation.

Traditional Catholic theology understands this participation in the priesthood of Christ to be something that permanently characterizes those who have been baptized. Unlike the gift of sanctifying grace and the indwelling of the Holy Spirit, it is not lost by a person who commits grave sin. It is a "character" or "spiritual mark" which distinguishes the baptized as persons consecrated to Christ and sharers in his priesthood. They retain the holiness of this consecration, despite any possible infidelity to their calling.

Since the church is made up of baptized believers in Christ, the whole church is marked with the holiness of consecration as a priestly people. This, then, is an indefectible holiness of the whole church. Needless to say, it calls for the personal response of a holy way of life. But, whether individual Christians live up to their calling or not, the whole church remains as a people consecrated to the worship of God, as a "spiritual house and a holy priesthood." In this sense, then, the church is indefectibly holy as a priestly people.

Holiness of Grace and Virtue

While holiness is always due to God's initiative, and is his gift, it also calls for a response on the part of those who are called into a closer relationship with God: it is their duty to live up to their calling by leading a holy life. As St. Paul put it at the beginning of his first letter to the Corinthians, Christians are "sanctified in Christ Jesus," but also "called to be saints." So, in the letter to the Ephesians, he exhorts his readers: "I, therefore, a prisoner for the Lord, beg you to lead a life worthy of the calling to which you have been called, with all lowliness and meekness, with patience, forbearing one another in love, eager to maintain the unity of the Spirit in the bond of peace" (Eph 4:1–3). There is no need to multiply such biblical citations; practically every book of the New Testament contains some such exhortation to the holiness of life that should characterize those who have been called to membership in the church.

What is the nature of the personal holiness to which all Christians are called? An authoritative answer to this question is found in the following passage of chapter 5 of *Lumen gentium* whose title is: "The Call of the Whole Church to Holiness":

> The Lord Jesus, the divine Teacher and Model of all perfection, preached holiness of life to each and every one of his disciples, regardless of their situation: "You therefore are to be perfect, even as your heavenly Father is perfect" (Mt 5:48). He himself stands as the author and finisher of this holiness of life. For he sent the Holy Spirit upon all men that he might inspire them from within to love God with their whole heart and their whole soul, with all their mind and all their strength (cf. Mk 12:3), and that they might love one another as Christ loved them (cf. Jn 13:34; 15:12).
>
> The followers of Christ are called by God, not according to their accomplishments, but according to his own purpose and

grace. They are justified in the Lord Jesus, and through baptism sought in faith they truly become sons of God and sharers in the divine nature. In this way they are really made holy. Then, too, by God's gifts, they must hold on to and complete in their lives this holiness which they have received. They are warned by the Apostle to live "as becomes saints" (Eph 5:3), and to put on "as God's chosen ones, holy and beloved, a heart of mercy, kindness, humility, meekness, patience" (Col 3:12), and to possess the fruits of the Spirit unto holiness (cf. Gal 5:22; Rom 6:22). Since we all truly offend in many things (cf. Jas 3:2), we all need God's mercy continuously and must daily pray: "Forgive us our debts" (Mt 6:12).

Thus it is evident to everyone that all the faithful of Christ of whatever rank or status are called to the fullness of the Christian life and to the perfection of charity (LG 40).

It is clear from this passage that holiness consists in the keeping of the two great commandments: of the love of God and the love of neighbor as oneself. Actually, such love is in the first place a gift bestowed in baptism. As St. Paul puts it: "The love of God has been poured into our hearts by the Holy Spirit who has been given to us" (Rom 5:5). The indwelling presence of the Holy Spirit is inseparable from this supernatural capacity to love God and our neighbor which we call the infused virtue of charity. It is likewise inseparable from the freedom from grave sin and friendship with God that we call "being in the state of grace."

Holiness, then, is a matter of "walking in love" (Eph 5:2). All growth in holiness is a matter of striving for "the perfection of charity." On the other hand, the reference in the text we have cited from the council, to the fact that we all truly offend in many things, need God's mercy continuously, and must daily pray for the forgiveness of our sins, reflects the Catholic understanding that "venial" sin does not deprive us of the holiness of "being in the state of grace" and having the Holy Spirit maintaining in us the infused virtue of charity.

It is important to recognize the fact that everyone in whom the Holy Spirit is dwelling is a holy person, indeed is a "saint" in the sense that St. Paul used this term. At the same time, we recall that the council spoke of Christians who "remain incorporated in the church, but do not persevere in charity. Such persons remain in the bosom of the church, but, as it were, only in a 'bodily' manner, and not 'in their hearts' " (LG 14). Here the council is speaking of those living in the state of unrepented grave sin. According to Catholic teaching, being in such a state deprives one of the indwelling presence of the Holy Spirit, and thus of the holiness of grace and charity. But, as the conciliar text states, people lacking such holiness can remain incorporated in the church. This is the case unless their sin involves renunciation of Christian faith or of their communion with the church. The consequence of this, as LG 14 indicates, is that one must distinguish two kinds of Catholics: those "possessing the Spirit of Christ" who are fully incorporated in the church, and those who "do not persevere in charity," and who remain in the church but are not fully members of it. The latter retain the holiness of their baptismal character, but they no longer have the holiness of sanctifying grace.

What is the consequence of this situation for the holiness of the church? If the church is really the people of God, its holiness cannot be independent of the holiness of the men and women who are its members. The conclusion is inescapable that as the holiness of those living in grace redounds to the holiness of the church, so the sinfulness of its members must also diminish the holiness of the people of which they remain a part. No doubt this is what the council had in mind when it said that on this earth the church is marked with imperfect holiness.

At the same time, the council described the church as indefectibly holy. This makes it obvious that by "indefectibly" they did not mean "perfectly." The meaning of "indefectibly" is well brought out by the phrase used in the Abbott translation: "holy in a way which can never fail." Indefectible holiness, then, is not such as to exclude all defect or imperfection, but it does exclude the loss of holiness, any ceasing to be truly holy.

The question we must now consider is whether the church can be said to be indefectibly holy not only in its formal elements and in its priestly consecration, but also with the holiness of grace and charity. In other words, we must ask whether there is a guarantee that the church will always be a holy people, a people "walking in love."

The problem is that no individual member of the church is indefectibly holy in this sense. The baptized cannot lose the holiness of their sharing in the priesthood of Christ, but they can fail to persevere in charity and thus lose the holiness of sanctifying grace and the indwelling of the Holy Spirit. No individual Christian has a guarantee of persevering in charity.

The question, then, is whether we can say of the church something we cannot say of any individual member of it. Can we say that even though no individual member is indefectibly holy, the church is? If each member can fail to persevere in charity, can the church do so? If an individual member can no longer have the Holy Spirit dwelling in him or her, can this ever happen to the church?

This last question would seem to require a decided "no" for an answer. It seems absurd to think that the church of Christ could ever lack the indwelling Spirit, the divine gift that the risen Christ poured out on his church at Pentecost. But we must ask how we can say of the people of God something that we cannot say about any one of its members.

To answer that question, I find it helpful to recall something that St. Thomas Aquinas said about the faith of the church, using the term "faith" not of what the church believes, but of the attitude or virtue of faith. Along with Catholic theologians generally, when speaking of the faith of individual Christians, he distinguished between "faith formed by charity" and "unformed faith," the latter being the kind of faith that can remain even when a person has lost the virtue of charity by grave sin. Of individual members of the church one cannot say that their faith will always be formed by charity; indeed it would be unrealistic to claim that at any time the faith of all the members of the church is formed by charity. Nevertheless, St. Thomas confidently asserts that the faith of the church is formed by charity.[56] One might ask whether, in saying this, he was thinking of the church as a kind of "mystical person," distinct from the concrete, historical people of God. From the explanation he gives it is quite certain that this is not what he had in mind. The reason he gives for saying that the faith of the church is formed by charity is that this is the faith that is had by those who belong to the church "both by number and by merit." The last phrase needs some explanation. To belong to the church only by number means to be numbered among its members, but to lack charity. To belong "by merit" is to be living the life of grace. It is the latter members of the church whose faith is formed by charity. The reader may have noticed that, with different terminology, St. Thomas is making the same distinction that Vatican II made between Catholics "possessing the Spirit of Christ" who are fully incorporated in the church, and others who fail to persevere in charity and hence are not fully incorporated, since they lack an essential bond of spiritual communion with the church (LG 14).

In the light of the reason that St. Thomas gives for saying that the faith of the church is formed by charity, we can draw two conclusions about his thinking: (1) the church is identified with the "congregation of believers," and the faith of the church is the faith of this concrete people, not of some mystical person; (2) it is correct to predicate of the church what is actually true of those who are really living its life, or, as Vatican II put it, of those who are fully incorporated in it. "Faith formed by charity" is rightly seen as an attribute of the church, because one can rightly characterize a corporate body by the quality of those who are fully its members. In other words, to describe the church as a community of living faith, it is not necessary that every single person who belongs to it should have living faith. It is enough that those who are fully its members have such faith. Since to have faith formed by charity is the essence of what it means to be holy, we can apply St. Thomas' thinking to our question, and say that we can call the church a "holy people" on the grounds that those who are fully incorporated in it are holy.

What then would it mean to say that the church is "indefectibly holy"? It would mean that the church can never cease to be a "holy people," and hence it can never lack fully incorporated members who are living the life of grace and charity. It does not seem necessary that such members would always and necessarily constitute the numerical majority in the church. Nothing St. Thomas says indicates that he thought this was the case. However, to speak realistically of the church as a "holy people," it would seem that those actually living holy lives would have to constitute a substantial proportion of the whole. Exactly how great a proportion this would have to be seems an unanswerable question.

However, a very real question still remains. We have said that for the church to be an indefectibly holy people, it would always have to consist, in sufficient proportion, of those fully incorporated members whose faith is formed by charity. The question is: what reasons do we have for believing that the church can never cease to be such a holy people?

Grounds for Belief That the Church Is an Indefectibly Holy People

The grounds for this belief are succinctly stated at the beginning of the chapter of *Lumen gentium* on the universal call to holiness.

> Faith teaches that the church, whose mystery is being set forth by this sacred Synod, is holy in a way which can never fail. For Christ, the Son of God, who with the Father and the Spirit is praised as being "alone holy," loved the church as his bride, delivering himself up for her. This he did that he might sanctify her (cf. Eph 5:25–26). He united her to himself as his own body and crowned her with the gift of the Holy Spirit, for God's glory.

On the basis of this text, we can distinguish at least three reasons for our confidence that Christ's church can never cease to be a holy people: (1) because its holiness is the fruit of Christ's sacrifice; (2) because Christ has united the church indissolubly to himself as his bride; (3) because Christ has endowed his body the church with the abiding gift of the Holy Spirit.

The first of these reasons involves our belief in the infinite value of the sacrifice which Christ offered to the Father on our behalf, and the definitive, "eschatological" nature of the victory which he won over the powers of evil by his death and resurrection. It was because of this definitive victory that Christ could say with absolute assurance that the "gates of hell" would never prevail over his church. For the church ever to cease being a holy people, a people of faith formed by charity, would mean that the powers of evil had prevailed over it.

The second reason, that the church is Christ's bride, assures us that he will never permit his church to become so unworthy of such an intimate relationship with him as to require his repudiation of her as an unfaithful wife. To put it another way, Christ, having won a definitive victory over sin, cannot fail to share the fruits of this victory with his spouse. To argue that if God could condemn the people of Israel to exile for their idolatry, Christ could some day cast off the church, is to deny something essential to the new covenant: its definitiveness.

Third, indefectible holiness is guaranteed to the church by the abiding presence in her of the Holy Spirit, the gift of the risen Christ to his church. It is unthinkable that the Holy Spirit could either abandon the church or abide in her without actually causing the church to be a holy people. Admittedly, individuals can resist the Holy Spirit and remain in unrepented grave sin. In such people the Spirit no longer dwells. But the Spirit cannot fail to dwell in Christ's church, or fail to make her the holy people God intends her to be. And the church cannot be such a holy people without holy members, and that means that the Spirit will always bring it about that there is in the church a decisive proportion of people whose faith is formed by charity.

We come now to the third quality which Vatican II attributes to the holiness of the church: it is not only "genuine" and "indefectible," it is also "imperfect."

Is the "Imperfectly Holy" Church
Also a "Sinful Church"?

We recall that the statement about the holiness of the church being "genuine though imperfect" occurs in the council's discussion of the "eschatological nature of the pilgrim church" (LG 48). It should be clear by now why we said that the genuine holiness of the church is a consequence of its eschatological nature: that is, it is a consequence of the definitiveness of Christ's victory over sin, which he shares with his church. On the other hand, the fact that its holiness is imperfect is a consequence of its being a "pilgrim church," still having to struggle to stay on the right road to its true home.

Again and again in the course of history, Christians have made the mistake of attributing to the church in this world qualities it will have only in the future kingdom of God. For instance, in the time of St. Augustine, the Donatists believed that the holiness of the church required that no sinner could be tolerated as a member of it. St. Augustine replied by recalling several parables of the Lord, such as the one about the cockle sown amid the wheat, and the net that brought up good fish and bad. In each case the point was that the separation of good and bad was to take place only at the final judgment; until then the church would contain both saints and sinners. Faithful to this teaching of the Lord, the magisterium has consistently rejected theories that would restrict membership in the church to those predestined to eternal life,[57] or to those actually in the state of grace.[58]

A passage of the letter to the Ephesians has sometimes been invoked to prove that the church cannot tolerate the presence of sinners among its members. "Christ loved the church and gave himself up for her, that he might sanctify her, having cleansed her by the washing of water with the word, that he might present the church to himself in splendor, without spot or wrinkle or any such thing, that she might be holy and without blemish" (Eph 5:25–27). St. Augustine's answer was that the church "without spot or wrinkle" is not the church as she is now, but as she will be in the kingdom of God.[59] Vatican II reflects this interpretation when, speaking of the Blessed Virgin Mary as exemplar of the church, it says: "In the most holy Virgin the church has already reached that perfection whereby she exists without spot or wrinkle" (LG 65). In other passages, the council has explicitly acknowledged that the church in her pilgrim state is not without "spot or wrinkle." Here are some of the pertinent texts where that is brought out.

> While Christ, "holy, innocent, undefiled" (Heb 7:26) knew nothing of sin (2 Cor 5:21), but came to expiate only the sins of the people (cf. Heb 2:17), the church, embracing sinners in her bosom, is at the same time holy and always in need of being purified, and incessantly pursues the path of penance and renewal (LG 8).

> Although the Catholic Church has been endowed with all divinely revealed truth and with all means of grace, her members fail to live by them with all the fervor they should. As a result, the radiance of the Church's face shines less brightly in the eyes of our separated brethren and of the world at large, and the growth of God's kingdom is retarded. Every Catholic must therefore aim at Christian perfection and, each according to his station, must play his part so that the church, which bears in her own body the humility and dying of Jesus, may daily be more purified

and renewed, against the day when Christ will present her to himself in all her glory, without spot or wrinkle (UR 4).

Christ summons the church, as she goes her pilgrim way, to that continual reformation of which she always has need, insofar as she is an institution of men here on earth (UR 6).

The explicit recognition by the council of the church's need to be purified, renewed and reformed shows that it does not want us to think of the church as remaining perfectly spotless, unstained by the sins committed by her members. The realism with which the council admits that the church itself, and not just some of its members, is in need of purification and reform is a consequence of the new emphasis which the council put on the nature of the church as the "pilgrim people of God." Focusing too one-sidedly on the idea of the church as mystical body of Christ, one could be led to identify the church so closely with Christ as to attribute to her the sinlessness that is unique to her head. Stressing the nature of the church as "pilgrim people" brings out the fact that the church consists of real people who throughout their earthly pilgrimage have to struggle with temptation and the weakness of the flesh.

We have insisted above that for the church to be indefectibly holy it must always have members who are holy. Realistically, we have to say that it will always have other members who are living in the state of unrepented grave sin. There is also a sense in which all the members of the church are sinners, because no one can avoid all venial sin, the kind of sin for which we must ask daily for forgiveness.[60] Keeping this in mind, we can describe the church as both a holy people and a sinful people, not only because some are holy and others are sinners, but because even the holy ones are also sinners.

The fact that the same people can be both holy and sinners at the same time is manifested when we celebrate the Eucharist. The celebration begins with the penitential rite, in which all confess themselves to be sinners and ask God's mercy. But at Communion time, the same sinners judge themselves holy enough to receive the Eucharist. The kind of sins they have confessed are not such as to deprive them of the holiness required for reception of the Eucharist.

Can we describe the church itself as both holy and sinful? If we take seriously the idea that the church is the concrete people of God, and therefore consists of real people who are both holy and sinful, we have to conclude that the church is both holy and sinful. However, several points need to be made, lest erroneous conclusions be drawn from this.

First, while those who preach the word of God and administer the sacraments can be personally corrupt, and can have a corrupting influence on others to whom they minister, still, the word of God, the sacraments, and in general all the "formal elements" by which the church is a "sacrament of salvation" can have only a positive influence for holiness; they can never be responsible for the sins which members of the church commit. On the contrary, they are always working against such sinfulness.

Second, although persons entrusted with leadership in the church, even at the highest levels, can be guilty of grave sin in their personal lives and even when they are acting in the name of the church, it is not correct to say that in such a case the church commits sin. The commission of sin is always the choice of a personal free will.

Of course it is a common enough mistake for people to say "The church has done this or that," when they really should say that "the Pope," or "the bishops," or "certain officials of the Vatican" have done such and such. The identification of the church with the clergy or the hierarchy is understandable, but it does not justify accusing the church as such of sins that members of its clergy commit.

On the other hand, there is sometimes reason to admit that the church at large shares in the guilt of sins that have been committed by its leaders. One example of this is the blame which the Catholic Church must share for the breakdowns of Christian unity which took place in the eleventh and sixteenth centuries. The bishops at Vatican II, in their Decree on Ecumenism, were clearly confessing the guilt of the Catholic Church for the sinful causes of Christian disunity when they said: "St. John has testified: 'If we say that we have not sinned, we make him a liar, and his word is not in us' (1 Jn 1:10). This holds good for sins against unity. Thus, in humble prayer, we beg pardon of God and of our separated brethren, just as we forgive those who trespass against us" (UR 7).

One might think of other examples of historical sins for which the church in some way shares a collective responsibility: such as ill-treatment of the Jewish people, racial discrimination, the exploitation of colonized nations, and the toleration of slavery. In many cases, these attitudes and ways of acting may not have been recognized as gravely sinful at the time. One can judge such things to have been objectively wrong, but we must not judge the consciences of people of the past in the light of modern sensibilities. However, it is not inappropriate for those authorized to speak in the name of the church to confess its share of guilt for attitudes and practices which have been so common among Christians as to justify the recognition that the church as a whole must accept a certain responsibility for the pain and harm that such things have caused.

We conclude this discussion of the holiness of the church on a somber note. But we must be realistic: we are talking about the holiness of the historical people of God. The confession of sin is not a denial of holiness; on the contrary, for sinful human beings, it is an essential ingredient of holiness. The church's holiness is indefectible, but it does not consist in immunity from weakness and sin. As Vatican II puts it:

> Moving forward through trial and tribulation, the church is strengthened by the power of God's grace promised to her by the Lord, so that in the weakness of the flesh she may not waver from perfect fidelity, but remain a bride worthy of her Lord, that moved by the Holy Spirit she may never cease to renew herself, until through the cross she arrives at the light which knows no setting (LG 9).

5 ‖ "The Catholic Unity of the People of God"

For the title of this chapter we are using a phrase of *Lumen gentium* n. 13, where the translator for the Abbott edition correctly spells the word "catholic" with a small "c." As we have remarked earlier, practically all Christians profess their belief in the church as "catholic," even though only about half of them would say that they belong to the Catholic Church, if written with a capital "C." It is our intention to write "Catholic" when referring to the Roman Catholic Church, and to write "catholic" when using the adjective as it is used in the creed. Similarly, Catholicism embraces all that is proper to the Catholic Church, while catholicity is one of the four properties that practically all Christians attribute to the church of Christ. In the light of our second chapter, we could say: "The church that subsists in the Catholic Church is catholic, but catholicity is not found exclusively in Catholicism."

The first question we must ask is: what do we mean when we profess our belief in the church as catholic?

The Meaning of the Term "Catholic"

The Greek adjective *katholikos* is derived from the two words *kath'holou*, meaning literally "according to the whole." The basic meaning of the adjective is "universal"; it was commonly used by the Greek philosophers of concepts like "goodness" and "beauty," as distinguished from particular good or beautiful things which exemplified such "universals."

The earliest known use of the term as applying to the church is found in the letter of St. Ignatius of Antioch to the church of Smyrna, in which he wrote: "Wherever the bishop appears, there is the community, just as where Jesus Christ is, there is the catholic church." Of the many interpretations that have been given of this sentence, the most probable seems to be that Ignatius is distinguishing between the local eucharistic assembly and the church "as a whole," "in its entirety."[62]

In the account of the martyrdom of St. Polycarp, bishop of Smyrna, written by the presbyters of his church around the year 160, there are four occurrences of the word "catholic" in reference to the church. The account, written in the form of a letter to the other churches, opens with a salutation to "all the congregations of the holy catholic church in every place."[63] It recounts how Polycarp, after his arrest, prayed "for the whole catholic church spread throughout the world."[64] It describes Jesus Christ as "the shepherd of the catholic church throughout the world."[65] In these instances, the word "catholic" would seem to be used in the sense of "universal" as contrasted with "local" or "particular." However, as J.N.D. Kelly observes, even here "catholic" is not simply synonymous with "geographically universal," for it contains, more or less latent, the further idea of oneness, uniqueness. To be truly "catholic," it has to be *one* church throughout the world.[66]

The fourth use of "catholic" in the *Martyrdom of Polycarp* introduces a strikingly new application of the word: Polycarp is described as "the bishop of the catholic church of Smyrna."[67] Here it is clearly the local church of Smyrna that is being described as "the catholic church." If one asks in what sense a local church could be designated by an adjective whose basic meaning is "universal," the answer seems to be found in the fact that in the course of the second century the orthodox Christians began to distinguish their church from the numerous heretical and schismatic sects on the ground of the oneness and universality of the true church, in contrast to the multiplicity and locally limited nature of the sects. Thus "catholicity" came to be recognized as a criterion of orthodoxy, and "catholic" came to mean the opposite of "sectarian" and "heretical." According to J.N.D. Kelly, "This is the dominant meaning of 'catholic' from the second half of the second century onwards in East and West alike;

it denotes the one, true church of Christ as opposed to all heretical and schismatic groups, and points to the universality of the former as the guarantee of its authenticity."[68]

Less frequently one finds the term "catholic" used in another application of the basic idea of universality, namely, that of "wholeness" or "plenitude." A good example of such a use of the term is found in the *Catecheses* of St. Cyril of Jerusalem, where he was explaining the various reasons why the church is called "catholic."

> The church is called "catholic" because it is spread throughout the world from end to end of the earth; also because it teaches universally and completely all the doctrines which men should know concerning things visible and invisible, heavenly and earthly; and also because it subjects to right worship all mankind, rulers and ruled, lettered and unlettered; further because it treats and heals universally every sort of sin committed by soul and body, and it possesses in itself every conceivable virtue, whether in deeds, words or in spiritual gifts of every kind.[69]

The notion of "wholeness" or "plenitude" is further developed in the sense in which "catholic unity" is contrasted with mere "uniformity." What makes the unity of the church "catholic" is the rich variety of components that make up the church. We shall have occasion to see that Vatican II insisted strongly on this sense of the catholicity of the church.

Catholicity As "Gift" and As "Task"

Lumen gentium declares that the universality which is proper to the church is a gift from the Lord, but a gift by virtue of which the catholic church "strives energetically and constantly to bring all of humanity, with all its riches, under Christ as its head, in the unity of his Spirit" (LG 13). From the fact that this is a gift from the Lord, his church must have been "catholic" or universal from the very beginning, even when it consisted of the one Jewish-Christian community of Jerusalem. At that time the church of Christ was already destined to be the church of all races and cultures. But the apostles did not yet know how or when they were to begin preaching the gospel to others than Jews. Peter had to be enlightened by a vision to know that he should go to preach the good news to the Roman centurion Cornelius (Acts 10). Even after the mission to the Gentiles had begun, it took strenuous efforts on the part of St. Paul to ensure for his Gentile converts the freedom from circumcision and the other burdens of the law that made possible a truly universal church, no longer identified with a particular people or its religion.

If then we say that the church of Christ was catholic from the beginning, we have to distinguish between catholicity as a gift, a tendency, a destiny, and catholicity as realized universality. In the latter sense, catholicity is still an unfinished task. The church has constantly to strive to actualize this gift. In pursuing the goal of realized universality, the church has many obstacles to overcome; among them the council mentions the divisions among Christians, which, it says, "prevent the church from effecting the fullness of catholicity proper to her" (UR 4).

Hence, while as a gift the church's catholicity is what the Lord intends it to be, one cannot say the same of its actual catholicity, either in the sense of universal expansion, or in the sense of the rich variety of races and cultures in which it ought to be embodied. The church's mandate to realize her own catholicity is the basic motive for her unceasing efforts to evangelize those who have not yet heard the gospel. In the light of the fact that the divided state of Christianity is a major obstacle to this realization, catholicity also offers motivation for wholehearted participation in the ecumenical movement.

Vatican II on the Church's Catholicity

Lumen gentium treats the property of catholicity most fully in the last five articles (nos. 13–17) of Chapter Two: "The People of God." In the first of these articles, the council provides a brief theology of catholicity, of which the principal headings are: (1) the trinitarian source of catholicity, (2) catholicity as universality of races, nations and cultures, (3) catholicity as unity is rich diversity, and (4) catholicity as relationship with all of humanity. The following three articles spell out the ways that various categories of people are related to the church; art. 14 speaks of Catholics, 15 of other Christians, 16 of those who are not Christian. The last article, n. 17, treats the church's mandate to actualize its gift of catholicity by evangelization. We shall follow the lead of the council, offering some comments on each of these headings.

The Trinitarian Source of the Church's Catholicity

The mandate of the church to be one people, embracing all races and cultures, is rooted in the will of God the Father, who, having created one human family, decreed that his scattered children should be gathered into one people (cf. Jn 11:52). The role of the Son is expressed in one sentence: "It was for this reason that God sent his Son, whom he appointed heir of all things (Heb 1:2), that he might be Teacher, King and Priest of all, the Head of the new and universal people of the sons of God" (LG 13). Something more needs to be said on this point, because the claim of Christianity to be a truly universal religion, intended by God for all races, peoples and cultures, is questioned by many on the ground that Jesus was a man of one particular people and its culture. The historically conditioned particularity of Jesus, as a man of one time, place and religious background, it is argued, would invalidate the claim of Christianity to be the one universal religion for all times and all peoples.

The Problem of Jesus' Particularity

In the first place the question is raised whether Jesus understood his message of salvation to be intended for people of other cultures than his own. Appeal is made to such sayings of Jesus as: "I was sent only to the lost sheep of the house of Israel" (Mt 15:24), and his instruction to his disciples: "Go nowhere among the Gentiles, and enter no town of the Samaritans, but go rather to the lost sheep of the house of Israel" (Mt 10:5f). There is no doubt about the authenticity of such sayings, or about the fact that Jesus did limit his ministry to his own people. The rare instances when he acceded to the requests of Gentiles for his ministry of healing do not contradict this, since in each case it was they who came to him, not he who went out to them (cf. Mt 8:5f; 15:22f). Furthermore, in the earliest period of the New Testament church, the initiative to preach the gospel to others than Jews was taken not by men who had been Jesus' disciples during his lifetime, but by "Hellenist" Christians like Philip, who evangelized the Samaritans, and the men of Cyprus and Cyrene who were the first to preach the good news about Jesus to the Greeks at Antioch (cf. Acts 8:4ff; 11:19ff). These facts suggest that Jesus' older disciples still felt themselves bound by the instruction to go only to the "lost sheep of the house of Israel," and renders it difficult to believe that they had heard Jesus himself tell them to "make disciples of all nations" (Mt 28:19), or to "go into all the world and preach the gospel to the whole creation" (Mk 16:15).

We have to reckon with the probability that such explicitly universal mandates attributed to the risen Jesus may have been the church's expression of what it only later came to understand that Jesus intended. There is no doubt that the early church recognized the opening to the Gentiles to have been accomplished under the guidance of the Spirit, and in that sense to be attributable to the risen Christ who sent his Spirit to the church to guide it into all truth.

The question remains whether, despite Jesus' limitation of his ministry to his own people, there are solid grounds for asserting that it really was his intention that his gospel and the salvation it offered should be preached to all nations. If this question is answered in the affirmative, we must also ask how such an intention can be reconciled with the limitations that he put on his own ministry and on that of his immediate disciples.

The evidence that Jesus understood the coming reign of God to offer salvation not only to Jews but to all nations is found in several authentic sayings of Jesus recorded in the gospels. One particularly significant passage is his praise of the faith of the Roman centurion: "Truly, I say to you, not even in Israel have I found such faith. I tell you, many will come from east and west and sit at table with Abraham, Isaac and Jacob in the kingdom of heaven, while the sons of the kingdom will be thrown into the outer darkness; there men will weep and gnash their teeth" (Mt 8:10–12). Another is Jesus' description of the judgment, where all nations will be gathered before the Son of Man, and all will be judged by the way they have treated people in need, without any distinction between Jew and Gentile (Mt 25:31–46). A prediction of the equal or even more favorable judgment that Gentiles will receive in comparison with that to be meted out to Jesus' own people is had in his warning: "The men of Nineveh will arise at the judgment with this generation and condemn it; for they repented at the preaching of Jonah" (Mt 12:41). On the basis of these and other authentic words of Jesus, such eminent Scripture scholars as Joachim Jeremias have concluded that Jesus' preaching did contain a promise of salvation for the Gentiles.[70]

Why Did Jesus Restrict His Ministry to the Jewish People?

The New Testament offers two answers to this question. The first is found in the episode toward the end of Jesus' public life in the fourth gospel, when "some Greeks" expressed their desire to meet Jesus. His response to this request was: "The hour has come for the Son of Man to be glorified. Truly, truly I say to you, unless a grain of wheat falls into the earth and dies it remains alone; but if it dies it bears much fruit" (Jn 12:23f). A little later in the same passage, Jesus declares: "I, when I am lifted up from the earth, will draw all men to myself" (Jn 12:32). In other words, the salvation which Jesus promises is intended also for the Greeks—indeed for all men—but first he must be "lifted up from the earth" and "glorified": both obvious references to his impending death and resurrection.

The second answer to our question, found in the letters of Paul and the Acts of the Apostles, is that the good news of salvation had to be announced first to the Jews before it could be shared with Gentiles, because of the priority they enjoyed as the people to whom the Redeemer had been promised. This was Paul's understanding of how things had to be, and his practice. For him, the gospel "is the power of God for salvation to everyone who has faith, to the Jew first, and also to the Greek" (Rom 1:16). So also he explains the ministry of Jesus: "Christ became a servant to the circumcised, in order to confirm the promises given to the patriarchs, and in order that the Gentiles might glorify God for his mercy" (Rom 15:8f). Paul's own ministry was also "first to the circumcised"; in each city he would go to the synagogue to preach the good news of Jesus before speaking to the Gentiles. Thus, in Pisidian Antioch, when the leaders of the synagogue rejected the preaching of Paul and Barnabas, they declared: "It was necessary that the word of God should be spoken first to you. Since you thrust it from you, and judge yourselves unworthy of eternal life, behold, we turn to the Gentiles"

(Acts 13:46). The same priority is expressed by Peter in his discourse after the healing of the cripple at the temple gate: "You are the sons of the prophets and of the covenant which God gave to your fathers, saying to Abraham, 'And in your posterity shall all the families of the earth be blessed.' God, having raised up his servant, sent him to you first, to bless you in turning every one of you from your wickedness" (Acts 3:25f).

There is every reason to believe that the priority observed by the apostles is a faithful reflection of the mind of Jesus, and is the reason why his own ministry was to "the lost sheep of the house of Israel." It was only after he had been "lifted up" that he would draw all people of all nations to himself.

Up to this point we have been replying to an objection that is raised against the claim of Christianity to universality on the grounds of the "Jewishness" of Jesus. We must now consider the positive reasons that Christians have for believing that the church has to be catholic precisely because it is the church of Christ, and has to reflect his own catholicity.

The "Catholicity" of Christ

By the catholicity of Christ I mean his role as the "one mediator between God and men, the man Christ Jesus, who gave himself as a ransom for all" (1 Tim 2:5f). Or as Peter put it: "There is salvation in no one else, for there is no other name under heaven given among men by which we must be saved" (Acts 4:12). His catholicity is his universal role as the one mediator, one redeemer, one hope of salvation for all of humanity.

For Christian faith, Jesus is no merely human founder of a religion; he is the eternal Word of God, who was with God from the beginning, and who "became flesh and dwelt among us," through whom "grace and truth have come" to mankind (cf. Jn 1:14,17). "No one has ever seen God; the only Son, who is in the bosom of the Father, he has made him known" (Jn 1:18). As the incarnate Word of God, Christ is the unique mediator between God and all of humanity.

St. Paul expressed the universality of Christ in terms of his headship over all creation, and of his being the one in whom "all the fullness of God was pleased to dwell." Thus, in the letter to the Colossians: "In him all the fullness of God was pleased to dwell, and through him to reconcile to himself all things, whether on earth or in heaven, making peace by the blood of the cross" (Col 1:19). And in Ephesians: "God has put all things under his feet and has made him head over all things for the church, which is his body, the fullness of him who fills all in all" (Eph 1:22f).

In this last text we see the connection between the "fullness" of Christ and the "fullness" of his church, recalling that fullness or plenitude is one way of expressing catholicity. The church as the body of him through whom God was pleased to reconcile all things to himself cannot fail to offer this reconciliation to people of all races and cultures; as the "fullness" of him who fills all things, it cannot lack anything of the plenitude of grace and truth which God has chosen should come through Christ to all of humanity.

The Holy Spirit As Source of Catholicity

The first paragraph of *Lumen gentium* 13 concludes with mention of the Holy Spirit as the one who, "on behalf of the whole church and each and every one of those who believe, is the principle of their coming together and remaining together in the teaching of the apostles and in fellowship, in the breaking of bread and in prayers (cf. Acts 2:42)." Here the stress is on the Spirit as the principle of the communion that binds all the faithful together in one church of Christ. But catholicity is unity in diversity, and we can point to the Spirit also as the source of the rich diversity of gifts with which the church is endowed. *Lumen gentium* speaks of the Spirit as the one who "furnishes the church with various gifts, both hierarchical and charismatic, and adorns her with the fruit of his grace" (LG 4). St. Paul, referring to the extraordinary variety of charisms found among the Corinthians, insisted that their multiplicity and diversity was no reason for disunity in the church, because "all these are inspired by one and the same Spirit, who apportions to each one individually as he wills" (1 Cor 12:11). It is a characteristic of the unity of which the Holy Spirit is the principle, that it be "catholic unity," that is, unity in diversity, the opposite of uniformity. It is the same Holy Spirit who provides the rich variety of gifts, and at the same time maintains the bond of communion among all those who receive and exercise them for the good of the whole body.

Universality of Races and Cultures

The second paragraph of LG 13 develops what we may call the "extensive" aspect of the church's catholicity: its reaching out to all races, nationalities, and cultures. In this context, it is obvious how contradictory to genuine catholicity any theory of racism or practice of racial discrimination would be. No class of persons can be treated as "second-class citizens" in a church that is truly catholic.

In speaking of the elements which comprise the cultural heritage of each people, the council twice uses the Latin word *assumere*, which the Abbott edition translates by "take to herself."

> Since the kingdom of Christ is not of this world (cf. Jn 18:36), the Church or People of God takes nothing away from the temporal welfare of any people by establishing that kingdom. Rather does she foster and take to herself, insofar as they are good, the ability, resources, and customs of each people. Taking them to herself she purifies, strengthens, and ennobles them.

In the light of the post-conciliar development of the notion of inculturation, one might find the council's emphasis on "taking to herself" somewhat one-sided. The church realizes her catholicity in the first place by her insertion into each culture, allowing herself to be taken into that culture, and not merely "taking to herself" what is there. Inculturation is a process that can be described as "incarnation with a view to redemption." As the Divine Word emptied himself, becoming flesh so that he might heal and restore mankind, so the church must become "enfleshed" in each culture, allowing herself to be emptied of what she brings with her of an alien culture, so as to be able to heal and restore whatever in the new culture needs redemption. The more fully inculturated its particular churches are, the more catholic the universal church will be, provided that in the process the essential bonds of communion are not weakened.

Catholicity As Unity in a Rich Diversity

The third paragraph of LG 13 speaks of what we can call the qualitative aspect of catholicity: the inner diversity of the church by reason of the variety of ways of life which are led within the church, and the variety of particular churches. Among those who follow different ways of life within the church, mention is made of those who exercise the sacred ministry (a term which in the language of Vatican II refers to the ordained clergy), and of those who enter the religious life. Needless to say, other examples could be cited, such as the variety of ministries now being exercised by lay people, and the different ways of life followed by members of secular institutes and of the new kinds of communities that have sprung up in the church, especially in the context of the charismatic renewal.

In a previous chapter we have already spoken of the various applications of the term "particular churches." In the paragraph on which we are now commenting, which stresses the different traditions proper to particular churches, and the legitimate differences between them, it seems likely that the term is being used not of local churches, but of larger groupings, such as the eastern churches, or others that share a particular tradition or culture.

The idea briefly mentioned here, that the diversity of traditions in particular churches is an aspect of the church's catholicity, is more explicitly brought out in the third chapter of *Lumen gentium*, in the following paragraph:

> By divine Providence it has come about that various churches established in diverse places by the apostles and their successors have in the course of time coalesced into several groups, organically united, which, preserving the unity of faith and the unique divine constitution of the universal church, enjoy their own discipline, their own liturgical usage, and their own theological and spiritual heritage. Some of these churches, notably the ancient patriarchal churches, as parent-stocks of the faith, so to speak, have begotten others as daughter churches. With these they are connected down to our own time by a close bond of charity in their sacramental life and in their mutual respect for rights and duties. This variety of local churches with one common aspiration is particularly splendid evidence of the catholicity of the undivided church (LG 23).

The reference to the undivided church here recalls the statement made in the Decree on Ecumenism to the effect that the divisions among Christians prevent the church from realizing the fullness of her catholicity (UR 4). One of the reasons for this is that the rich

traditions of the separated eastern churches belong to the full catholicity of the church. Historically the differences in theology and
practice between the eastern and the western churches were largely
responsible for the tragic split between them. The Decree on Ecumenism sees these differences rather as manifestations of the rich
variety that belongs to the catholicity of the church. The following
passages illustrate the ecumenical approach that Vatican II has taken
to the question of pluralism within the one church.

> All should realize that it is of supreme importance to understand,
> venerate, preserve, and foster the exceedingly rich liturgical and
> spiritual heritage of the Eastern Churches, in order faithfully to
> preserve the fullness of Christian tradition, and to bring about
> reconciliation between Eastern and Western Christians (UR 15).

> From the earliest times, moreover, the Eastern Churches fol-
> lowed their own disciplines, sanctioned by the holy Fathers, by
> synods, even ecumenical councils. Far from being an obstacle to
> the Church's unity, such diversity of customs and observances
> only adds to her comeliness, and contributes greatly to carrying
> out her mission (UR 16).

> What has already been said about legitimate variety we are
> pleased to apply to differences in theological expressions of doc-
> trine. In the investigation of revealed truth, East and West have
> used different methods and approaches in understanding and
> proclaiming divine things. It is hardly surprising, then, if some-
> times one tradition has come nearer than the other to an apt ap-
> preciation of certain aspects of a revealed mystery, or has
> expressed them in a clearer manner. As a result, these various
> theological formulations are often to be considered as comple-
> mentary rather than conflicting. With regard to the authentic the-
> ological traditions of the eastern Christians, we must recognize
> that they are admirably rooted in holy Scripture, fostered and
> given expression in liturgical life, and nourished by the living tra-
> dition of the apostles and by the writings of the Fathers and spir-
> itual authors of the East; they are directed toward a right ordering
> of life, indeed, toward a full contemplation of Christian truth
> (UR 17).

In the period since Vatican II, theological pluralism has come
more and more to be seen as a legitimate and necessary aspect of

what is now termed the "inculturation" of the Christian faith: that is, its "incarnation" into the diverse cultures of humankind. In 1972 the International Theological Commission produced a statement on this issue, of which the following passage is especially significant.

> Because the Christian faith is universal and missionary, the events and words revealed by God must be each time rethought, reformulated, and lived anew within each human culture, if we wish them to inspire the prayer, the worship and the daily life of the people of God. Thus, the gospel of Christ leads each culture towards its fullness and at the same time submits it to a creative criticism. Local churches which, under the guidance of their shepherds, apply themselves to this difficult task of incarnating the Christian faith, must always maintain continuity and communion with the universal Church of the past and of the present. Thanks to their efforts they contribute as much to the deepening of the Christian life as to the progress of theological reflection in the universal Church, and guide the human race in all its diversity towards that unity wished by God.[71]

Catholicity As Relationship with All of Humanity

We come now to the final paragraph of LG 13: a brief paragraph which merits being quoted in full:

> All men are called to be part of this catholic unity of the People of God, a unity which is harbinger of the universal peace it promotes. And there belong to it or are related to it in various ways, the Catholic faithful as well as all who believe in Christ, and indeed the whole of mankind. For all men are called to salvation by the grace of God.

The paragraph begins by repeating the opening statement of article 13, which reads: "All men are called to belong to the new People of God." This "call to membership" establishes a relationship with the church that is presented as absolutely universal: all without exception are thus "called." We shall have to consider in what such a call consists, and how it can be said that everyone receives it. The translation which describes the church's unity as a "harbinger of the universal peace it promotes" does not bring out as clearly as does the original Latin—*praesignat et promovet*—that reference is being made to the role of the church as "sacrament, that is to say, both sign and instrument, of the unity of all mankind" (cf. LG 1).

Having asserted a universal call to membership in the church, our text goes on to distinguish the various ways in which people either belong to or are related to the church. Since the call is universal, these different relationships must depend on how the call is given and received. The two verbs used, *pertinent vel ordinantur*, are certainly not synonyms; they indicate two quite different ways of being related to the church, as we shall see. Three categories of people are then distinguished: Catholics, other Christians, and then, instead of non-Christians, as one might have expected, there follows: "absolutely all men" (*omnes universaliter homines*), of whom a new assertion is made: "who are called to salvation by the grace of God." We shall have to ask whether "being called to salvation" is exactly the same thing as being called to belong to the people of God.

As we have indicated, the following three articles spell out the ways that the different categories of people are related to the church. We shall consider each of them in turn.

The Catholic Faithful (LG 14)

The first paragraph of this article introduces the question of the necessity of belonging to the Catholic Church, and offers an interpretation of the dictum: "Outside the church no salvation." We shall postpone discussion of this question to the next chapter.

The second paragraph distinguishes two ways in which Catholics can belong to the church: either as "fully incorporated," or as remaining incorporated, but without charity. We have already discussed this distinction in an earlier chapter. One could think of other categories of Catholics whose ways of belonging to the church differ considerably from one another, since being fully incorporated requires not only charity, but the bonds of professed faith, of the sacraments, of ecclesiastical government, and of communion. Here one must surely reckon with degrees of membership that would fall somewhere between full incorporation, and a clean break with the Catholic Church by apostasy, heresy or schism. In the post-conciliar period there are many Catholics who have no intention of leaving the church, but whose communion with it in terms of professed faith and acceptance of the directives of the magisterium is hardly such as could be called "full communion." And it is notorious that there are many who have been baptized in the Catholic Church and would call themselves Catholics who have never received the Eucharist and rarely if ever participate in the public worship of the church. One could also mention the large number of Catholics who are divorced and remarried, whose participation in the sacramental life of the church is gravely impaired. So there are various degrees of incorporation by which Catholics themselves belong to their church.

A final category is mentioned at the close of art. 14: catechumens who intend to receive baptism in the Catholic Church. Since it is through baptism "as through a door" that one enters the church (cf. LG 14), catechumens are not yet members; nevertheless "Mother Church already embraces them as her own."

Other Christians (LG 15)

In our third chapter we have already explained the notion of ecclesial communion, and the distinction between "juridical" and "theological" communion. We can sum up the contents of article 15 by saying that it explains the various bonds of theological communion that link to the Catholic Church those Christians who are not in juridical communion with her. The lack of juridical communion is expressed by the phrase: "they do not preserve unity of communion with the successor of Peter." One common bond of theological communion is the fact that all are baptized Christians. Over and above baptism, there are various elements and degrees of theological communion that link other Christians to the Catholic Church. Some, like the Orthodox, share practically every element of ecclesial life with Catholics except the Petrine ministry. Others share much less of Catholic faith and its sacramental system. As we have already mentioned, the Decree on Ecumenism also describes the various bonds of communion linking other Christians with the Catholic Church (UR 14–18 for eastern Christians, and 20–23 for those of the west). Here again it is a question of communion with the Catholic Church: "For men who believe in Christ and have been properly baptized are brought into a certain, though imperfect, communion with the Catholic Church" (UR 3).

The council has treated this question only in terms of the communion that links other Christians to the Catholic Church. But the notion of communion admits of other applications, of which we shall mention some here. For instance, by Christian faith and baptism, Christians are in theological communion not only with Catholics, but with all other Christians. Furthermore, Christians who are fully incorporated members of their respective churches and ecclesial communities are in juridical communion with those whom they recognize as their pastors. Another kind of ecclesial communion would be that linking all the churches of the Anglican Communion together in shared faith and traditions, even though they are juridically independent of one another.

One way to approach the question of ecclesial communion is to consider the various aspects of the communion that is established by the reception of baptism. Vatican II describes baptism as "the door by which people enter the church." We have seen above that the church of Christ is no longer to be exclusively identified with the Catholic Church. We have proposed that one can understand the church of Christ, in its broadest sense, as the communion, at various levels both of "communion" and of "church," of all the Christian churches and ecclesial communities in the world. I suggest that every valid sacrament of baptism has the effect of incorporating a person into the church of Christ.

However, as LG 15 points out, people receive sacraments in their own churches and ecclesiastical communities. To request baptism from the minister of a particular church establishes a bond between the person baptized and the church of which the one administering the sacrament is an authorized pastor. Hence, to request baptism from a Catholic priest establishes a bond of juridical communion with the Catholic Church; to request it from an Orthodox priest makes one a member of that Orthodox Church, and so on. Hence, one can distinguish different aspects of the communion established by baptism: with the Catholic Church, with all other Christians in the church of Christ, and with one's own particular church. But an even more important bond of communion is established by receiving the sacrament fruitfully: with Christ himself. "By the sacrament of baptism, whenever it is properly conferred in the way the Lord determined, and received with the appropriate dispositions of soul, a man becomes truly incorporated into the crucified and glorified Christ and is reborn to a sharing of the divine life" (UR 22).

"Those Who Have Not Yet Received the Gospel" (LG 16)

We recall that in the last paragraph of art. 13, it was stated that all men either belong to or are related to the people of God. It is surely significant that the opening sentence of art. 16 says of "those who have not yet received the gospel" only that they are *related* in various ways to the people of God. The omission of the other term, "belong to," in this context indicates that in the mind of the council it is only Christians who can be said to belong to the church, and this is a logical consequence of the fact that it is by baptism that one is incorporated into the church. Of all the baptized one can say that in various ways they belong to the church; of all others the council says that they are related, in various ways, to the people of God.

One point that is immediately worth noting is that the term "people of God" as used here is a synonym for "the church." It is true that all of humanity can be called "God's people" by reason of creation, and even more by reason of the new relationship of all humanity with God established by the incarnation of his Son. But if the term "people of God" were being used here in that sense, there would be no basis for the distinction between those who belong to it and those who are only related to it. Apart from references to Israel, there is no instance in the documents of Vatican II where the term "the people of God" is not correctly understood as a synonym for "the church of Christ."

The term "those who have not yet received the gospel" includes all those who are not members of the church either in fact, by baptism, or in desire, as are catechumens. It is sobering to recall that about two-thirds of all the people in the world are included here. Of all these people, it is stated that "in various ways they are related to the people of God." The rest of art. 16 spells out the grounds on which various groups of people can be described as "related to the church." Five groups of people are distinguished on the basis of the source and kind of knowledge of God that is characteristic of each group. They are listed in a descending order, from those whose knowledge of God is closest to Christian revelation, to those who have not yet arrived at an explicit knowledge of God.

First to be mentioned are the Jewish people, whose knowledge of God is based on divine revelation. They are related to the church of Christ since they are "the people to whom the covenants and the promises were given, and from whom Christ was born according to the flesh." Indeed they are still a "people most dear to God." St. Paul asks: "Has God rejected his people?" and answers: "By no means! God has not rejected his people whom he foreknew" (Rom 11:1f). Being still "God's dear people," the Jews are uniquely related to the people of the new covenant, whom St. Paul described as wild olive shoots, grafted onto the olive tree of which the Jews are the natural branches (cf. Rom 11:17–21). What is very briefly set forth in two sentences in LG 16 is more amply developed in art. 4 of the council's Declaration on the Relationship of the Church to Non-Christian Religions (*Nostra aetate:* NA).

The next group are the Moslems, who are mentioned first among those "who acknowledge the Creator." The Moslems are described as people who, "professing to hold the faith of Abraham, along with us adore the one and merciful God who on the last day will judge mankind." Again, we can refer to *Nostra aetate*, which devotes a full paragraph to the reasons why the church "looks upon the Moslems with esteem" (NA 3).

After the Moslems come "those who in shadows and images seek the unknown God." Presumably the council is here referring to members of other non-Christian religions, without mentioning any of them by name. In *Nostra aetate* specific mention is made of Hinduism and Buddhism among religions whose "ways of conduct and of life, whose rules and teachings . . . often reflect a ray of that Truth which enlightens all men" (NA 2).

The following paragraph seems best understood as referring to people who do not practice any specific religion. Some are described as those "who sincerely seek God"; others as "those who, without blame on their part, have not yet arrived at an explicit knowledge of God." Of both groups it is said that they strive, with the help of grace, to live a good life according to the dictates of their conscience.

The question remains as to how these various categories of people are "related to the church." There is no problem on this score about the Jewish people, who are in a unique relationship to Christ and to his church. But, after the mention of the Jews, the basis of the relationship of all the other groups seems to lie in the fact that all are included in God's plan of salvation, and all receive the offer of his grace. This idea is expressed again and again, in a variety of ways: "But the plan of salvation also includes those who acknowledge the Creator." "God as Savior wills that all men be saved (cf. 1 Tim 2:4)." "Those also can attain to everlasting salvation . . . " "Nor does divine Providence deny the help necessary for salvation . . . " It seems clear that the reason why all these people are said to be related to the church is the fact that "all men are called to salvation by the grace of God" (cf. LG 13, the last sentence).

If one asks in what, concretely, this universal "call to salvation" consists, the answer suggested by the text is: it consists in the universal offer of grace, the divine help which makes it possible for all these people to attain salvation. It is obvious that the offer of grace does not automatically guarantee salvation; this depends also on the free response a person makes to grace. It is also clear that the grace necessary and sufficient for salvation in a great many cases does not include the grace that makes it possible for the person to arrive at explicit Christian faith and incorporation in the church by baptism. The text certainly speaks of the hope of salvation for people who will live and die as "non-Christians." This of course involves the real possibility of their attaining supernatural justification and living in the state of grace. But whether or not they respond to God's grace in such a way as to attain salvation, they all remain, to the end of their lives, the object of God's sincere offer of grace, and this offer, the concrete expression of the divine will that all be saved, is what is meant by the "universal call to salvation."

It would seem to be the mind of the council that this universal call to salvation is the basis for the assertion that all men are called to belong to the people of God (LG 13, first sentence). But one has to admit that there is an important difference between these two "calls." The grace in which the call to salvation consists makes the attainment of the state of grace and of eternal salvation a real possibility for everyone. But the call to belong to the church does not make membership in the church by the profession of Christian faith and baptism a real possibility for everyone. There are millions of people for whom this is certainly not a real possibility; one has only to think of the fact that one fourth of the world's population lives in the Republic of China.

If, then, one asks how such people can be said to receive a "call to belong to the people of God," the answer would seem to be that every offer of grace that makes salvation possible is in some real way *directed toward* the church, even when this "directedness" will not result in actual membership in it. There are several reasons for saying that all grace for salvation is in some way directed toward the church. One is that the ultimate goal of all such grace is that a person may be numbered among the just, and thus, to be among all those "just men from the time of Adam, from Abel, the just one, to the last of the elect, who will be gathered together with the Father in the universal Church" (cf. LG 2). The grace whose goal is participation in the "universal church" of the kingdom of God must also be intrinsically ordered toward the church in its earthly state. Secondly, the grace that brings a person to supernatural justice must include the grace that makes possible an act of saving faith. Such faith, however incomplete it may be in content, is intrinsically directed toward the full profession of faith that is had in the church. Thirdly, the grace of salvation includes the gift of supernatural love of God and neighbor, and this is intrinsically ordered toward the fullness of communion in charity that is the inner life of the church.

We have taken the conciliar statement that all men are related to the church to be a conclusion from the truth that all receive the grace by which they can be saved. The council specified that all those who are not Christian are related in various ways to the church, and distinguished various groups according to their knowledge of God. Besides this criterion, there is another basis for distinguishing between ways that non-Christians can be related to the church: namely, according to whether or not they have so responded to God's grace as to be living in the state of grace. To say that non-Christians can attain salvation certainly means that in the course of this life they can enjoy the supernatural friendship with God that we call the state of grace.

Now it is a basic tenet of Christian faith that there is no grace by which men can be saved but the grace which Christ won for all by the paschal mystery of his death and resurrection. The grace which God offers to everyone is none other than the grace of Christ. In the Pastoral Constitution on the Church in the Modern World the council declares: "Since Christ died for all men, and since the ultimate vocation of man is in fact one, and divine, we ought to believe that the Holy Spirit in a manner known only to God offers to every man the possibility of being associated with the paschal mystery" (GS 22).

Here again it is a question of the universal offer of grace. We do not know whether everyone will respond to this grace in such a way as to attain salvation. But those who do will at some point in their lives begin to live a supernatural life in the grace of Christ, even without explicit faith in Christ. Such are the people whom Karl Rahner has called "anonymous Christians." He called them "Christians," in the sense that their life in grace is truly life in Christ; "anonymous," because, lacking explicit Christian faith, they do not have the name of being Christian, and do not know the author of their grace.[72]

As Rahner himself insisted, it is not so important whether one thinks the term "anonymous Christians" appropriate or not; the important truth at stake is that there is no grace for salvation but the grace of Christ, and that, without knowing Christ, many people can be living by his grace.[73]

What about the relationship that such "anonymous Christians" have with the church? Being "anonymous," they cannot be numbered among those who "belong to the church." But their relationship to the church consists of their sharing in the same gift of grace and charity which is the spiritual life of the church. The same Holy Spirit who gives life to the church is also dwelling in them. So their relationship to the church is one of spiritual communion: a sharing in the life of Christ.

God alone knows how many persons in the world, Christians and non-Christians alike, at any moment in time, are actually living in grace, sharing this spiritual communion. The fact that this is a purely spiritual reality, knowable only to God, is one of several reasons for not identifying this "sphere of grace" with the church. The church in this world is a complex reality, at the same time a spiritual community and a visible society structured by sacraments and ministry. The spiritual communion of all who at any moment are in the state of grace is something real, but it is not the same thing as the church. To identify it with the church would be to make the mistake of applying to the church on earth what will be true only of the future kingdom of God, where all the just, and only the just, will be gathered together with the Father in the universal church (cf. LG 2). The church here on earth is a community of Christian faith and sacraments, not all of whose members share fully in the life of grace, on the other hand, some who lack the faith and baptism necessary for membership in the church do share in the life of grace.

At this point the question may be raised: how then should we understand the relationship between the spiritual communion of all those, baptized or not, who at any moment are in the state of grace, and the Christian community of faith and sacraments, not all of whose members may be in the state of grace? Various solutions have been offered to this question in the past. Some have related them as "invisible church" to "visible church"; some as "soul of the church" to "body of the church"; some as "mystical body" to "institutional church." Let us look briefly at each of these solutions, before proposing the solution that we believe corresponds to the ecclesiology of Vatican II.

The distinction between "visible" and "invisible" church is commonly associated with Lutheran ecclesiology.[74] It was a distinction which Luther and the Lutheran tradition used to distinguish between the church in an empirical sense, the church that includes all baptized Christians, both saints and sinners, and the church in a vision of faith, consisting only of "true believers" or saints. A modern Lutheran theologian assures us: "The intention was never to bifurcate the church, as if visible and invisible referred to two churches that existed side by side."[75] It would seem that one could translate the Lutheran idea into the language of Vatican II by saying that their "visible church" includes all who are incorporated in the church by baptism, while their "invisible church" consists only of those who are "fully incorporated," as "having the Spirit of Christ" (cf. LG 14). In the Lutheran sense, the "invisible church" is found only within the "visible church," since they would recognize as "true believers" only baptized Christians who are justified by sincere faith in God's mercy. In that sense, their "invisible church" is "hidden" within the visible church; it does not exist apart from it, and does not extend beyond it, at least as far as this world is concerned.

It is quite a different application of the distinction between an invisible and a visible church, when some modern Catholic writers have sought to reconcile the possibility of salvation for non-Christians with the axiom "No salvation outside the church," by extending the limits of the church so as to include all those who are in the state of grace. This necessitated distinguishing between the visible boundaries of the church and its invisible boundaries, and thus between the visible church of the baptized and the invisible church of all who are actually living in grace.[76] We shall see in our next chapter that there is a better way to handle the problem caused by the axiom "No salvation outside the church" than by enlarging the church so as to include within the "invisible church" all those who are on the way to salvation.

In this connection it should be noted that while Rahner speaks of non-Christians in the state of grace as "anonymous Christians," he does not extend the limits of the church in such a way as to identify "anonymous Christianity" with an invisible church.

The distinction between the "soul" and "body" of the church was used by Robert Bellarmine as a way of expressing the difference between the spiritual elements in the make-up of the church, such as faith, hope, charity, and grace, on the one hand, and the visible bonds by which people are linked to the church, such as the profession of the same faith, the reception of the sacraments, and communion with the pastors under the Pope. Thus, he said that some people could be "of the body" of the church and not "of the soul" (such as Catholics lacking charity); while others could be "of the soul" without being "of the body" (people who are not actually members of the church, but have the virtues of faith and charity, and thus have such dispositions as can be interpreted as an implicit desire of being in the church).[77] Bellarmine's use of the distinction between "soul" and "body" of the church is analogous to the distinction made in LG 8 between the "divine" and the "human" elements of the complex reality which is the church. His description of Catholics living without grace as being of the "body" but not of the "soul" of the church is not unlike the way that LG 14 speaks of such people as remaining in the church only in a "bodily" manner and not "in their hearts."

Unfortunately, Bellarmine's distinction has often been misused, when more recent Catholic writers have identified the "soul" of the church not with the internal, spiritual elements of the church, but with all those people whom Bellarmine would describe as being "of the soul" without being "of the body." In other words, the distinction between "soul" and "body" becomes really a distinction between the visible church as "body" and the invisible church of all those in the state of grace, as "soul."[78] Here we have a "soul" that extends far beyond the limits of the body, depending on how optimistic one is about the number of non-Christians who are living in the state of grace. While it is not inappropriate to speak of the formal principle of the life of the church as its "created soul,"[79] it does seem altogether incongruous to say that Christians constitute the "body" of the church, while non-Christians in grace constitute its "soul."

In any case, in the period following the first world war, this way of speaking was largely abandoned in favor of the distinction between the "mystical body" and the "visible church." In our first chapter we have mentioned the fact that prior to the encyclical *Mystici corporis* of Pius XII in 1943, the notion of the "mystical body of Christ" had most often been treated by Catholic theologians in their treatise on grace, whereas their ecclesiology had to do with the institutional church as a "perfect society." Membership in the mystical body was understood to depend on the degree to which one shared in the life of Christ by grace, while membership in the church required professing Catholic faith, receiving the sacraments and being in communion with the Catholic bishops and the Pope. The consequences of this way of distinguishing between "mystical body" and "church" are well brought out in the following passage of one of the most important studies of the theology of the mystical body of that period: Emile Mersch's *The Theology of the Mystical Body*.

> In the ordinary language of the Church, "mystical body" connotes the entire multitude of those who live the life of Christ, with a life that admits of degrees (cf. St. Thomas, *Summa* III, 8, 3), whereas the word "Church" represents the society of the baptized faithful as organized under their lawful pastors.
> The two realities are closely related, and the present chapter will show how the one necessarily involves the other. But the two are not absolutely identified on this earth. A person can be a member of the visible society of the Church without actually living the life of Christ as a perfect member of the mystical body; this is the case with a Catholic hardened in sin. Likewise, one can truly live the life of Christ without being actually attached to the visible society that is His Church; an example is a pagan who

would have received grace and charity without being aware of the Church, or a fervent catechumen.

It is quite true that the Church visible alone, as established over the entire earth, fully represents what Jesus Christ desires. But it is also true that the visible Church is far from having achieved that position, and Jesus Christ foresaw this. Accordingly the great number of souls effectively living the life of Christ is one thing, and the visible Church is another; in a matter so delicate, dealing with such important objects, we shall find it useful to have two different words to designate two realities that differ *de facto*, however closely they may be related *de jure*.[80]

Emile Mersch died in 1940; the work from which we have just quoted was issued posthumously in 1942.[81] The following year saw the publication of Pius XII's encyclical *Mystici Corporis*, which insisted that the mystical body of Christ and the Roman Catholic Church are one and the same reality. The Second Vatican Council has followed Pius XII in rejecting the separation of mystical body and church into two distinct realities, but has nuanced his teaching in several respects. Describing the church as both "a society furnished with hierarchical agencies" and "mystical body of Christ," it has brought out the fact that these terms connote very different aspects of the one complex reality which is the church.[82] Secondly, while continuing to identify mystical body and church, it no longer exclusively identifies the church with the Roman Catholic Church, thus leaving open the possibility of our recognizing all baptized Christians, and not Catholics alone, as being really members of the body of Christ.[83] On the other hand, the doctrine of Vatican II gives no support to the distinction between a visible church and a mystical body of Christ that would be, as Mersch put it, "the entire multitude of those who live the life of Christ."

If, then, none of the former solutions we have just briefly outlined is really compatible with the teaching of Vatican II, we must now ask what the council offers as a better key to understanding and expressing the relationship between the church and the "sphere of grace" in the world. I suggest that such a key is to be found in the council's description of the church as the "universal sacrament of salvation." It is to this notion that we must now turn our attention.

6 | "Universal Sacrament of Salvation"

In our first chapter we have already seen that to speak of the church as "sacrament of salvation" is an effective way to express the nature of the church as a mystery of faith. The fact that the Latin word *sacramentum* came into Christian usage as the translation of the Greek New Testament word *musterion* is already an indication that if the church is a sacrament, it is also in some sense a mystery. But, when *Lumen gentium* begins by describing the church as "a kind of sacrament," it is applying to the church, by analogy, the notion of sacrament as it is used of the seven sacraments. It is asserting that the church itself is, in its own way, a "visible sign of invisible grace," being an effective instrument of the salvation which it signifies.

In three important documents, Vatican II has further developed this concept by speaking of the church as the *universal* sacrament of salvation. In *Lumen gentium* we read: "Christ, having been lifted up from the earth, is drawing all men to himself (Jn 12:32). Rising from the dead, he sent his life-giving Spirit upon his disciples and through this Spirit has established his body, the church, as the universal sacrament of salvation" (LG 48). *Gaudium et spes* declares: "While helping the world and receiving many benefits from it, the church has a single intention: that God's kingdom may come, and that the salvation of the whole human race may come to pass. For every benefit which the People of God during its earthly pilgrimage can offer to the human family stems from the fact that the church is 'the universal sacrament of salvation,' simultaneously manifesting and exercising the mystery of God's love for man" (GS 45). Finally, the Decree on the Church's Missionary Activity (*Ad gentes:* AG)

109

opens with the statement: "The church has been divinely sent to all nations that she might be 'the universal sacrament of salvation' " (AG 1).

The appearance of the word "universal" in these texts suggests that we are dealing with an aspect of the catholicity of the church. If the role of the church as sign and instrument of salvation really means that the church not only signifies but helps to bring about the salvation of everyone who is saved, we have another important reason for professing our belief in the church as "catholic." In this chapter we shall have to see in what sense the church can be said to be both sign and instrument of salvation, and what grounds there are for claiming a universal role for it in the salvation of all humanity.

In the previous chapter we have seen that there is no salvation without the grace of Christ, and that every offer of grace is intrinsically directed toward the church, even when it does not bring about actual membership in the church on earth. In this sense, the catholicity of the church consists in the fact that the universal offer of grace involves a relationship to the church on the part of every human person—a relationship, to be sure, that will vary according to the response each person makes to God's grace. In some cases, as we have seen, people can respond to grace in such a way as to enter into spiritual communion with the church, living in Christ without knowing him as the source of their supernatural life. In other cases, a person may not have responded, and yet the offer continues to be made. The common factor here is that everyone without exception is placed in some relationship to the church. All those who do not actually belong to her are at least "ordered toward her" (*ad eam ordinantur*).

The new aspect of catholicity that is expressed when the church is described as "universal sacrament of salvation" is that all grace of salvation is not only ordered *toward* the church, but in some way comes *from* and *through* the church. As sign and instrument of all salvation, the church is not merely the goal toward which grace is directed, it is the channel or medium through which grace is given.

It is not difficult to see that if the church is the medium or instrument through which all salvation is obtained, it follows that no one can be saved except through the church. This has certainly been the mind of the church from its earliest period. The traditional expression of this belief has been the saying: "No salvation outside the church." While it is put negatively, this axiom is really a way of expressing the catholicity of the church as universally necessary for salvation. But it is a way of expressing the necessity of the church that is terribly misleading If It is not understood in the light of its historical context. Our view is that this negative formula is so open to misunderstanding that it would be better to avoid its use, and rather to express the truth about the necessity of the church by describing it as the universal sacrament of salvation.

However, since the saying "No salvation outside the church" has such a long tradition in the teaching of the church, and has been affirmed by ecumenical councils and by Popes, it seems necessary to explain first how this negative formula should be understood in the light of its historical context, before going on to discuss the positive formula we would prefer to use.

"No Salvation Outside the Church" in Its Historical Context

In treating this question we shall distinguish between two periods of church history: first the patristic and medieval period up to the end of the fifteenth century, and second the period since the beginning of the sixteenth century. The dividing line between these two periods was the discovery of the new worlds, both of America and of Asia, which shattered what had until that time been the common Christian assumption that the whole world had heard the gospel, and that everyone (with extremely rare exceptions) had had ample opportunity to embrace the Christian faith.

We shall also distinguish between the several categories of people whom those who used this axiom had in mind as being "outside the church" and thereby excluded from salvation.

No Salvation for Christian Heretics and Schismatics

During the patristic period, we find the axiom "No salvation outside the church" most often being used with reference to Christians who have separated themselves from the "great church," the *catholica*, by joining some heretical or schismatic sect. St. Cyprian introduced this saying, and St. Augustine followed him in using it as a salutary warning to such Christians that there was no hope for salvation for them as long as they persisted in their adherence to their sect. But it is important for us to understand that in the eyes of both of these great African bishops, anyone who had broken off communion with the true church and joined a heretical or schismatic group was guilty of a grave sin against charity. For them, ecclesial communion and charity were synonymous; whoever sinned against one sinned against the other, and there was no hope for salvation for anyone who persisted in grave sin.[84]

Cyprian and Augustine were convinced that the Holy Spirit could not remain where charity was grievously offended, and hence the sacraments that were administered in heretical or schismatic sects could not confer the Holy Spirit or his saving gifts of grace. St. Cyprian drew the conclusion that their sacraments would not even be valid; St. Augustine corrected this opinion, agreeing with Rome that their sacraments could indeed be valid, but denying that they could be fruitful for grace or salvation, since those who received them were not properly disposed to receive grace as long as they persisted in the sin against ecclesial charity.[85]

What emerges from this consideration of the context in which they said "No salvation outside the church" is that they were thinking of people whose very being outside the church they judged to be gravely sinful. We might nowadays question their judgment that everyone adhering to a schismatic sect is personally guilty of grave sin. As a matter of fact, St. Augustine did recognize the difference between those who had been responsible for the separation and those who were brought up in a family that was separated from the church.[86] But he still held out no real hope for the salvation of such people unless they returned to the communion of the church. We must reckon with the fact that the negative judgment expressed by Cyprian and Augustine and by the early Fathers generally on the chances of salvation for Christians separated from the church by heresy or schism was the common view of the medieval theologians as well. But we have to keep in mind that this judgment included the presumption that such people were all guilty of grave sin against the basic virtues of faith or charity.

No Salvation for Unbelievers:
Jews, Pagans, and (Later on) Moslems

With regard to the possibility of salvation for Jews and pagans, the Fathers and medieval theologians distinguished between the time before Christ and the time since the gospel had been promulgated. Before Christ, they recognized that the Hebrew religion had been a way of salvation for the Jews, through faith in the true God and in his promised Messiah. They also saw the possibility of salvation for Gentiles during that time: not, to be sure, for those who worshiped idols and flouted the law written in their hearts (cf. Rom 1:18–32), but for those who followed the light which they received from the Divine Word "who enlightens every man" (cf. Jn 1:9). Such people had also been saved through faith, believing "that God exists and that he rewards those who seek him" (Heb 11:6). Some of the Fathers, like Augustine, would say that Jews and Gentiles who had lived justly before the coming of Christ had not really been "outside the church," since one could speak of a church of all the just, that had existed since the time of Abel, the first man whose life had been wholly pleasing to God.

Once the gospel had been preached, however, the Fathers saw no hope of salvation for anyone who had heard about Christ and failed to believe in him. They took very literally the words attributed to Jesus in the ending of Mark: "Go into the whole world and preach the gospel to every creature. He who believes and is baptized will be saved; but he who does not believe will be condemned" (Mk 16:16). They applied this text to all the Jews and pagans of their own day, as well as other texts, like the following one from the fourth gospel: "He who believes is not condemned; he who does not believe is condemned already, because he has not believed in the name of the only Son of God" (Jn 3:18). There was no question in their minds about the guilt of the Jews, who had heard the gospel message and had rejected it. With regard to unbelievers among the Gentiles, it is astonishing to learn how soon the Fathers came to believe that the gospel had already been preached everywhere, and that pagans no longer had any excuse for not believing in Christ and entering the church. Of course we have to keep in mind that their knowledge of geography was limited to what they knew of the Roman Empire. They also relied on the word of St. Paul, who even in his own day could say: "I ask, have they not heard? Indeed they have, for 'their voice has gone out to all the earth, and their words to the end of the world' " (Rom 10:18). Whatever St. Paul may have meant by this, the Fathers had no hesitation in taking this to be literally true in their own day, especially by the fourth century, when the Roman Empire became officially Christian. St. John Chrysostom, for example, was convinced that in his time no one could be inculpably ignorant of the Gospel, and hence there was no hope of salvation for those who persisted in their unbelief.

Chrysostom's view that the exclusion of Jews and pagans from salvation was in every case the just consequence of their own sinful refusal to believe in Christ was a conviction shared by most of the Fathers, and then by the medieval theologians. They were convinced that everyone had a sufficient opportunity to come to Christian faith, and that it was their own fault if they rejected it. St. Augustine, in the course of his controversy with the Pelagians about original sin and the need of grace, came to have an exceptional view, namely, that even such unbelievers as had never had a chance to hear the gospel would be condemned, and that this would be a just punishment for original sin. One of his most faithful disciples, Bishop Fulgentius of Ruspe in North Africa, shared the pessimistic view of his great master about the fate of all unbelievers, even of those who had never heard the gospel, when he wrote: "Hold most firmly, and by no means doubt, that not only all pagans, but also all Jews, and all heretics and schismatics, who end this present life outside the catholic church, will go to the eternal fire prepared for the devil and his angels."[87]

However, the common view of the medieval theologians was that no one would be condemned for unbelief that was not personally culpable. They shared the Fathers' belief that the gospel had been preached everywhere and saw it as an extremely rare and exceptional case if anyone had been brought up in a place where there was no opportunity to hear about Christ. Indeed they were convinced that God would provide even extraordinary means to make it possible for such a person to come to Christian faith, on the condition that he was living according to the dictates of his conscience. On the other hand, they agreed with the Fathers that there was no hope for the salvation of anyone who persisted in unbelief, and they now added the Moslems to the list of those who had heard the gospel message and had culpably rejected it.

The teaching of the Fathers and theologians was confirmed by the medieval councils and Popes. The Fourth Lateran Council, in 1215, declared: "There is one universal church of the faithful, outside of which no one at all is saved."[88] Pope Boniface VIII, in his famous bull *Unam sanctam* of 1302, compared the church to the ark of Noah, insisting that as all living things that remained outside the ark were lost in the flood, so there could be no salvation for those who remained outside the Catholic Church. Furthermore, since no one could be a member of the Catholic Church who did not recognize the authority of the Pope, he concluded that salvation was impossible for those who were not in obedience to the Bishop of Rome.[89]

In the middle of the fifteenth century, the ecumenical Council of Florence gave conciliar authority to what we have seen was the doctrine of Fulgentius, incorporating his statement into its Decree for the Jacobites. The council declared:

> (The Holy Roman Church) firmly believes, professes and proclaims, that none of those living outside the Catholic Church, neither pagans nor Jews nor heretics nor schismatics, can become sharers in eternal life; rather they will go into the eternal fire prepared for the devil and his angels, unless they join the church before the end of their lives. . . . No one, no matter how great alms he has given, even though he has shed his blood for Christ, can be saved, unless he remains in the bosom and unity of the Catholic Church.[90]

Within the century that followed the Council of Florence, explorers from Europe discovered that there were vast numbers of people in Africa, Asia and America who had never heard the gospel. This necessitated a new approach to the question of the possibility of salvation for non-Christians. But various approaches to the problem were taken. After the Reformation, most Protestants took a very negative view toward the possibility of salvation without explicit faith in Christ. Many of them took the lack of faith, even if not culpable, to be a sign that a person simply was not predestined to be saved.

Within the Catholic Church two opposing points of view were championed: by the Jansenists, and by the Jesuits. The Jansenists held rigidly to the medieval position, and went beyond it, insisting that the "infidels" could only commit sin and deserve condemnation. Some went so far as to hold that there was no grace given outside the church: a proposition that was condemned by Pope Clement XI in 1713.[91]

The Jesuits, many of whom were missionaries who had firsthand knowledge of the peoples who had recently been discovered, took a more optimistic view, holding that God did not deny to anyone the grace necessary for salvation. Since so many millions of these people had had no opportunity until now to hear the gospel and enter the church, there must be a possibility of salvation for them without explicit Christian faith and actual membership in the church. The leading Jesuit theologian of the time, Robert Bellarmine, offered this solution to the problem: "The saying that no one is saved outside the church should be understood of those who belong to her neither in fact nor in desire, just as theologians commonly say with regard to baptism."[92]

The idea of "baptism in desire" was not new; even the Fathers of the church had said that catechumens who died unexpectedly before baptism could be saved by their desire of the sacrament. What was new in the sixteenth century was the application of this idea to vast numbers of people who obviously had known nothing of baptism or the church. In order to credit such people with a desire of baptism, one would have to invoke the notion of an implicit desire: i.e. such dispositions of soul as could be interpreted as the will to do whatever was required for their salvation. Centuries before, Thomas Aquinas had already said that before receiving the sacrament, a person might have obtained the remission of sin through an implicit desire of baptism.[93] Francis Suarez appealed to this teaching of Aquinas when he offered his solution to the problem raised by the discovery of so many people for whom explicit Christian faith and membership in the church had been impossible. He explained that when explicit faith was not possible, implicit faith would suffice, and when the explicit desire of baptism and membership in the church was not possible, the implicit desire would suffice.[94]

While not all Catholic theologians accepted the interpretation given by Bellarmine and Suarez, their view was never condemned, whereas the rigid interpretation of the Jansenists did meet with official condemnation. Passing over the various approaches that were taken to this question in the intervening centuries, we shall consider some official statements that have been made in the present century by the teaching authorities of the Catholic Church.

In the encyclical *Mystici corporis*, Pius XII, referring to those "who do not belong to the visible Catholic Church," urged them "to seek to extricate themselves from a situation in which they cannot be sure of their eternal salvation, since, even though they may be related to the Mystical Body of the Redeemer by an unconscious desire and wish, they still lack so many and so important heavenly gifts and aids which can be enjoyed only in the Catholic Church."[95]

Several points are worth noting about this statement of Pope Pius. First, it has to be understood in the light of his strict identification of the mystical body of Christ with the Catholic Church. Second, while he does not say so explicitly, he does imply that non-Catholics can be saved if they are related to the Catholic Church by an "unconscious" (*inscio*) desire of belonging to it. This would seem to give papal approval to the solution that Suarez had offered to this problem centuries before. The Pope did not explain what dispositions of soul would be understood as containing such an unconscious desire of belonging to the Catholic Church. Third, the Pope made no distinction between the situation of baptized non-Catholics, and the unbaptized, as far as their relationship to the mystical body of Christ is concerned. In either case, their salvation would depend on their having such dispositions as can be interpreted as an implicit desire to belong to the Catholic Church.

The second official statement on this question came six years later in a letter which the Holy Office, the Vatican body dealing with questions of doctrine, addressed to the archbishop of Boston, Cardinal Cushing.[96] The occasion of this letter was the controversy in Boston over the rigid interpretation which the Jesuit Leonard Feeney and his followers were putting forth as the authentic Catholic position on the question of salvation outside the Catholic Church. Feeney insisted that the pronouncements of the medieval church, such as those of Pope Boniface VIII and the Council of Florence, were still binding, and had to be understood in their literal sense. He rejected the idea that Protestants and Jews had any unconscious or implicit desire to belong to the Catholic Church, or that they could be saved by any such desire. In his opinion, only catechumens and others sincerely intending to become Catholics could be saved as members of the church by desire.

Needless to say, the Holy Office based its reply on the teaching of Pope Pius XII concerning the possibility of salvation by an "unconscious desire" of membership in the Catholic Church. However, it further clarified this teaching in several respects. It explained that what was meant by an "unconscious desire" was the implicit desire that was contained in the good dispositions of a person's soul, whereby the person intended to have his will in conformity with the will of God. It further specified that a disposition of soul sufficient for salvation would have to include "perfect charity" and the supernatural virtue of faith.

Finally, we come to the interpretation of the axiom "No salvation outside the church" given by the Second Vatican Council. We have already seen that in art. 16, *Lumen gentium* repeatedly affirmed the possibility of salvation for "those who had not yet received the gospel." It declared that all such persons were related to the church in various ways. But it never specified that in order to be saved, non-Christians had to be related to the church by a desire to belong to her. It did, however, spell out the kind of dispositions that would be needed for non-Christians to be saved: namely, that they "sincerely seek God, and, moved by grace, strive by their deeds to do his will as it is known to them, through the dictates of their conscience" (LG 16). Now these are the very dispositions in which the Holy Office had recognized an implicit desire of membership in the church, and a footnote at this point in LG 16 refers to the letter to Cardinal Cushing in which this point had been clarified.

The fact remains, however, that there is no explicit reference in the conciliar text to the idea that non-Christians must have an implicit desire of belonging to the church in order to be saved. Nor is there any reference, in *Lumen gentium* or in the Decree on Ecumenism, to the idea of such an implicit desire of belonging to the Catholic Church on the part of other Christians. I am not aware of any official explanation of what seems to have been a deliberate decision on the part of the theological commission not to use this terminology.

How, then, did Vatican II handle the question of the interpretation to be given of the axiom "No salvation outside the church"? The answer is found in the first paragraph of LG 14, which reads:

> This sacred Synod turns its attention first to the Catholic faithful Basing itself upon sacred Scripture and tradition, it teaches that the Church, now sojourning on earth as an exile, is necessary for salvation. For Christ, made present to us in His Body, which is the Church, is the one Mediator and the unique Way of salvation. In explicit terms, He Himself affirmed the necessity of faith and baptism, and thereby affirmed also the necessity of the Church, for through baptism as through a door men enter the Church. Whosoever, therefore, knowing that the Catholic Church was made necessary by God through Jesus Christ, would refuse to enter her or to remain in her could not be saved.

Analyzing this paragraph, we see that two reasons are given why the church is necessary for salvation: first, because it is in the church that we come into contact with Christ, the unique way of salvation, and, second, because it is in the church that we receive faith and baptism. The conclusion of the paragraph is the council's interpretation of the axiom "No salvation outside the church." It means, in effect: "No salvation for those who are *culpably* outside the church." The terms "knowing" and "would refuse" clearly indicate the conditions for mortal sin. Only those who are personally guilty of mortal sin in their decision not to be in the church are thereby excluded from salvation.

The converse would also be true: those can be saved who are inculpably outside the church. This side of the coin is amply developed in LG 16, as we have already seen. There it is a question of those who "through no fault of their own do not know the gospel of Christ or his church"; of those "who without blame on their part have not yet arrived at an explicit knowledge of God." No mention is made of their also being inculpably outside the church, but this is clearly the presumption of the article.

The question that arises at this point, then, is whether the Catholic Church has changed its doctrine on the question of the necessity of being in the church for salvation. On the face of it, there certainly seems to be a contradiction between the Council of Florence, on the one hand, and the position taken by the Second Vatican Council. According to Florence, no pagan, Jew, heretic or schismatic can be saved unless he enters the Catholic Church before he dies. According to Vatican II, salvation is possible for all these people, and even for those who have no religion at all. Is there any way of reconciling these positions?

I believe that they can be reconciled on the grounds that what has changed is not really the basic doctrine that is at stake, but the way Christians judge those who do not belong to the church. We have seen that when Sts. Cyprian and Augustine said that there was no salvation for heretics and schismatics, it was because they judged all such people personally guilty of grave sin against charity by their break with the communion of the church. When Fulgentius and the medieval church declared that all pagans and Jews were doomed to be condemned to hell if they did not become Catholics before they died, their belief was that they were all guilty of refusing to accept Christian faith, on the grounds that the gospel had been sufficiently presented to them, and that therefore they had no excuse for not believing it.

If I am not mistaken, the underlying dogma has always really been what Vatican II explicitly declared it to be: "There is no salvation for those who are culpably outside the church." The difference between Florence and Vatican II is that Florence judged all those outside guilty, and Vatican II presumed them to be innocent. What has changed is a way of judging other people.

One thing we have to keep in mind about our Christian forefathers who thought that God was going to condemn all pagans and Jews to eternal punishment in hell is that they also believed that God is good and that he judges justly. It is inconceivable that they really thought that God would condemn innocent people to eternal punishment. One indication of their refusal to accept such an idea is their invention of limbo as a state where infants dying without baptism would escape even the mitigated form of punishment that St. Augustine thought they would have to suffer as a consequence of original sin. Hardly any Christian theologians followed St. Augustine in thinking that a good and just God would punish in hell anyone who had never committed personal sin. Hence, if these same people thought that God would condemn all pagans and Jews to eternal punishment, we can hardly doubt that they thought that God would be just in doing so.

While we cannot agree with their judgment that all pagans and

Jews were guilty of grave sin in not being Christians, it is possible to understand how they could have judged them in that way; on the other hand, if they had not thought them all guilty, it is impossible to understand how they could have thought that God was going to condemn them all to hell.

For these reasons, we conclude that when the saying "No salvation outside the church" is invoked to exclude any group of people from salvation, the supposition must be, and I believe always has been, even though for the most part unspoken, that such people are guilty of grave sin by the very fact that they are not in the church.

From this discussion of the history of the axiom "No salvation outside the church," it should be clear why we have suggested that it would be better to abandon this way of expressing the necessity of the church for salvation. This is all the more true, since Vatican II has provided us with a better way of expressing it when it described the church as the "universal sacrament of salvation." It is this term that we now wish to explain. We begin with the idea that the whole economy of salvation is "sacramental."

The Sacramental Economy of Salvation

When we speak of the "economy of salvation," we mean the particular way that God has chosen to accomplish the reconciliation of sinful humanity to himself. Without doubt it would have been possible for God to choose some other plan of salvation than the one he did choose. However, the way he did choose was by the incarnation of the eternal Son of God in the man Jesus, and by Jesus' obedience unto death for our redemption, being "put to death for our trespasses and raised for our justification" (Rom 4:25).

Why do we call this a "sacramental" economy of salvation? As we have seen, a sacrament is a visible sign which effects the invisible grace which it signifies. Sacraments are certain actions which men perform, using ordinary created things like water, bread, wine and oil, while speaking human words. It is the nature of a sacrament to be something visible, concrete, a part of our world of created reality—and it is only by faith that we know that it signifies and effects something in the supernatural order of divine grace.

We call the economy of salvation which God has chosen a sacramental economy, because it is only by faith that we could know that the crucifixion of Jesus of Nazareth was not just another act of human injustice, but was the sublime expression of God's love for sinful humanity, since it meant that "God did not spare his own Son but gave him up for us all" (Rom 8:32). In other words, Jesus himself, all his human acts, his suffering, and death, were all visible, concrete elements of our world and of our history—and at the same time, by faith, we know that they signified and brought about our reconciliation with God.

When God chose to accomplish our redemption through the man Jesus, he chose an economy of salvation in which something created, of our finite nature, namely the humanity of Jesus, was going to play an essential role in the working out of his plan. When Jesus, in his turn, chose a group of men as his disciples, and prepared them to carry the good news of redemption to the world, and especially when, before he died, he took bread and wine and gave it to them, telling them that this was his body and blood that they were to eat and drink, and to do this in memory of him—in all this he showed that the economy of salvation was going to continue to be "sacramental." God was going to keep on making use of creatures to accomplish his plan. Ordinary men and women, and ordinary things like bread and wine, were going to be signs and instruments of divine grace. And if we think of all the men and women, and all the things, that God has specially chosen as signs and instruments of grace, what we have is the church. That is why we call the church the sacrament of salvation; it is the continuation of the sacramental economy that God instituted with the incarnation of his Son.

We must now consider the reasons we have for calling the church the *universal* sacrament of salvation.

The Universal Sacrament of Salvation

A sacrament is an efficacious sign of grace. If the church is the universal sacrament of salvation, it must stand forth as a sign of the total work of salvation that God is accomplishing in the world, and somehow be involved as God's instrument in that work. The first question to be asked then is: in what sense is the church the sign of that total work of salvation that God is accomplishing in the world? Using the language of St. Paul, we can describe God's work as "reconciling the world to himself." "In Christ, God was reconciling the world to himself, not counting their trespasses against them, and entrusting to us the message of reconciliation. So we are ambassadors for Christ, God making his appeal through us. We beseech you on behalf of Christ, be reconciled to God" (2 Cor 5:18–20).

The first sense in which the church is a "sign" of God's work is that the church is entrusted with the message of reconciliation. It is the church's role to proclaim to the whole world that God is offering his peace and mercy to sinful humanity, and that he wants all men and women to be reconciled with him and with one another.

But "actions speak louder than words." If the church is to be a convincing ambassador of reconciliation, it must show the world a concrete example of what it means to be a people reconciled to God. The clearest proof that people are at peace with God is that they are at peace with one another. We recall how the early church used such terms as "peace" and "love" as synonyms for ecclesial communion. The church is a sign of salvation for the world by being a community that manifests in its very life the things in which St. Paul tells us the kingdom of God consists: "The kingdom of God is not food and drink, but justice and peace and joy in the Holy Spirit" (Rom 14:17). Another way of putting it is to say that the church is a sign of salvation by being a holy people, since holiness consists in the love of God and of neighbor. Jesus told his disciples that their love for one another would be the sign that would bring people to know that they were his disciples (Jn 13:35).

Vatican II sees in the fact that the church on earth is "marked with a genuine though imperfect holiness" a sign that "the renovation of this world has been irrevocably decreed and in this age is already anticipated in some real way" (LG 48). The fact that the church is marked with a "genuine holiness," and that this holiness, while imperfect, is something she can never lose, is the most effective way that the church is a sign of what salvation is all about. The fact that this holiness is imperfect, of course, means that the church is always an imperfect sign of salvation as well. The more effectively it realizes its gifts of holiness, unity, love and peace among its own members, the more convincing a sign it will be of the reconciliation that God is offering to the world.

At this point the question can be raised: how can the church be a "universal sign of salvation" if there are many people who have no knowledge of the church? One might think of the millions of people in China today. Can the church, which is not present and visible to them, be a sign of salvation for them too? One thing is certain: the church can never renounce its universal mission to strive to become present and visible everywhere in the world. There are some areas of the world where, at present, the church can be present but it cannot publicly preach the gospel and seek to convert people to the Christian faith. The reason why missionaries persist, under great handicaps, to maintain the presence of the church in such places is precisely so that even without the freedom to preach the message of Christ in words, it can be a sign to the people there of reconciliation with God by being a community at peace, sharing God's peace and love in whatever way it can.

There are other places, however, where the church is not allowed to be present at all, yet the council assures us that even there "the Holy Spirit, in a manner known only to God, offers to every man the possibility of being associated with the paschal mystery" (UR 22). There is still a sense in which the church is the outward sign of this invisible grace: the church has been established by God as the unique social and public sign of salvation for all of humanity. The church, then, remains as the visible sign even of the work of salvation that the Holy Spirit is doing in the hearts of men, "in a manner known only to God."

For the church to be the universal sacrament of salvation, it is not enough that it be a sign: it must also serve as an instrument; in some way it must be actively involved in the accomplishment of God's purpose to reconcile the world to himself. The first reason for describing the church as "universal instrument of salvation" is suggested by the statement made in the Decree on Ecumenism that "it is through Christ's Catholic Church alone, which is the universal help toward salvation (*generale auxilium salutis*), that the fullness of the means of salvation can be obtained" (UR 3). In claiming the fullness of the means of salvation for the Catholic Church, the council did not intend to deny that many such means of salvation are found and fruitfully exercised in other Christian churches. The Decree on Ecumenism explicitly recognized this, in the preceding paragraph of the same article, when it said: "The brethren divided from us also carry out many of the sacred actions of the Christian religion. Undoubtedly, in ways that vary according to the condition of each church or community, these actions can truly engender a life of grace, and can be rightly described as capable of providing access to the community of salvation" (UR 3). In the light of this, we can say that while the fullness of the means of salvation is found only in the Catholic Church, the totality of ecclesial means of salvation is to be found in the church of Christ, taking this term in its most inclusive sense.

The fact that all the ecclesial means which God has established for the accomplishment of his plan of salvation enter into the very structure of the church, as constitutive of it, justifies describing the church as "universal sacrament of salvation." Here the term "universal" refers to the plenitude of those elements with which the church is equipped in order to be an effective instrument in the work of reconciling humanity with God.

The question remains whether the church can be called "universal instrument of salvation" in the sense that it is actually involved in bringing about the salvation of everyone who is saved. *Lumen gentium* suggests such a universal instrumental role for the church in God's plan of salvation when it says: "Established by Christ as a fellowship of life, charity and truth, it is also used by him as an instrument for the redemption of all . . . " (LG 10).

It is not difficult to recognize such an instrumental role of the church in the salvation of all those who are reached by its ministry of word and sacraments. We have seen that such a role is played not only by the Catholic Church but by other Christian churches and communities as well, which "the Holy Spirit has not refrained from using as means of salvation" (UR 3). Hence, the church as "universal sacrament of salvation" has to be understood as including all the churches and ecclesial communities which share this instrumental role.

A further question is whether the church can be said to have an instrumental or mediating role in the salvation of the great many people whom it does not actually reach with its ministry. We recall that in LG 16, the council insisted that God offers the help necessary for salvation to those "who do not know the gospel of Christ or his church," and even to those who "have not arrived at an explicit knowledge of God." It declared that all such people were, in various ways, "related to the church," but it did not say anything about the church as playing an instrumental role in their salvation. Likewise, when the council tells us that "the Holy Spirit, in a manner known only to God, offers to every one the possibility of being associated with the paschal mystery" (GS 22), it does not suggest that the church is associated with the Holy Spirit as his instrument in every offer of saving grace.

However, there is a statement of *Lumen gentium* that can throw some light on this question. It is the passage that proposes an analogy between the mystery of the church and the mystery of the Incarnate Word. "Just as the assumed nature inseparably united to the divine Word serves Him as a living instrument of salvation, so, in a similar way, does the communal structure of the Church serve Christ's Spirit who vivifies it, by way of building up the body" (LG 8). This would suggest that as the humanity of Christ is the instrument of the divine Word in the total work of salvation, so also the church can be seen as the instrument of the Holy Spirit in the total work of bringing Christ's grace to every human person.

We still have to ask in what way the church can be said to exercise an instrumental or mediatory role in the salvation of all those people who apparently have no contact with the church. The answer to this question can be found in the role of the church as "priestly people." The letter to the Hebrews tells us: "Every high priest chosen from among men is appointed to act on behalf of men in relation to God, to offer gifts and sacrifices for sins" (Heb 5:1). What was true of the individual high priest of the old law is now true of all the new people of God, who, "like living stones, are built into a spiritual house, to be a holy priesthood, to offer spiritual sacrifices acceptable to God through Jesus Christ" (1 Pet 2:5). Pope Pius XII, in his encyclical *Mystici corporis*, speaking of how the Savior "wishes to be helped by the members of his Mystical Body in carrying out the work of redemption," said:

> Dying on the cross He left to his Church the immense treasury of the redemption; toward this she contributed nothing. But when these graces are to be distributed, not only does He share this work of sanctification with his spouse, but He wishes that it be due in a way to her activity, A truly awe-inspiring mystery this, and one unceasingly to be pondered: that the salvation of many depends on the prayers and voluntary penances which the members of the Mystical Body of Jesus Christ offer for this intention.[97]

Going beyond this statement of Pius XII that the "salvation of many" depends on the prayers and penances which are the exercise of the priesthood of all the faithful, we have all the more reason to attribute to the sacrifice of the Eucharist a universal role in the salvation of all humanity. On the basis of our belief that what is made present in the celebration of the Eucharist is the unique sacrifice which obtained the grace of redemption for the whole world, and that the Eucharist is the principal channel through which that grace is now mediated to each generation, we have good reason to conclude that all the grace which the Holy Spirit distributes throughout the world is in some way also mediated through the church's offering of the Eucharist. Vatican II, referring to the prayer over the offerings for the ninth Sunday after Pentecost, declares that "it is through the liturgy, especially the divine eucharistic sacrifice, that the work of our redemption is exercised" (SC 1). Later on in the same document, we read: "From the liturgy, therefore, and especially from the Eucharist, as from a fountain, grace is channeled into us, and the sanctification of men in Christ and the glorification of God, to which all other activities of the church are directed as toward their goal, are most powerfully achieved" (SC 10).

The new eucharistic prayers, which are a fruit of the council's renewal of the liturgy, express in various ways the church's understanding that this sacrifice is offered not just for those present at it, nor only for the Christian faithful, but for the salvation of all people, both Christian and non-Christian, both living and dead. In the third eucharistic prayer we find the following expressions of such universality: first in the prayer for the living, and then in the prayer for the dead. "Lord, may this sacrifice, which has made our peace with you, advance the peace and salvation of all the world." "Welcome into your kingdom our departed brothers and sisters, and all who have left this world in your friendship." Here the "departed brothers and sisters" are all those who have been members of the Christian family of faith; "all who have departed this world in your friendship" would include all those mentioned in LG 16, who, without Christian faith and baptism, can still have departed this life in the state of supernatural friendship with God.

The fourth eucharistic prayer likewise expresses the fact that the Eucharist is offered for the salvation of the whole world. "We offer you his body and blood, the acceptable sacrifice which brings salvation to the whole world." "Remember those who take part in this offering, those here present and all your people, and all who seek you with a sincere heart." "Remember those who have died in the peace of Christ, and all the dead whose faith is known to you alone." It is obvious that it is the optimism of Vatican II about the possibility of salvation for non-Christians that is being expressed in these last two prayers.

On the basis of the teaching of the council, and the eucharistic prayers which reflect this teaching, we have sound reason for affirming that because of the church's role as priestly people, offering to the Father with Christ the High Priest the sacrifice from which the grace of salvation flows to the whole world, the church is rightly termed the universal sacrament of salvation in the sense that it plays an instrumental role in the salvation of every person who is saved.

Is the Church the Only Instrument of Salvation?

At this point the question may be raised whether, when we describe the church as "universal sacrament of salvation," we intend to assert that apart from the church, there is nothing else in the world that the Holy Spirit can make use of as an instrument in his work of bringing people to share the life of grace. It is already clear that we are not making such an exclusive claim for the Catholic Church, since, along with Vatican II, we recognize that the Holy Spirit is using the other churches and ecclesial communities as effective means of grace and salvation. What we can say is that it is only the church of Christ that can offer the specifically ecclesial means of salvation, by which we mean things like Christian faith, sacraments and ministry, which are the formal elements of the church. The question then is whether the Holy Spirit can make use of any other means of salvation than those that are strictly ecclesial.

When we described the economy of salvation as "sacramental," we explained that in this context, the term "sacramental" referred to the fact that God had chosen a plan of salvation in which, beginning with the humanity of Jesus, certain created realities were going to be God's instruments in his saving work. For the people whom the church reaches with its ministry of word and sacraments, the created realities that God uses are what we have called the ecclesial means of salvation. But there are a great many people in the world whom the church does not reach. If we have reason to believe that there is only one economy of salvation for the whole of humanity, and that it is consistently "sacramental," then we ought to expect that where the ecclesial means of salvation are not available, God will make use of other created realities as channels of his grace. In the first place, God will make use of other persons, such as good parents, good teachers, good community leaders, to exert a wholesome influence, especially on the younger generation. He will make use of the positive elements in cultures to instill ideals of justice, and loving care for the young, the poor, the sick, the aged.

This line of thought leads us to the question how the non-Christian religions fit into the divine economy of salvation. It is certain that God's salvific will includes all the millions of people who belong to one or another of these religions. How ought we to think about their religions as such? Are they simply irrelevant or useless as far as salvation is concerned? Can some of them even be obstacles in the way of salvation? Or, in God's providence, can they serve as means of salvation, helping people to be open and responsive to the inner working of grace in their lives?[98]

It would no doubt be unwise to lump all non-Christian religions together and give one answer that would apply to all of them. Most likely the right answer would be that in varying degrees almost all religions possess elements that are capable of serving as positive helps toward salvation. We certainly should not hesitate to affirm this of the religions that are singled out for special mention in the Declaration on the Relationship of the Church to Non-Christian Religions of the Second Vatican Council (*Nostra aetate*). As we could expect, the Islamic and Jewish religions are recognized as positive influences, leading people to the knowledge of the true God who revealed himself to Abraham and Moses. But the declaration speaks very positively of other religions as well, as in the following passage of article 2.

> From ancient times down to the present there has existed among diverse peoples a certain perception of that hidden power which hovers over the course of things and over the events of human life; at times, indeed, recognition can be found of a Supreme Divinity and of a Supreme Father too. Such a perception and such a rec-

ognition instill the lives of these peoples with a profound religious sense. Religions bound up with cultural advancement have struggled to reply to these same questions with more refined concepts and in more highly developed language.

Thus in Hinduism men contemplate the divine mystery and express it through an unspent fruitfulness of myths and through searching philosophical inquiry. They seek release from the anguish of our condition through ascetical practices or deep meditation or a loving trusting flight toward God. Buddhism in its multiple forms acknowledges the radical insufficiency of this shifting world. It teaches a path by which men, in a devout and confident spirit, can either reach a state of absolute freedom or attain supreme enlightenment by their own efforts or by higher assistance. Likewise, other religions to be found everywhere strive variously to answer the restless searchings of the human heart by proposing "ways" which consist of teachings, rules of life and sacred ceremonies.

The Catholic Church rejects nothing which is true and holy in these religions. She looks with sincere respect upon those ways of conduct and of life, those rules and teachings which, though differing in many particulars from what she holds and sets forth, nevertheless often reflect a ray of that Truth which enlightens all men. . . .

The Church therefore has this exhortation for her sons: prudently and lovingly, through dialogue and collaboration with the followers of other religions, and in witness of Christian faith and life, acknowledge, preserve, and promote the spiritual and moral goods found among these men, as well as the values in their society and culture.

In the light of the positive approach taken by the council, we can conclude that the "spiritual and moral good" that non-Christians find in their own religions, as well as the genuine "values in their society and culture," all of which Christians are urged to "acknowledge, preserve and promote," are such created realities as the Holy Spirit can use as means for disposing people to respond to the grace which he offers to them. Needless to say, such means are not sufficient in themselves to accomplish anyone's salvation, nor can anyone save himself by sheer good will. Salvation, whatever the created helps may be, will always be the fruit of the grace of Christ, offered and made effective in human hearts by the Holy Spirit. But since

God has chosen an economy of salvation in which creatures play a helping role, we have reason to believe that where ecclesial means are not at hand, the Holy Spirit will find other means that will serve his purpose.

Does this mean that the church would be justified in abandoning its effort to evangelize the non-Christian world? If there is salvation without Christian faith and membership in the church, and if non-Christian religions can be used by God as means of salvation, what motive is left for carrying on the arduous and unrewarding missionary task?

Catholicity As a Motive for Evangelization

A further consideration of the church's property of catholicity is to look at it as a motive which the church will always have to continue its effort to bring the message of the gospel to those who have not yet received it. It is doubtless true that a great effort is needed to rekindle Christian faith and practice among those already baptized. But the church can never limit its ministry to its own members. Catholicity is a gift to the church but it is also a mandate: to "strive energetically and constantly to bring all of humanity under Christ as its head" (cf. LG 13). For the church ever to renounce its effort to evangelize the non-Christian world would be to renounce the realization of its own catholicity—and this it can never do.

It is not a question of a realistic expectation that someday the whole world will be Christian. Statistics after two thousand years of missionary effort do not favor such a hope. But the church can never allow Christianity to be satisfied to be the religion of some continents and not others, of some cultures and not others, of some peoples and not others. It is true that in some continents, cultures and peoples Christians may still be a small minority for a long time to come. But the church can never give up its effort to be present, as a vital Christian community, no matter how small in numbers, in order to give witness to Christ, at least by its example, wherever there are people for whom Christ died. The catholicity of the church demands nothing less than this.

7 || Sacrament of "Integral Salvation"

In the previous chapter we have seen that one way to express the catholicity of the church is to describe it as the "universal sacrament of salvation." It will be recalled that at the very beginning of *Lumen gentium*, when the council proposed that the church is a "kind of sacrament," it explained this as meaning that the church is "sign and instrument" of two things: "intimate union with God" and "the unity of the whole human race." Up to now we have focused our attention on the notion of salvation as "intimate union with God," achieved through the reconciliation won for all by Christ and offered as grace to all by the Holy Spirit. We have proposed that the church is the "universal sacrament" of this intimate union with God, inasmuch as it plays a role as sign and instrument of the saving work that the Holy Spirit accomplishes in the heart of every single person who is brought into communion with God in this life and thus prepared for eternal communion with him in the next. We have suggested that the universality of the church's mediating role: her being involved in the offer of Christ's grace to everyone who is saved, if not by her ministry of evangelization, at least by her celebration of the eucharistic sacrifice, is an essential aspect of her catholicity. In this sense, there is no salvation without the church.

What we wish to do in this chapter is to look at the second part of that twofold object of which the council said that the church is sign and instrument: namely, "the unity of the whole human race." Among the questions we wish to discuss are these: (1) what are the causes of the disunity that presently afflicts humanity? (2) how can

132

the causes of this disunity be overcome, so that the whole human race might enjoy the blessings of unity? (3) what role can the church play as sign and instrument, to overcome disunity and bring about unity? (4) does the "salvation" of which the church is "sacrament" include both "intimate union with God" and "the unity of the whole human race"?

Briefly, the answers we propose will be: (1) the major cause of the disunity of the human race at the present time is the objectively unjust situation in which relatively few people enjoy the advantages of prosperity while the great majority of the people in the world suffer all the disadvantages of poverty; (2) the unity of the whole human race can only be achieved by the establishment of a just global society; (3) the church is called upon to be a sign to the world of what a truly just society would be, and to work, with all the resources proper to it, to overcome the causes of injustice and to promote justice in the world; (4) the "unity of the whole human race" that can come about only through the achieving of a truly just global society is correctly understood to be a component of the "salvation" of which the church is sacrament; (5) it is this concept of salvation, as embracing both communion with God and the achieving of unity and justice among all the people in this world, that recent official documents of the Catholic Church have described as "integral salvation." Our thesis, then, is that the church is the "sacrament" of this "integral salvation," and that the "integrity" or "totality" of the salvation which the church seeks for humanity is a further aspect of her catholicity.

It must be admitted that some of the ideas just expressed may seem novel; indeed I am not aware of anyone who has previously described the church as "sacrament of integral salvation." However, I am convinced that this term does correspond to the way the Catholic Church, in the documents of Vatican II and in official pronouncements issued since then, has expressed its mind about the full meaning of the salvation of which the Lord intends his church to be sign and instrument.

The procedure we shall follow in this chapter, then, will be, first, to show how our thesis is at least implicitly contained in the teaching of Vatican II, and then to follow its explicit development in statements issued by bearers of teaching authority in the Catholic Church in the period since the council.

Lumen Gentium

As we have already seen, *Lumen gentium* begins by describing the church as sacrament both of "intimate union with God" and "the unity of the whole human race." From the fact that the *res* of which the church is *sacramentum* is elsewhere identified as "salvation" (cf. LG 48), we can conclude that, in the mind of the council, the notion of salvation includes both a "vertical dimension" and a "horizontal dimension." Since "intimate union with God" is a salvation which, while it begins in this life, can reach its fullness only in the next, whereas "the unity of the whole human race" would seem to refer, at least primarily, to a goal to be sought in this world, there is also a distinction between an eschatological and a temporal dimension of salvation.

These different aspects of the salvation of which the church is "sacrament" are also suggested when the council describes the church as "a lasting and sure seed of unity, hope and salvation for the whole human race" (LG 9). A bit later on, the same article, having named Jesus as "the author of salvation and the source of unity and peace," goes on to describe the church as "the visible sacrament of this saving unity." While it first distinguished between "salvation" (no doubt in the sense of "intimate union with God") and "unity and peace," it then brought these two dimensions of salvation together in the term "saving unity."

The unity and peace of which Jesus is the source is later on identified with the *res* of which the church is *sacramentum*, when LG 13 declares that "the catholic unity of the people of God prefigures and promotes universal peace." These two verbs (*praesignat* and *promovet*) express the functions of a sacrament, as a sign that effects what it signifies. "Universal peace," while it may have eschatological fulfillment, surely refers to a salvation that the church is intended to signify and promote in this world. If the question is raised as to what "universal peace" has to do with "salvation," one need only ask how the human race can be saved from the utter destruction that a nuclear war would inflict on it if it were to give up the effort to achieve universal peace.

In the texts that we have seen thus far, the "horizontal dimension" of salvation has been described in terms of unity and peace. That the salvation that Jesus has brought into the world, and that his church must propagate, also includes liberty and justice is brought out in the following passage of the chapter on the laity (LG 36).

> The Lord wishes to spread his kingdom by means of the laity also, a kingdom of truth and life, a kingdom of holiness and grace, a kingdom of justice, love and peace. . . . The faithful, therefore, must learn the deepest meaning and the value of all creation, and how to relate it to the praise of God. They must assist one another to live holier lives even in their daily occupations. In this way the world is permeated by the spirit of Christ, and more effectively achieves its purpose in justice, charity and peace. . . . Let them work to see that created goods are more fittingly distributed among men, and that such goods in their way lead to general progress in human and Christian liberty. In this manner, through the members of the church, Christ will progressively illumine the whole of human society with his saving light.

Since the council does not hesitate to use the adjective "saving" of the light with which Christ progressively illumines the whole of human society, we conclude that the council recognizes the promotion of justice, peace and liberty as aspects of the salvation that Christ wishes to bring to the world through his church.

Gaudium et Spes

As one might expect, it is in the Pastoral Constitution on the Church in the Modern World that we find the most explicit statements of the council on the temporal dimensions of the salvation of which the church is called to be both sign and instrument. We find the first such statement in the preface: "The council intends to bring to humanity the light which it draws from the gospel, and to provide it with those saving resources which the church herself, under the guidance of the Holy Spirit, receives from her founder. For it is the human person that needs to be saved; it is human society that needs to be renewed" (GS 3). One could hardly have put more strongly the conviction that the church's saving mission is not limited to the eternal salvation of "souls."

The church's saving mission is modeled on that of her founder, whose work in the world is described in the following way:

Appointed Lord by his resurrection and given plenary power in heaven and on earth, Christ is now at work in the hearts of men through the energy of his Spirit. He arouses not only a desire for the age to come, but, by that very fact, he animates, purifies, and strengthens those noble longings too by which the human family strives to make its life more human and to render the whole earth submissive to this goal (GS 38).

That the church, like Christ, is concerned not only with the age to come, but with making life on this earth more human as well, and that this forms part of her saving mission, is brought out in the following passage:

Pursuing the saving purpose that it proper to her, the church not only communicates divine life to men, but in some way casts the reflected light of that life over the entire earth. This she does most of all by her healing and elevating impact on the dignity of the person, by the way in which she strengthens the bonds of human society and imbues the everyday activity of men with a deeper meaning and importance. Thus, through her individual members and her whole community, the church believes she can contribute greatly toward making the family of man and its history more human (GS 40).

It is true, of course, as the council insists, that "Christ gave his church no proper mission in the political, economic or social order. The purpose which he set before her is a religious one. But out of this religious mission itself come a function, a light, and an energy which can serve to structure and consolidate the human community according to the divine law" (GS 42).

The climax of the teaching of *Gaudium et spes* on the church as "sacrament of salvation" is found in the final article of part one of the constitution:

While helping the world and receiving many benefits from it, the church has a single intention: that God's kingdom may come, and that the salvation of the whole human race may come to pass. For every benefit which the people of God during its earthly pilgrimage can offer to the human family stems from the fact that the church is "the universal sacrament of salvation," simultaneously

manifesting and exercising the mystery of God's love for man."
(GS 45).

We have already seen that among the "benefits" that the church
wishes to offer to the human family during its earthly pilgrimage are
the blessings of unity, justice and peace. Now we are told that the
capacity and desire of the church to work for such benefits for humanity belong to her nature as "universal sacrament of salvation."
In striving to communicate such benefits to humanity, the church
fulfills its calling to be both sign and instrument of God's saving
love.

The whole argument of *Gaudium et spes* assures us that when it
asserts that "the single intention of the church is that God's kingdom
may come and that the salvation of the whole human race may come
to pass," it is not looking exclusively to the final coming of the kingdom, or to a salvation to be achieved in the next world only. If God's
kingdom is a "kingdom of truth and life, of holiness and grace, of
justice, love and peace," as the preface of the feast of Christ the King
tells us, then the promotion of all these values in human society must
be "of vital concern to the kingdom of God. For after we have
obeyed the Lord, and in his Spirit nurtured on earth the values of
human dignity, brotherhood and freedom, and indeed all the good
fruits of our nature and enterprise, we will find them again, but
freed of stain, burnished and transfigured. This will be so when
Christ hands over to the Father a kingdom eternal and universal: 'a
kingdom of truth and life, of holiness and grace, of justice, love and
peace.' On this earth that kingdom is already present in mystery.
When the lord returns, it will be brought into full flower" (GS 39).

Pope Paul VI, "Octogesima Adveniens" (1971)

To mark the eightieth anniversary of *Rerum novarum*, the first
of the great papal encyclicals on social issues, Pope Paul VI made
an important statement on the church's role in promoting justice, in
the form of a letter addressed to the cardinal president of the Pontifical Commission on Justice and Peace.[99] In this letter, Paul VI
insisted that the church must not only teach norms of social justice,
it must take effective action to bring it about.

In the social sphere, the church has always wished to assume a double function: first to enlighten minds in order to assist them to discover the truth and to find the right path to follow amid the different teachings that call for their attention; and secondly to take part in action and to spread, with a real care for service and effectiveness, the energies of the Gospel. . . . It is to all Christians that we address a fresh and insistent call to action. . . . Let each one examine himself, to see what he has done up to now, and what he ought to do. It is not enough to recall principles, state intentions, point to crying injustices and utter prophetic denunciations; these words will lack real weight unless they are accompanied for each individual by a livelier awareness of personal responsibility and by effective action. It is too easy to throw back on others responsibility for injustices, if at the same time one does not realize how each one shares in it personally, and how personal conversion is needed first. This basic humility will rid action of all inflexibility and sectarianism; it will also avoid discouragement in the face of a task which seems limitless in size. The Christian's hope comes primarily from the fact that he knows that the Lord is working with us in the world, continuing in his Body which is the Church—and through the Church, in the whole of mankind—the Redemption which was accomplished on the Cross and which burst forth in victory on the morning of the Resurrection. This hope springs also from the fact that the Christian knows that other men are at work, to undertake actions of justice and peace working for the same ends.[100]

The last part of this quotation is a striking indication that, in the thinking of Paul VI, Christians are not only called upon to undertake actions for justice and peace, but that in doing so, they are collaborating with the Lord in his work of redemption. Here is a concept of redemption that means the freeing of men and women not only from the bondage of personal sin, but also from the misery and oppression that are the consequences of the sins of injustice that others commit against the poor and defenseless of this world. Through the church the Lord continues his redeeming work, which, in the synagogue at Nazareth, he himself described as "preaching good news to the poor, proclaiming release to captives, setting at liberty those who are oppressed" (Lk 4:18).

In that same letter, Pope Paul VI announced his intention that one of the tasks of the Synod of Bishops to be held in 1971 would be to "study more closely and to examine in greater detail the church's mission in the face of the grave issues raised today by the question of justice in the world."[101]

Synod of Bishops, 1971: "Justice in the World"

The bishops who met for their third synod, September 30 to November 6, 1971, accomplished what, in the light of subsequent synods, seems the remarkable feat of preparing, discussing, voting on and promulgating, a highly significant document: "Justice in the World."[102] Undoubtedly much of the credit for this achievement must be attributed to the work done by the Pontifical Commission on Justice and Peace, which had been established by Paul VI in January 1967.

It is not our intention to offer anything like a complete analysis of the contents of this document. (For that purpose one can consult the "Overview" prepared by Philip Land, S.J. and the whole series of brochures published after the synod by the Commission on Justice and Peace.)[103] Our purpose here is simply to point out how clearly and emphatically the bishops of that synod expressed their understanding that the redeeming and saving mission of the church must include the church's full participation in the effort to rid the world of the prevailing systems of injustice which condemn so many millions of people to conditions of misery and oppression.

In the introduction to their document the bishops already expressed their recognition that in focusing their attention on the role of the church in promoting justice in the world, they would be dealing with an aspect of the divine plan for the salvation of the world.

> Scrutinizing the 'signs of the times' and seeking to detect the meaning of emerging history, while at the same time sharing the aspirations and questionings of all those who want to build a more human world, we have listened to the Word of God that we might be converted to the fulfilling of the divine plan for the salvation of the world.[104]

It is striking that the bishops saw this as calling for conversion on their part, through an attentive listening to the word of God. This same word of God, the gospel, they went on to say, "through the power of the Holy Spirit, frees men from personal sin and from its consequences in social life."[105] Looking to sacred history, they found that "God has revealed himself to us, and made known to us, as it is brought progressively to realization, his plan of liberation and salvation which is once and for all fulfilled in the Paschal Mystery of Christ."[106] The introduction concludes with the dramatic assertion:

> Action on behalf of justice and participation in the transformation of the world fully appear to us as a constitutive dimension of the preaching of the Gospel, or, in other words, of the Church's mission for the redemption of the human race and its liberation from every oppressive situation.[107]

In part 2 of their text, entitled "The Gospel Message and the Mission of the Church," the bishops explain more fully the reasons that justify their understanding of the church's redemptive mission.[108]

> Christian love of neighbor and justice cannot be separated. For love implies an absolute demand for justice, namely, a recognition of the dignity and rights of one's neighbor.[109] . . . The mission of preaching the Gospel dictates at the present time that we should dedicate ourselves to the liberation of man even in his present existence in the world. . . . The Church has received from Christ the mission of preaching the Gospel message which contains a call to man to turn away from sin to the love of the Father, universal brotherhood, and a consequent demand for justice in the world. This is the reason why the Church has the right, indeed the duty, to proclaim justice on the social, national and international level, and to denounce instances of injustice, when the fundamental rights of man and his very salvation demand it. The Church, indeed, is not alone responsible for justice in the world; however, she has a proper and specific responsibility which is identified with her mission of giving witness before the world of the need for love and justice contained in the Gospel message, a witness to be carried out in the Church institutions themselves and in the lives of Christians.[110]

Declaration of the Fourth Synod of Bishops (1974)

This synod, which focused on the theme of evangelization, was not so successful as the third synod had been, in managing to produce a synodal document. Actually, the majority of the bishops rejected the draft of the document that was supposed to have summed up the fruits of their deliberations, and time did not allow the preparation of another full-length document. However, in the closing days of the synod, a brief declaration was prepared which, when presented to the bishops, was approved by a majority of 182 to 11.[111] The size of this majority gives us good reason to assume that this brief declaration did reflect the views that the bishops had been expressing, both in the general assemblies and in their discussion groups.

The following passage of this declaration shows how the bishops had taken what the 1971 synod had said about the church's role in the promotion of justice, and had applied it specifically to their understanding of the full dimensions of the church's task of evangelization.

Among the many matters treated at the Synod we paid particular attention to the problem of the inter-relation between evangelization and integral salvation, or the full liberation of man and peoples. It is a matter of considerable importance and we were profoundly at one in reaffirming the close link between evangelization and liberation. We were led to this conclusion because we ourselves share the lives and the common fate of our fellow-Christians and of other men. Most of all, however, it is the gospel, which God's mercy has entrusted to us, which convinced us. For every man and for the whole of society the gospel is the good news of a salvation which must commence and be manifested on earth, for all that its full achievement must await the after-life. Prompted by the love of Christ and enlightened by the gospel, let us hope that the Church, by setting about the work of evangelization more faithfully, will announce man's total salvation, or full liberation, and will at one commence to achieve it. . . . [112]

Faithful to her mission to evangelize, the Church, as a truly poor, praying and fraternal community, can do much to achieve men's

full liberation. The gospel itself furnishes her with the most profound reasons and ever-fresh incentive for generous dedication to
the service of all men, especially the poor, the weak and oppressed, and for eliminating the social consequences of sin which
find expression in unjust social and political structures. The
Church, relying on Christ's gospel and strengthened by his grace,
can save from distortion these very aspirations towards liberation
and those efforts to achieve it. The Church is not confined to political, social and economic matters, though she must, of course,
take them into consideration. Rather does she lead towards freedom in all its forms, freedom from sin, from individual and collective egoism, towards full communion with God and with men
as brothers. In this way, the Church, acting in the spirit of the
gospel, promotes the true and full liberation of all men, groups
and peoples.[113]

In the passages that we have just quoted, the alert reader will
have noticed the term "integral salvation," which we have used in
the title of this chapter. Later on the term "total salvation" is used;
both terms are followed by the explanatory expression "full liberation." While the 1971 synod had described God's plan as a "plan of
liberation and salvation,"[114] the 1974 declaration is the first official
statement, to my knowledge, to have used the term "integral salvation" of the goal which the church seeks: to save men and women
not only from the consequences of personal sin, but also from the
consequences of the sins of injustice that others commit against
them. This is seen as a present realization of salvation: a salvation
that is "integral" because it involves both reconciliation with God
with a view to a future fulfillment of communion with him, and also
reconciliation of all classes of people with one another, on the basis
of a just social order in which the human dignity and fundamental
rights of all are respected.

"Evangelii Nuntiandi" of Pope Paul VI

Since the 1974 synod found itself unable to produce its own
full-length document, it turned over the fruits of its labors to Pope
Paul VI, with the request that he make use of that material in the
preparation of an encyclical or other such document on the subject
of evangelization. Paul VI responded to this request with the pub-

lication, on December 8, 1975, of what he termed his "apostolic exhortation to the episcopate, to the clergy, and to all the faithful of the entire world on evangelization in the modern world."[115]

While Pope Paul did not make use of the term "integral salvation," his treatment of the "links between liberation and evangelization" shows his basic agreement with what the bishops meant by that term. In our opinion, *Evangelii nuntiandi* contains the clearest and most effective statement which the Catholic Church has made to date on the part which Christians should be playing in the struggle for liberation in which the oppressed peoples of the world are engaged. As I see it, the key statement of *Evangelii nuntiandi* on this question is the following: "The Church strives always to insert the Christian struggle for liberation into the universal plan of salvation which she herself proclaims."[116] Here we see that Pope Paul does not hesitate to describe the struggle for liberation as "Christian," and that he identifies this as something that belongs to a "universal plan of salvation." Surely we are not far here from the notion of an "integral salvation," which would include liberation from situations of injustice and oppression, as well as from personal sinfulness.

Given the importance of this papal document, it will be worth our while to present the thought of Paul VI in some detail, so as to see how he wishes Catholics to understand the full meaning of the salvation which the church proclaims and strives to bring about through her task of evangelization.

It is noteworthy that the very first time the word "salvation" appears in *Evangelii nuntiandi*, it is explained in terms of "liberation":

> As the kernel and center of his Good News, Christ proclaims salvation, this great gift of God which is liberation from everything that oppresses man but which is above all liberation from sin and the Evil One, in the joy of knowing God and being known by him, of seeing him and of being given over to him.[117]

A salvation which is "liberation from everything that oppresses man" is precisely the salvation which the bishops of the 1974 synod described as "integral." The Pope's insistence that this is above all liberation from sin and the Evil One in no way limits the notion of salvation to personal reconciliation with God; it simply indicates an order of priorities in the church's mission.

This order of priorities is again expressed when the Pope insists in the first place on the transcendent and eschatological dimensions of the salvation which Christ won for all by his death and resurrection:

> Evangelization will also always contain—as the foundation, center and at the same time summit of its dynamism—a clear proclamation that, in Jesus Christ, the Son of God made man, who died and rose from the dead, salvation is offered to all men, as a gift of God's grace and mercy. And not an immanent salvation, meeting material or even spiritual needs, restricted to the framework of temporal existence and completely identified with temporal desires, hopes, affairs and struggles, but a salvation which exceeds all these limits in order to reach fulfillment in a communion with the one and only divine Absolute: a transcendent and eschatological salvation, which indeed has its beginning in this life but which is fulfilled in eternity.[118]

However, Paul VI is far from thinking that the church's mission is limited to proclaiming a future "salvation of souls." The following passage of his exhortation, while rather long, is worth quoting at length, as it provides clear and strong papal confirmation of the views expressed by the majority of the bishops at the synod of 1974 to the effect that evangelization must include participation in the struggle for liberation, since this is an aspect of the salvation which it is the church's mission to proclaim and to promote in the world.

> Evangelization would not be complete if it did not take account of the unceasing interplay of the Gospel and of man's concrete life, both personal and social. This is why evangelization involves an explicit message, adapted to the different situations constantly being realized, about the rights and duties of every human being, about family life without which personal growth and development is hardly possible, about life in society, about international life, peace, justice and development—a message especially energetic today about liberation.
>
> It is well known in what terms numerous bishops from all the continents spoke of this at the last Synod, especially the bishops from the third world, with a pastoral accent resonant with the voice of the millions of sons and daughters of the church who

make up those peoples. Peoples, as we know, engaged with all their energy in the effort and struggle to overcome everything which condemns them to remain on the margin of life: famine, chronic disease, illiteracy, poverty, injustices in international relations and especially in commercial exchanges, situations of economic and cultural neo-colonialism sometimes as cruel as the old political colonialism. The church, as the bishops repeated, has the duty to proclaim the liberation of millions of human beings, many of whom are her own children—the duty of assisting the birth of this liberation, of giving witness to it, of ensuring that it is complete. This is not foreign to evangelization.

Between evangelization and human advancement—development and liberation—there are in fact profound links. These include links of an anthropological order, because the man who is to be evangelized is not an abstract being but is subject to social and economic questions. They also include links in the theological order, since one cannot dissociate the plan of creation from the plan of Redemption. The latter plan touches the very concrete situations of injustice to be combatted and of justice to be restored. They include links of the eminently evangelical order, which is that of charity: how in fact can one proclaim the new commandment without promoting in justice and peace the true, authentic advancement of man? We ourself have taken care to point this out, by recalling that it is impossible to accept that "in evangelization one could or should ignore the importance of the problems so much discussed today, concerning justice, liberation, development and peace in the world. This would be to forget the lesson which comes to us from the Gospel concerning love of our neighbor who is suffering and in need."

The same voices which during the Synod touched on this burning theme with zeal, intelligence and courage have, to our great joy, furnished the enlightening principles for a proper understanding of the importance and profound meaning of liberation, such as it was proclaimed and achieved by Jesus of Nazareth and such as it is preached by the church.[119]

In the following section of *Evangelii nuntiandi*, Paul VI warns against the tendency on the part of some to reduce the mission of the church to a purely temporal project, as though the salvation of which the church is the messenger could consist in merely material well-being. He goes on to say:

The church links human liberation and salvation in Jesus Christ, but she never identifies them, because she knows through revelation, historical experience and the reflection of faith that not every notion of liberation is necessarily consistent and compatible with an evangelical vision of man, of things and of events; she knows too that in order that God's Kingdom should come it is not enough to establish liberation and to create well-being and development.[120]

On the other hand, it is obviously the mind of Paul VI that it would not be enough either if the church were to restrict herself to preaching a future salvation, ignoring the present need of liberation and development for so many millions of people. Human liberation cannot be simply identified with salvation in Jesus Christ, but it cannot be separated from it either, because "the liberation which evangelization proclaims and prepares is the one which Christ himself announced and gave to man by his sacrifice."[121] It is this that justifies speaking of the "Christian struggle for liberation," which, as we have already seen, Pope Paul VI says "the church strives always to insert into the universal plan of salvation which she herself proclaims."[122]

We conclude that in *Evangelii nuntiandi*—which we believe will be recognized as one of the great papal documents of this century—we find firm grounds for our description of the church as "sacrament of integral salvation."

The Extraordinary Synod of 1985

The extraordinary synod held to celebrate the twentieth anniversary of the conclusion of Vatican II and to evaluate its implementation in the life of the church managed, despite the brevity of its session, to prepare and approve for publication a "Final Report," in which are summed up the major points that had been discussed.[123] In this document we find the term "integral salvation" again used in the sense in which the synod of 1974 had introduced it into the vocabulary of official church statements. Here is the paragraph in which the term appears.

In this paschal perspective that asserts the unity of Cross and Resurrection, one discerns the true and the false sense of so-called
aggiornamento. There is excluded the merely facile adjustment
that would lead to the secularization of the Church. There is also
excluded a rigid closing of the community of the faithful upon
itself. What is affirmed is a missionary opening-up for the integral
salvation of the world. Through this all truly human values are
not only accepted, but fiercely defended: the dignity of the human person; the fundamental rights of men; peace; freedom from
oppressions, misery and injustice. Integral salvation, however, is
obtained only if these human realities are purified and further
raised by grace to familiarity with God through Jesus Christ in
the Holy Spirit.[124]

The Synod's "Final Report" also contains a section under the
title "Preferential Option for the Poor, and Human Development,"
in which there is another reference to the integrity of the church's
saving mission.

After Vatican II, the Church became more aware of her mission
for service of the poor, the oppressed and the marginalized. In
this preferential option, which is not to be understood as exclusive, the true spirit of the Gospel shines out. Jesus Christ declared
the poor blessed (cf. Mt 5:3; Lk 6:20) and himself willed to be
poor for our sake (cf. 2 Cor 8:9). . . .

The Church must in prophetic fashion denounce every
form of poverty and oppression and defend and support everywhere the fundamental and inalienable rights of the human
person. . . .

We must grasp in its integrity the Church's saving mission
in relation to the world. Although the Church's mission is spiritual, it involves promotion of human progress even in the temporal field. . . . False and useless oppositions as, for example,
between spiritual mission and service for the world are to be dis-
carded and ignored.

As the world is in a state of continual evolution, we must
analyze the signs of the times over and over again, so that the message of the Gospel may be heard more clearly and the Church's
activity for the salvation of the world may become more intense
and alive.[125]

CDF: Instruction on Christian Freedom
and Liberation (1986)

In September 1984, the Congregation for the Doctrine of the Faith issued an "Instruction on Certain Aspects of the 'Theology of Liberation' " which was severely critical of that theology.[126] However, at the same time the Congregation announced that it was preparing a second instruction in which it would deal in a more complete and positive manner with the theme of Christian freedom and liberation. In this second document, released by the Congregation on April 5, 1986, we find further support for our proposal that the church can rightly be described as "sacrament of integral salvation." Since that support was somewhat unexpected, it is all the more important to present it here.[127]

Chapter 4 of the Instruction is entitled: "The Liberating Mission of the Church"; its first sub-section has the heading: "For the Integral Salvation of the World." Some of the major assertions of that sub-section are the following.

> The church's essential mission, following that of Christ, is a mission of evangelization and salvation. She draws her zeal from the divine love. Evangelization is the proclamation of salvation, which is a gift of God. Through the word of God and the sacraments, man is freed in the first place from the power of sin and the power of the Evil One which oppress him; and he is brought into a communion of love with God. . . .
>
> But the love which impels the church to communicate to all people a sharing in the grace of divine life also causes her, through the effective action of her members, to pursue people's true temporal good, help them in their needs, provide for their education and promote an integral liberation from everything that hinders the development of individuals. The church desires the good of man in all his dimensions, first of all as a member of the city of God and then as a member of the earthly city.[128]

> Therefore, when the church speaks about the promotion of justice in human societies or when she urges the faithful laity to work in this sphere according to their own vocation, she is not going beyond her mission. . . . The church is being faithful to her mission when she condemns the forms of deviation, slavery and oppression of which people are victims.[129]

Chapter 5 of the Instruction is entitled "The Social Doctrine of the Church: For a Christian Practice of Liberation." Under the heading "Nature of the Social Doctrine of the Church" we find the following description of the purpose of the church:

> The purpose of the church is to spread the kingdom of Christ so that all men may be saved and that through them the world may be effectively ordered to Christ. The work of salvation is thus seen to be indissolubly linked to the task of improving and raising the condition of human life in this world. The distinction between the supernatural order of salvation and the temporal order of human life must be seen in the context of God's singular plan to recapitulate all things in Christ. [130]

In the second sub-section of the same chapter 5 we find another use of the term "integral salvation."

> Faith inspires criteria of judgment, determining values, lines of thought and patterns of living which are valid for the whole human community. Hence the church, sensitive to the anxieties of our age, indicates the lines of a culture in which work would be recognized in all its full human dimensions and in which all would find opportunities for personal self-fulfillment. The church does this by virtue of her missionary outreach for the integral salvation of the world, with respect for the identity of each people and nation. [131]

In its concluding section, the Instruction again links "efforts for liberation" with the "mystery of salvation":

> It is the truth of the mystery of salvation at work today in order to lead redeemed humanity toward the perfection of the kingdom which gives true meaning to the necessary efforts for liberation in the economic, social and political orders and which keeps them from falling into new forms of slavery. [132]

With this recent Instruction of the Congregation for the Doctrine of the Faith we conclude our series of testimonies from magisterial statements of the Catholic Church since Vatican II, which provide authoritative support for our thesis that the church can rightly be understood as "sacrament of integral salvation." These documents witness to the acceptance of a broader, more comprehensive concept of salvation than was previously typical of Catholic thought. Even in the documents of Vatican II, the term "salvation" consistently refers to reconciliation and communion with God in this life, leading to eternal happiness in the next. Characteristic of the use of the term "salvation" at Vatican II is the following passage of the Decree on the Apostolate of the Laity:

> Christ's redemptive work, while of itself directed toward the salvation of men, involves also the renewal of the whole temporal order. Hence the mission of the Church is not only to bring to men the message and grace of Christ, but also to penetrate and perfect the temporal sphere with the spirit of the gospel. In fulfilling this mission of the Church, the laity, therefore, exercise their apostolate both in the Church and in the world, in both the spiritual and the temporal orders (AA 5).

Here we see that while it is indeed part of the church's mission to "penetrate and perfect the temporal sphere with the spirit of the gospel," this is seen as something quite distinct from "salvation," which is a matter of "the spiritual order" alone.

What has happened since Vatican II is a broadening of the concept of salvation, so that, besides the "vertical dimension" of reconciliation with God, it also includes the "horizontal dimension" of reconciliation of people with one another through the overcoming of systems of oppression and the establishment of a just social order in the world, recognizing this also as an indispensable foundation for the achieving of durable peace. As we have shown, there are inklings of such a concept of salvation already present in *Lumen gentium* and *Gaudium et spes*, but the explicit use of the term "integral salvation" to express this broader concept is found only in subsequent documents. Since this idea and terminology are so new, it has seemed useful to devote most of this chapter to the documentation of its acceptance in official statements of the teaching authorities of the church. At the same time, the texts we have cited at some length also provide a clear explanation of the meaning of "integral salvation," and of the active part that the church is called to have in working to achieve it. While these texts have not actually described the church as "sacrament of integral salvation," I am confident that this term does reflect the Catholic Church's present understanding of the task which its Lord has assigned it for the salvation of the world. It is the "integrity" or fullness of that concept of salvation that justifies its consideration as an aspect of the church's catholicity.

8 || The Church Is Apostolic

In the development of the article about the church in the baptismal creeds of the early church, "apostolic" was the last of the four properties to be added. The baptismal creed of the western church—the one we know as the "Apostles' Creed"—has never mentioned more than two attributes: "holy" and "catholic." About the middle of the fourth century the baptismal creed in use at Jerusalem, as we know from the catecheses given by the bishop St. Cyril, described the church as "one, holy and catholic."[133] The first baptismal creed we know of that added "apostolic" is the one that was in use in the church of Salamis in Cyprus, after the middle of the fourth century. St. Epiphanius, bishop of that city, gives us the text of this creed in his work *Ancoratus*, which is dated 374.[134] It was this or a similar eastern baptismal creed that the Council of Constantinople followed, when it described the church as "one, holy, catholic and apostolic" in the creed which has become the common liturgical creed of most Christian churches.

While the term "apostolic" made a late entrance into the official Christian creeds, it was by no means a new word in the Christian vocabulary. We find it used early in the second century in the letter of Ignatius of Antioch to the Trallians.[135] In the middle of the second century the presbyters of the church of Smyrna, recounting the martyrdom of their bishop, Polycarp, described him as "an apostolic and prophetic teacher."[136] The word is found exclusively in Christian literature, and with a variety of specific meanings, the common factor being the expression of a relationship to the apostles, whether it be origin, similarity, fidelity, succession or some other way that persons or things would be "of the apostles" or "like the apostles."

In this chapter we are concerned with the reasons that justify our profession of faith in the church as "apostolic." The chapter will be divided into two parts. In the first part we shall focus on the church during the period of the New Testament, to see why that church is properly called "apostolic." Secondly, we shall see how the early, post-New Testament church understood itself to continue to be apostolic. In the next chapter we shall look at various notions of apostolicity that are current in Christian thinking today.

I. THE CHURCH OF THE NEW TESTAMENT PERIOD WAS APOSTOLIC

It is obvious that the description of the New Testament church as apostolic is a consequence of the importance of the role which the apostles played in the life of that church. We must begin, then, with some questions about these men who are called "apostles": about their identity, their calling, their mission and ministry.

Who Were the Apostles?

The expression "the twelve apostles" is so familiar to us that one might think that the question we have posed here would be easily answered by giving the names of these twelve men. But things are not quite that simple. It is a relatively minor problem that the names given in the several lists that we find in the New Testament are not in every case identical. Thus Luke (Lk 6:16 and Acts 1:13) has an apostle named "Judas the son of James," whereas the lists given by Mark and Matthew have no "Judas son of James" but have a man named Thaddeus instead (Mk 3:18; Mt 10:3). However, it was not uncommon for people to be known by more than one name (thus Simon came to be known as Cephas and then as Peter, and Saul of Tarsus came to known as Paul). So it may well be that Thaddeus and Judas were different names of the same man.

However, there are some more serious problems about simply identifying "the apostles" with "the twelve." First of all, while there are solid grounds for accepting as historical the fact that Jesus chose a special group of twelve disciples, it is not right to think of them as apostles until they received their mission from the risen Lord. Secondly, and more importantly, Paul certainly was an apostle, and was accepted as such by the leaders among the twelve (cf. Gal 2:7–9), even though he could not have met the conditions laid down in Acts (1:21–22) for the man who would make up the number twelve after the defection and death of Judas Iscariot. Furthermore, when Paul lists the appearances of the risen Christ, the second appearance is to the twelve, while the fifth is to "all the apostles." If Paul included the twelve among "all the apostles," it is hardly likely that he thought of these two groups as simply identical. Of course he did not include himself in that group of "all the apostles," because his own calling came only later, "out of due time," as he put it (1 Cor 15:8). But there is reason to take Paul's term "all the apostles" to include others than the twelve. Perhaps Barnabas would be one of them; Luke refers to him as an apostle, even though he tended to identify the apostles with the twelve (cf. Acts 15:4,14). James "the brother of the Lord," who was the recipient of a special appearance of the risen Christ (1 Cor 14:7), was probably also included among the apostles by Paul (cf. Gal 1:19).

Some New Testament critics have questioned whether Paul recognized the twelve as apostles. It is true that he never explicitly identifies the whole group as apostles. But shortly after his conversion to Christian faith he knew that there were, in the church at Jerusalem, men "who were apostles before him" (cf. Gal 1:17), and he certainly recognized the leaders among the twelve, Peter and John, as apostles (cf. Gal 2:7–9). Indeed he saw his own claim to be an apostle confirmed by the fact that they recognized him to have been entrusted with the mission of the gospel just as they had been. So we are safe in concluding that when Paul spoke of "the apostles before him," who he knew could be found at Jerusalem, he had at least some of the twelve, if not all of them, in mind. We also have to note that Paul speaks of two kinds of apostles: the "apostles of Jesus Christ" and "the apostles of the churches." The latter are envoys or messengers sent by one or another local church (cf. 2 Cor 8:23; Phil 2:25). While Paul could use the word "apostle" of them, in its generic meaning of "one sent out," it is obvious that their role in the church could not be compared with that of the men whom Paul calls "apostles of Jesus Christ." So we must now see what Paul understood to be the criteria by which certain persons were recognized as "apostles of Jesus Christ," and what role such apostles played in the life of the New Testament church. Then we shall compare what we

find in the letters of St. Paul with what we find in the rest of the
New Testament.

The Qualifications of "Apostles of Jesus Christ"

A fortunate consequence of the fact that Paul's adversaries chal-
lenged his right to be recognized as an apostle is that he was forced
to spell out the basis for his own claim to be an apostle, and thus to
provide the criteria by which he would have recognized others as
apostles as well. We shall look at the texts and see what light each
one sheds on our question.

In 1 Cor 9:1–2, Paul asks: "Am I not free? Am I not an apostle?
Have I not seen Jesus our Lord? If to others I am not an apostle, at
least I am to you; for you are the seal of my apostleship in the Lord."
Here we can distinguish two criteria: to have seen the risen Lord,
and to have founded a church by the effective preaching of the gospel. Regarding the first of these criteria, we can note that to have
seen the risen Lord, while a requirement, was not sufficient in itself
to make someone an apostle, since the "more than five hundred
brethren" to whom the Lord appeared are hardly to be numbered
among "all the apostles" (cf. 1 Cor 15:6–7). On the second criterion
we can observe a certain pragmatism in Paul's thinking: for him the
fruitfulness of a mission is a sign of its authenticity. We shall see
other indications of this.

In 1 Cor 15:8–11 we can see the same two criteria of apostleship
in Paul's mind when he says: "Last of all, as to one untimely born,
he appeared to me. For I am the least of the apostles, unfit to be
called an apostle, because I persecuted the church of God. But by
the grace of God I am what I am, and his grace toward me was not
in vain. On the contrary, I worked harder than any of them, though
it was not I, but the grace of God which is with me. Whether then
it was I or they, so we preach and so you believed." Here again we
see that Paul saw the effectiveness of his preaching as a confirmation
of his apostleship.

In 2 Cor 11:22–29 Paul compares himself with the men whom
he calls "false apostles" who "disguise themselves as apostles of
Christ." Here he bases his claim to be a "better servant of Christ
than they" on the far greater sufferings he has undergone in his missionary work. The detail with which he lists his sufferings for the

gospel suggests how important a criterion of his apostleship he considered them to be.

In the following chapter (2 Cor 12:12) Paul speaks of "the signs of a true apostle" which the Corinthians had witnessed in his ministry to them: "signs and wonders and mighty works" that were performed among them "in all patience." Paul's thinking here is echoed by the canonical ending of Mark: "And they went forth and preached everywhere, while the Lord worked with them and confirmed the message by the signs that attended it" (Mk 16:20).

When presenting himself to the Romans as "a servant of Jesus Christ, called to be an apostle, set apart for the gospel of God," Paul declares that it is "Jesus Christ our Lord through whom we have received grace and apostleship to bring about the obedience of faith for the sake of his name among all the nations" (Rom 1:1,5). Here we see that Paul's credentials include both the source and the goal of his apostleship.

In the letter to the Galatians we find a more lengthy exposition of the grounds on which Paul based his claim to be an apostle. He begins by describing himself as "an apostle, not from men or through man, but through Jesus Christ and God the Father who raised him from the dead" (Gal 1:1). The divine source of Paul's call is again brought out in vv. 15–16: "But when he who had set me apart before I was born, and had called me through his grace, was pleased to reveal his Son to me, in order that I might preach him among the Gentiles . . . " Here three points can be distinguished: (1) the call is from God; (2) it involves being a recipient of divine revelation; (3) it is a call and mission to preach Christ (in Paul's case, to the Gentiles).

In chapter 2 of Galatians, Paul mentions the criteria by which those who had been apostles before him recognized him as an apostle: "When they saw that I had been entrusted with the gospel to the uncircumcised, just as Peter had been entrusted with the gospel to the circumcised (for he who worked through Peter for the mission to the circumcised worked through me also for the Gentiles), and when they perceived the grace that was given to me, James and Cephas and John, who were reputed to be pillars, gave to me and Barnabas the right hand of fellowship, that we should go to the Gentiles and they to the circumcised" (2:7–9). We can sum this up by saying that the call to be an apostle means having been "entrusted with the gospel" and having the Lord "work through" one's ministry (evidently making it effective by his grace.)

From these texts of St. Paul we can draw out these basic criteria of an apostle of Jesus Christ: (1) to have seen the risen Christ, (2) to have received from him a mission to preach the gospel, and (3) to have one's ministry confirmed by its fruitfulness, by signs and wonders, and by one's sufferings for the sake of the gospel.

Thus far we have looked to the letters of St. Paul for his concept of an apostle. Now we must see whether his view was shared by the other writers of the New Testament.

The Apostles in the Gospels

The four gospels are unanimous in their witness that Jesus formed a special group of twelve disciples during his public ministry (cf. Mt 10:1–4; Mk 3:13–19; Lk 6:12–16; Jn 6:70). Luke's account brings out most clearly the fact that these twelve were selected out of a much larger number of disciples: "He called his disciples and chose from them twelve. . . . And he came down with them and stood on a level place, with a great crowd of his disciples" (Lk 6:13,17). All four Gospels testify that the initiative came from Jesus; it was he who chose them, not they who chose him (cf. Jn 15:16). Mark's expression of this is particularly vigorous: "He called to himself those whom he wished, and they came to him, and he appointed (literally: "he made") twelve . . . " (Mk 3:13–14). Mark also indicates the purpose for which he chose them: " . . . to be with him, and to be sent out to preach with authority to cast out demons" (Mk 3:14–15). Here we can distinguish their two roles: first as disciples (to be with him) and second as apostles (to be sent out to preach). It is significant that the only time Mark speaks of the twelve as "apostles" is when they returned from the preaching mission on which Jesus sent them during his public ministry (Mk 6:30; cf. 6:7–13). Otherwise they are "the disciples" or "the twelve." Matthew likewise calls them "apostles" once, when giving the names of "the twelve apostles" (10:2). Luke, on the other hand, speaks of the twelve as "apostles" six times in his Gospel, and of course far more frequently in Acts. The way that Matthew and Mark use the term suggests their consciousness of the fact that it was only when they had been "sent out" that they were properly called by the name that means "men sent out."

The Mission of the Twelve

The three synoptic gospels record that at least on one occasion Jesus sent his twelve disciples out on a mission to do what he himself was doing: to preach repentance in view of the coming kingdom of God, and to heal the sick (Mt 10:1–21; Mk 6:7–13; Lk 9:1–6). Each of these passages brings out the idea that their mission is an extension of Jesus' own ministry. They share his message and his power over illness and evil spirits, and the consequences for those who refuse to listen to them are as serious as they are for those who refuse to listen to Jesus himself (cf. Mt 10:14–15: "And if anyone will not receive you or listen to your words, shake off the dust from your feet as you leave that house or town. Truly, I say to you, it shall be more tolerable on the day of judgment for the land of Sodom and Gomorrah than for that town"). This is expressed more succinctly in the saying of Jesus: "He who receives you receives me, and he who receives me receives him who sent me" (Mt 10:40; cf. Jn 13:20). The converse is also true: "He who rejects you rejects me, and he who rejects me rejects him who sent me" (Lk 10:16).

While such sayings of Jesus are recorded in the gospels as having been said to the disciples on the occasion of their temporary mission, the early church certainly understood that they applied to the apostles when they were fully commissioned by the risen Christ.

A number of passages in the gospels indicate that one of the reasons why Jesus chose out the twelve was that he might teach them privately and instruct them more more fully than he did the rest of his hearers (cf. Mt 11:1; 13:36ff; Mk 4:10ff; 8:31; 9:30–37; 10:32; Lk 18:31). This suggests that Jesus was preparing them for a future ministry of teaching, when they would be like "scribes trained for the kingdom of God" (cf. Mt 13:52).

Other passages of the gospels, especially that of Matthew, record instructions which Jesus gave to the twelve that suggest a future role of leadership, with authority over a community. The clearest example of such sayings are found in Matthew 18, where the disciples are warned against giving scandal to the "little ones" or despising them. Rather, they are to be like the shepherd who goes after the straying sheep. In this context we find the saying: "Truly I say to you, whatever you bind on earth shall be bound in heaven, and whatever you loose on earth whall be loosed in heaven" (Mt 18:18). We know from contemporary Semitic literature that the terms "binding and loosing" were commonly used to express the idea of making authoritative decisions, declaring something forbidden or permitted by the law. Since this involved the interpretation of scripture, the expression also referred to authoritative teaching.

We have already seen that Paul recognized Peter as the leader of those who had been "apostles before himself." The words that Matthew's gospel records as having been addressed to Peter confirm the idea that the twelve were to play an important role in the life of the future community. Here Jesus speaks of this future community as "my church": "And I tell you, you are Peter, and on this rock I will build my church, and the powers of death shall not prevail against it. I will give you the keys of the kingdom of heaven, and whatever you bind on earth shall be bound in heaven, and whatever you loose on earth shall be loosed in heaven" (Mt 16:18–19). The image of Peter as the "rock" on which Jesus would build his church is best understood in the light of the parable of the wise man who "dug deep and laid the foundation of his house upon rock" (cf. Lk 6:48). Peter is to be a source of stability for the future church. The image of the "keys" suggests the role of the major-domo in a royal palace; Isaiah has the Lord say of Eliakim: "I will place on his shoulder the key of the house of David; he shall open and none shall shut; and he shall shut and none shall open" (Is 22:20–22). The fact that the authority to "loose and bind" is here promised to Peter confirms the interpretation we have given of Mt 18:18, namely, that these words are addressed to the twelve, in view of the role they are to have in the future community of disciples. (Some commentators take Mt 18:18 as spoken to the whole community, but this would be hard to reconcile with the fact that such authority is elsewhere promised to Peter alone.)

The Mission of the Eleven by the Risen Christ

All four gospels and Acts bear witness to the belief of the early church that the eleven men who had been Jesus' special disciples during his public ministry were sent out by the risen Christ, to be the primary witnesses to his life, his teaching, and above all to his resurrection (cf. Mt 28:18–20; Mk 16:15–16; Lk 24:45–49; Jn 20:21–23; Acts 1:8). It is possible, even likely, that the actual wording of these passages may in some cases reflect subsequent developments in the Christian community, but one can hardly question their unanimous witness to the understanding of the New Testament church that the eleven received their mandate as apostles directly from the risen Christ.

This mandate, besides the commission to "preach the Gospel to the whole creation," involved a role of authority in the community of disciples that would be formed by their preaching: "Go therefore and make disciples of all nations . . . teaching them to observe all that I have commanded you" (Mt 28:19–20). "As the Father has sent me, even so I send you. . . . If you forgive the sins of any they are forgiven; if you retain the sins of any, they are retained" (Jn 20:21–23). It would seem impossible to explain the presence of such sayings of the risen Christ in all four gospels except in the light of the experience of the early church that the men who had been Jesus' special disciples actually played a leading role in the early Christian community, and that the community attributed their authority to a mandate given them by Christ himself.

The Role of the "Twelve Apostles" in the New Testament Church

The book called "The Acts of the Apostles" focuses almost exclusively on the ministry of Peter and Paul, telling us nothing about the individual ministry of any of the others among the twelve. However, in several places Luke speaks in general about the role of "the apostles." Thus, in Acts 2:14 he has Peter deliver his Pentecost address "standing with the eleven." Those who were "cut to the heart" by his sermon "said to Peter and the rest of the apostles: 'Brethren, what shall we do?' " (2:37). Those who were baptized that day "devoted themselves to the apostles' teaching" (2:42). Subsequently Luke tells us: "Many signs and wonders were done through the apostles" (2:43), and that "with great power the apostles gave their testimony to the resurrection of the Lord Jesus" (4:33). The pastoral role of the apostles in the Jerusalem community is suggested by the fact that the people who sold their possessions "laid the proceeds at the apostles' feet and distribution was made to each as any had need" (4:35). When the Hellenists complained that their widows were being neglected, Luke tells us that it was "the twelve" who summoned the body of the disciples to solve this problem, and it was "the apostles" who prayed and laid hands on the seven who were presented to them (6:1–6). The same passage attributes to the twelve a special role of "prayer and the ministry of the word."

There are a number of indications of a special association of the twelve with the church at Jerusalem. We saw earlier that when Paul was converted he knew that there were "apostles before him" at Jerusalem (Gal 1:17). When, after the martyrdom of Stephen, many were scattered to escape the persecution, Luke tells us that the apostles remained at Jerusalem. It was in Jerusalem that "the apostles" heard that Samaria had received the word of God, and responded by sending Peter and John to them (Acts 8:14). When the dispute over the circumcision of Gentile converts broke out in Antioch, "Paul and Barnabas were appointed to go up to Jerusalem to the apostles and elders about this question" (15:2). However, a later episode in Acts suggests that at some point the apostles must have left Jerusalem, because when Paul went up to deliver the money he had collected for the church in Jerusalem, he was received "by James and all the elders" (21:18). We know that Peter left Jerusalem after his miraculous release from prison (12:17), and that he spent some time with the community of Antioch (Gal 2:11ff). He may well have visited Corinth also, judging from the presence of a "Cephas party" in that church (1 Cor 1:12). And there is convincing evidence from post-biblical sources that he suffered martyrdom at Rome.

Summing up what we know from the New Testament about the role which "the twelve apostles" played in the early church, we have to admit that, apart from what we know about Peter, our information is limited to what we find in Acts about their ministry as a group in the primitive church of Jerusalem. Luke focuses on the ministry of Peter, much as he and the other evangelists focus on Peter as the spokesman of the twelve in their gospels. Whatever the subsequent missionary work of the others among the twelve may have been, we are on solid ground if we take the first chapters of Acts as evidence of the memory, kept alive in the church, of a "patriarchal" role played by the twelve in the very first years of the life of the church at Jerusalem. Having been the specially chosen disciples of Jesus during his lifetime on earth, they provided the primary link between Jesus and the post-resurrection church. Their witness to Jesus' teaching, his miracles, and above all to his death and resurrection were foundational for the church. The earliest Christian community was the fruit of their witness and grew under their leadership. Their confirmation of the authenticity of the missionary work done by others—by Philip in Samaria, by the men of Cyprus and Cyrene at Antioch, and eventually by Paul—testifies to their openness to unexpected initiatives, and their role of oversight beyond the limits of the Judean church. Whatever missionary work they may have undertaken after leaving Jerusalem, the fact remains that their major contribution to the life of the church, at least as we know it from the New Testament, was made by their founding and leading the church of Christ during its infancy at Jerusalem. Given that this was to be "the mother of all the churches," their role in it is a good reason for describing the New Testament church as "apostolic."

The Ministry of the Apostle Paul

By far the greater part of our information about the ministry of an apostle in the New Testament church is based on what we know about Paul, both from his own writings and from the second part of Acts. As this is so well known, we shall not need to dwell on it at great length. Paul understood that his calling and mission was to preach the gospel to the Gentiles in regions where Christ was not yet known (cf. Rom 15:20). He saw the confirmation of his calling in the fruitfulness of his preaching, manifested in the formation of the Christian communities over which he continued to devote his pastoral care. In some of these communities he carried on his ministry for a considerable period of time. Thus, we are told that after founding the church at Corinth "he stayed a year and six months, teaching the word of God among them" (Acts 18:4). Similarly, at Ephesus his ministry "continued for two years, so that all the residents of Asia heard the word of the Lord, both Jews and Greeks" (Acts 19:10). Luke puts the following description of Paul's ministry at Ephesus into his farewell address to the elders of that church: "I did not shrink from declaring to you anything that was profitable, and teaching you in public and from house to house, testifying both to Jews and Greeks of repentance to God and of faith in our Lord Jesus Christ" (Acts 20:20–21). Later in the same speech he says: "Therefore be alert, remembering that for three years I did not cease day or night to admonish every one of you with tears" (20:31). This suggests the special care that Paul took in the formation of the elders, those whom "the Holy Spirit has made overseers, to care for the church of God" (21:28).

Paul frequently speaks of his ministry in the churches which he founded as "teaching" (cf. 1 Cor 4:17; Rom 6:17; 2 Th 2:15; Col 1:28). Paul also speaks of handing on traditions which he himself had received: for instance, concerning the Eucharist (1 Cor 11:23ff) and concerning the resurrection (1 Cor 15:3ff). We have first-hand evidence of Paul's ministry of teaching in the letters which he wrote to his churches. The letters equally show the kind of pastoral care that he gave to his communities. This care included the exercise of authority, as is particularly evident in the two letters to the Corinthians. Paul did not hesitate to invoke his authority in dealing with the disobedient: "authority," he tells them, "which the Lord gave for building you up, and not for destroying you" (2 Cor 10:8). If need be, he could be severe in the use of this authority (cf. 2 Cor 13:10). But he preferred to be able to treat them as a father treats his beloved children (cf. 2 Cor 12:14 15). When he had to write a strong admonition, it was "out of much affliction and anguish of heart, and with many tears" (2 Cor 2:4). The pain that he felt was like that of a woman in labor, such was his feeling toward those whom he had brought to birth in Christ (cf. Gal 4:19).

When Paul moved on from a community which he had founded, he did not leave it without leaders to exercise pastoral care in his absence. Thus, in the first letter to the Thessalonians, he urges them "to respect those who labor among you and are over you in the Lord, and admonish you, and to esteem them very highly because of their work" (1 Thes 5:12–13). Similarly, at the close of 1 Corinthians, commending Stephanas and his household as people who had "devoted themselves to the service of the saints," he urges the Corinthians "to be subject to such men and to every fellow-worker and laborer" (1 Cor 16:15–16). It is not certain that Paul "appointed elders in every church" as Luke asserts he did during his first missionary journey (Acts 14:23); however, the presence of "bishops and deacons" in the church at Philippi suggests the development of a structure of ministry in a Pauline church that can hardly have taken place without his approval if not at his initiative (cf. Phil 1:1).

While much more could be said about the ministry of the "apostle of the Gentiles," this should suffice to indicate how appropriately the churches which owed their faith, their Christian practice, their structure of ministry to Paul can be described as "apostolic" churches. Indeed, they continued to be "apostolic" even after the death of the founding apostle. We must now see how the later books of the New Testament witness to the consciousness of the early church of its abiding apostolic character.

The Heritage of Paul: The Pastoral Letters

The letters to Timothy and Titus are particularly important evidence of the continuing influence of the apostle Paul in the early church. We are following the more common opinion that these letters were written two or three decades after the death of St. Paul. The fact that they are presented as letters addressed by Paul to his disciples and co-workers, with detailed instructions regarding the pastoral care they were to exercise in the churches of Ephesus and Crete, shows the weight which the authority of Paul continued to enjoy. For the author of these letters, Paul is simply "*the* teacher" (cf. 1 Tim 2:5–7; 2 Tim 1:1; 3:10). Timothy is to hand on the tradition he had received from Paul (2 Tim 1:13; 2:2); indeed in every respect he is to follow the example that Paul had given him (2 Tim 3:10–11). Timothy and Titus are to follow the pattern of apostolic ministry that Paul had laid down: teaching the sound doctrine they had heard from him; exercising the same pastoral care that they had witnessed him lavishing on his churches. While they were not apostles, not having received their mandate directly from the risen Christ, they were "apostolic men," and the churches under their pastoral care had every right to be called "apostolic."

The role which the pastoral letters attribute to Timothy and Titus raises the question whether they are rightly considered to have been "successors" of the apostle Paul. It is true that the letters present them as Paul's co-workers rather than as his successors, since it is Paul himself who has sent them to Ephesus and Crete, just as the authentic letters show him sending them on various missions to his churches. But, as we have indicated above, it is more likely that the pastorals were actually written after Paul's death. In any case, the last chapter of 2 Timothy, in which Paul says that the time of his departure has come (2 Tim 4:6), clearly indicates that Timothy is expected to carry on his ministry after Paul has gone to his reward.

There is every reason to believe that men like Timothy and Titus, who shared Paul's ministry during his lifetime, carried it on after his death, continuing the work that they had already been doing with the authority they had received from him. Of course Timothy and Titus were not the only such co-workers with Paul. The Pauline letters speak of a number of other such men: Sosthenes (1 Cor 1:1), Apollos (1 Cor 16:12), Silvanus (2 Cor 1:19; 1 Thes 1:1), Epaphroditus (Phil 2:25), Epaphras (Col 1:7) and Tychicus (Eph 6:21). These were men who shared Paul's missionary labors and helped him found churches, or even founded churches on their own, as Epaphras seems to have done in his native town of Colossae (cf. Col 1:3–8; 4:12–13).

In the event of Paul's death, therefore, there was a considerable body of men, both missionaries and local church leaders, who would carry on his ministry. The letters to Timothy and Titus provide sound reason to believe that such men were recognized by the church as Paul's successors. The same letters, it must be added, make it seem highly unlikely that the second-generation church numbered among Paul's successors in the ministries of leadership and teaching any of the women whom Paul himself had mentioned among his co-workers.

In the final chapter of his letter to the Romans, Paul speaks of several women who in one way or another had helped him in his apostolic labors. First there is Phoebe, described as *diakonos* of the church at Cenchreae, whom Paul praises as one who has helped many, including himself (Rom 16:1–2). Next there is Prisca, wife of Aquila, both of whom Paul describes as his fellow-workers in the service of Christ (16:3). Another is Mary, who has worked hard for the people to whom Paul is writing. There follows the pair Andronicus and Junias (or Junia), who are "outstanding among the apostles." A respectable body of opinion today opts for the feminine name Junia; one would also like to know whether Paul numbered them among the "apostles of Christ" or among the "apostles of the churches" (cf. 2 Cor 8:23). Three other "workers in the Lord" have clearly feminine names: Tryphaena, Tryphosa and Persis (16:12). Except for Prisca (Priscilla in Acts 18), nothing is known about any of these women beyond what Paul says here.

I have said that the pastoral letters make it seem highly unlikely that the second-generation church would have numbered any of these women among Paul's successors in the ministry of leadership and teaching. My reason for saying this is the peremptory tone of the assertion in 1 Tim 2:12: "I permit no woman to teach or to have authority over men." At the same time, it is quite possible that the same letter attests to the role of women as deacons in the second-generation church: see 1 Tim 3:11, which can be taken as referring either to the wives of deacons or to women deacons. In any case, it is certain that the post-New Testament church did have deaconesses, especially for ministry to women on the occasion of baptism. But all indications are that the post-New Testament church followed the norm laid down in the pastoral letters excluding women from roles of leadership and teaching. These were ministries assigned to the men called *episkopoi* and *presbuteroi*, and it is only the people who carried on such ministries as these that one can call "successors of the apostles."

Of course it has to be kept in mind that there are important limits to the sense in which anyone could be the successor to an "apostle of Jesus Christ." Such an apostle received his mission directly from the risen Christ, so as to be a first-hand witness to his resurrection, and thus provide a direct link between Christ and his church. The apostles of Christ had a unique, foundational role in the church that no one in the following generations could have.

On the other hand, if the church was to continue until Christ's return in glory, as Christians certainly expected it would, then the commission that Christ had given to his apostles—to preach the gospel, make disciples, baptize, teach, forgive sins, and celebrate the Eucharist—would have to continue, since such ministry was essential to the very life of the church. During their own lifetime, the apostles shared this commission and ministry with others. As the local churches multiplied, more and more people were given a share in the pastoral ministry, receiving their mandate either directly from an apostle or from someone who had received it from him. We can speak of the apostolic mandate as having been shared collegially:

first among the original apostles, then with their co-workers, and then with all those who were called and appointed to pastoral ministry in the churches.

Within the period of the New Testament, the sharing of the apostolic mandate came to be expressed by the laying-on of hands, as we see in Acts (6:6) and the letters to Timothy (1 Tim 4:14; 5:22; 2 Tim 1:6). One of the principal responsibilities of Timothy and Titus, according to the letters addressed to them, was to choose men qualified for ministry in the churches of Ephesus and Crete, and to appoint them to their office by the laying-on of hands (cf. 1 Tim 3:1–13; 5:22; Tit 1:5–9). It would seem that at the period of the writing of the pastorals, those exercising the ministry in the local churches were most often called *presbuteroi* (elders); thus we read: "Let the elders who rule well be considered worthy of double honor, especially those who labor in preaching and teaching" (1 Tim 5:17). However, the term *episkopos* (overseer), which Paul used in his salutation to the church at Philippi, was also used (cf. 1 Tim 3:2), and apparently of the same individuals (cf. Tit 1:5–7). A similar use of both terms referring to the same persons is found in Acts, in Paul's farewell address to those whom Luke calls the elders of the church at Ephesus (Acts 20:17), but whom Paul describes as men whom the Holy Spirit has appointed as *episkopoi* to shepherd the church of the Lord (20:28). There is no clear evidence in the New Testament that the apostles or their missionary co-workers appointed one man in each church as its "bishop" with authority over the presbyters. As far as we can tell, local leadership during the period of the New Testament was collegial in structure, although the beginning of the development toward the historical episcopate can perhaps be seen in the role of James, "the brother of the Lord" at Jerusalem at the time of Paul's final visit to that church (Acts 21:18), and possibly in that of Diotrephes in 3 John 9.

Although we do not find what we know as the historical episcopate in the New Testament, the principle of apostolic succession in the ministry is clearly present there, in the pastorals and in Acts—writings that belong to the second generation of Christianity. As Timothy is to take what he has heard from Paul and "entrust it to faithful men who will be able to teach others also" (2 Tim 2:2), so also the elders whom Paul leaves in charge of the church at Ephesus are to do in their turn what he had done while with them (Acts

20:18–35). Men like Timothy and Titus who had been the apostles' co-workers would undoubtedly have been recognized as their principal successors in the work of founding churches. Such men also shared their pastoral ministry with those whom they appointed in each church as elders and *episkopoi*.

It is only in the post-New Testament period that we find a single bishop in each local church. Second-century Christian documents do not provide a clear picture of how the transition took place from the collegial structure we see in the New Testament to the episcopal structure that eventually prevailed. What we can affirm with reasonable certitude is that toward the close of the second century, each church was being led by a single bishop, and that these bishops were being recognized as the successors of the apostles in their pastoral ministry. This recognition, which only the gnostic heretics refused to give, was a crucial element in the church's consciousness of its apostolicity. We shall now begin the second part of this chapter by seeing some expressions of this consciousness in early Christian literature.

II. THE APOSTOLICITY OF THE POST-NEW TESTAMENT CHURCH

Our first witness is the *First Letter of Clement to the Corinthians*, an undoubtedly authentic document of the last decade of the first century. While this letter presents itself as sent by the Roman church, without mention of the name of its individual author, it is attributed to Clement on the testimony of Dionysius, who was bishop of Corinth a half-century later.[137] The occasion of this letter was the strife at Corinth caused by the expulsion of some of its *episkopoi* from their office. Clement urges the restoration of these men to their rightful position in the church, appealing to the fact that they had been installed in office according to a pattern of succession in ministry that was apostolic in origin. Here are the pertinent sections of the letter.

> The apostles received the gospel for us from the Lord Jesus Christ. Jesus Christ was sent from God. The Christ therefore is from God and the apostles from Christ. In both ways, then, they were in accordance with the appointed order of God's will. Having therefore received their commands, and being fully assured

by the resurrection of the Lord Jesus Christ, and with faith confirmed by the word of God, they went forth in the assurance of
the Holy Spirit, preaching the good news that the kingdom of
God is coming. They preached from district to district, and from
city to city, and they appointed their first converts, testing them
by the Spirit, to be bishops and deacons of the future believers
(42:1–4).

Our apostles also knew through our Lord Jesus Christ that there
would be strife for the title of bishop. For this cause, therefore,
since they had received perfect foreknowledge, they appointed
those who have been already mentioned, and afterwards added
the codicil that if they should fall asleep, other approved men
should succeed to their ministry. We consider therefore that it is
not just to remove from their ministry those who were appointed
by them, or later on by other eminent men, with the consent of
the whole church, and have ministered to the flock of Christ
without blame, humbly, peaceably, and disinterestedly, and for
many years have received a universally favorable testimony. For
our sin is not small, if we eject from the episcopate those who
have blamelessly and holily offered its sacrifices (44:1–4).[138]

Among the many points that are worthy of note in this section
of 1 Clement, we shall mention the following. First, there is the
striking sequence of missions: Christ sent from God, and apostles
from Christ, receiving from him the gospel which they handed on
to the church. Second, there is the apostolic origin of the ministry,
and of the principle of succession in such ministry. Clement uses the
Pauline vocabulary, speaking of the *episkopoi* and *diakonoi* (cf. Phil
1:1) as the "first converts" (literally "first fruits") (cf. 1 Cor 16:15)
whom the apostles "tested in the Spirit" and placed in charge of the
churches they had founded. The apostles also provided for an orderly succession in the ministry: after the apostles, other "eminent
men" would continue to appoint local leaders. We can hardly be far
wrong if we identify Clement's "eminent men" with apostolic co-
workers like Timothy and Titus.

It seems clear that the leadership of the church at Corinth was
still collegial in structure at this time; there was a group of *episkopoi*,
but no one "bishop" in the later sense of this term. The situation
resembles that of the pastoral letters, where also "eminent men"

were carrying on the ministry of the founding apostle and providing for local leadership in the churches.

While Clement clearly sees the church of his generation as apostolic in its faith (since it has received the gospel from the apostles, who received it from Christ), his concern is rather with the apostolic origin of the ministry, and of the principle of orderly succession in such ministry. His letter provides striking witness to the church's consciousness of its apostolicity toward the end of the first century.

In the course of the second century the church had to face a serious challenge to its faith in the form of gnosticism, whose proponents rejected the doctrine that was being taught in the churches by the bishops, claiming to possess a more perfect knowledge of revelation through a secret tradition to which only they had access. Irenaeus, bishop of Lyons, responded to this danger with his great work *Against the Heresies*, dated about 185.

The question which Irenaeus poses is: where is the authentic tradition of the apostles to be found? His answer is: it is to be found in the churches of apostolic origin, since it was to their churches, and to those to whom they entrusted the care of their churches, that the apostles committed all that they had received from Christ. The agreement of all the apostolic churches in proclaiming the same doctrine is the proof that they have preserved the authentic apostolic teaching.

> It is within the power of all, therefore, in every church, who may wish to see the truth, to contemplate clearly the tradition of the apostles manifested throughout the whole world, and we are in a position to reckon up those who were by the apostles instituted bishops in the churches, and the succession of these men to our own times: those who neither taught nor knew of anything like what these heretics rave about. For if the apostles had known hidden mysteries, which they were in the habit of imparting to the "perfect," apart and privily from the rest, they would have delivered them especially to those to whom they were also committing the churches themselves. For they were desirous that these men should be very perfect and blameless in all things, whom also they were leaving behind as their successors, delivering up their own place of government to these men.[139]

Irenaeus then goes on to name those who had handed on the apostolic tradition in the church of Rome, where the teaching of the two greatest of the apostles, Peter and Paul, had been preserved and transmitted through the orderly succession of bishops down to Irenaeus's own day. He concludes:

> In this order, and by this succession, the ecclesiastical tradition from the apostles and the preaching of the truth have come down to us. And this is most abundant proof that there is one and the same vivifying faith, which has been preserved in the church from the apostles until now and handed down in truth.[140]

> Since therefore we have such proofs, it is not necessary to seek the truth among others which it is easy to obtain from the church, since the apostles, like a rich man (depositing his money) in a bank, lodged in her hands most copiously all things pertaining to the truth, so that everyone, whosoever will, can draw from her the water of life.[141]

Our third witness is Tertullian, in his work *De praescriptione haereticorum*, dated about the year 200, when Tertullian was still a defender of the Catholic faith. His argument in this work against the heretics is that they had no right to argue for their doctrines from the scriptures, since the scriptures were the property of the apostolic churches, where alone one could find their authentic meaning and interpretation. He wrote:

> The apostles, after first bearing witness to the faith in Jesus Christ throughout Judea, and founding churches there, went forth into the world and preached the same doctrine of the same faith to the nations. They then in like manner founded churches in every city, from which all the other churches, one after another, derived the tradition of the faith and the seeds of doctrine, and are every day deriving them that they may become churches. Indeed it is on this account only that they will be able to deem themselves apostolic, as being the offspring of apostolic churches.[142]

> It is then manifest that all doctrine which agrees with the apostolic churches—those moulds and original sources of the faith— must be reckoned for truth, as undoubtedly containing that which the said churches received from the apostles, the apostles from Christ, Christ from God.[143] (The doctrine of the heretics) after comparison with that of the apostles, will declare, by its

own diversity and contrariety, that it had for its author neither an apostle nor an apostolic man, because, as the apostles would never have taught things which were self-contradictory, so the apostolic men would not have inculcated teaching different from the apostles. To this test, therefore, will the heretics be submitted for proof by those churches who, although they derive not their founder from an apostle or apostolic man (as being of much later date, for in fact they are being founded daily), yet, since they agree in the same faith, they are accounted as not less apostolic, because they are akin in doctrine (*pro consanguinitate doctrinae*).[144]

Looking back over the passages we have cited from Irenaeus and Tertullian we can see that for both of them the essential question was: where is the authentic teaching of the apostles to be found? Neither of them was content with the reply: "It is to be found in their writings," because they knew that the heretics also claimed that their doctrines were supported by scripture. They insisted that scripture must be understood in the light of the authentic teaching of the apostles, as it is found in the concordant witness of the apostolic churches. Three arguments were invoked to support their position. First, it was to the churches, and to those to whom they committed the pastoral care of the churches, that the apostles entrusted their teaching (and not to some special group of the "perfect," as the heretics claimed). Second, the apostolic doctrine has been faithfully preserved and handed down in the churches through the succession of bishops from the apostles and apostolic men. Third, the fact that all the Christian churches throughout the world teach the same doctrine proves that they all derive their teaching from the same apostolic source.

It is clear, then, that for these writers the essential apostolicity of the church was its fidelity to the apostolic faith. This apostolicity was essential, because the apostles provided the link with Christ; hence, Christian faith was necessarily apostolic faith. Apostolic succession in ministry was also important in their thinking, but primarily as the guarantor of fidelity to the apostolic tradition of faith. In their writings, the concept of apostolic succession was the regular succession of one teacher of the faith after another in the pastoral leadership of the churches. We do not find them stressing the idea of the transmission of sacred power through sacramental ordination. However, we have good reason to presume that in their day the procedure by which bishops were chosen and installed in office was actually such ordination. The chief witness to this at that period is Hippolytus, with his work entitled *The Apostolic Tradition*, written about the year 215.[115] The importance of the testimony which this work bears to the recognition by the late second-century church of the apostolic origin of the office and authority of its bishops warrants our treating this work in some detail.

First of all, a word about the author, who was a presbyter of the church of Rome under Pope Zephyrinus (190–217). When Callistus, who had been Zephyrinus' archdeacon, was elected as his successor, Hippolytus refused to recognize his election, and formed a schismatic group which considered him its bishop. However, he eventually seems to have been reconciled with the second successor of Callistus, the martyr Pope Pontian, with whom he shared exile and martyrdom. The Roman church subsequently honored him among its martyrs, with no reference to the fact that he had for a time been an anti-pope.

Hippolytus was still a presbyter in good standing when he wrote *The Apostolic Tradition,* but his work is not to be taken as though it were the official liturgical book of the Roman church. On the other hand, there are good reasons to accept it as a reliable description of the practice of the church of his day. Gregory Dix points to the particular significance of the presence of many indications of a Jewish origin of the liturgical practices that Hippolytus describes.

> Hippolytus reveals clearly for the first time how firmly the Jewish liturgical basis persisted in the Catholic cultus after a century and a half of Gentile Christianity. That is a fact—not yet adequately appreciated—which must have great weight in such questions as the alleged influence of Hellenistic Mysteries on primitive Christianity. And it reveals, too, something of the immense importance of *paradosis*, "tradition," in the formation of the Christian *spirit*. "Tradition" for the early Church, as Hippolytus' title indicates, meant much more than the mere process of instruction or "handing on." It stood for the whole Christian *via vitae*, belief, ethics, worship, "the Way," the established and received Christian *life*. In an age when the "Apostolic" documents of the New Testament were only slowly making good their position as an authoritative Canon beside the old Jewish scriptures, the importance of the Christian "tradition" was incalculable in

preventing the distortion of authentic "Apostolic" Christianity into a mere theosophy by Hellenistic influences. The appearance of these Jewish features in the *Apostolic Tradition* is in itself some justification for styling its tradition "Apostolic." They do bring us at second hand into contact with the Church Order and devotional practice of the Apostolic age itself.

This is not to say that every phrase of Hippolytus can be taken at once as likely to be endorsed by the whole of the second-century Great Church. . . . We can watch Hippolytus at work on his material, adapting and supplementing a little here and there with his own comments, perhaps in one or two cases misunderstanding the origin and intention of the practices already ancient which he describes. But making all due allowance for these cases, there remains a much larger part of the contents, some of it supported by allusions in other writers, of which we can safely say that his material comes to him rather than from him. It represents the mind and practice not of St. Hippolytus only but of the whole Catholic Church of the second century. As such it is of outstanding importance.[146]

Apostolic Origin of Episcopal Ministry

Hippolytus begins his work with a description of the ordination of a bishop. Because of the importance of the witness which this document gives to the consciousness of the apostolic origin of episcopal office and authority toward the end of the second century, we shall quote this part of the text in full, in the English version provided by Dom Gregory Dix.[147]

II. 1. Let the bishop be ordained being in all things without fault, chosen by all the people.

2. And when he has been proposed and found acceptable to all, the people being assembled on the Lord's day together with the presbytery and such bishops as may attend, let the choice be generally approved.

3. Let the bishops lay hands on him and the presbytery stand by in silence.

4. And all shall keep silence praying in their heart for the descent of the Spirit.

5. After this one of the bishops present at the request of all, laying his hand on him who is ordained bishop, shall pray thus, saying:

III. 1. "O God and Father of our Lord Jesus Christ, Father of mercies and God of all comfort," "Who dwellest on high yet hast respect unto the lowly," "Who knowest all things before they come to pass";

2. Who didst give ordinances unto Thy church "by the Word of Thy grace"; Who "didst foreordain from the beginning" the race of the righteous from Abraham, instituting princes and priests and leaving not Thy sanctuary without ministers; Who from the foundation of the world hast been pleased to be glorified in them whom Thou hast chosen:

3. And now pour forth that Power which is from Thee, of "the princely Spirit" which Thou didst deliver to Thy Beloved Child Jesus Christ, which He bestowed on Thy holy Apostles who established the Church which hallows Thee in every place to the endless glory and praise of Thy Name.

4. Father "who knowest the hearts of all," grant upon this Thy servant whom Thou hast chosen for the episcopate to feed Thy holy flock and serve as Thine high priest, that he may minister blamelessly by night and day, that he may unceasingly behold and propitiate Thy countenance and offer to Thee the gifts of Thy holy Church.

5. And that by the high priestly Spirit he may have authority "to forgive sins" according to Thy command, "to assign lots" according to Thy bidding, to "loose every bond" according to the authority Thou gavest to the Apostles, and that he may please Thee in meekness and a pure heart, "offering" to Thee "a sweet-smelling savour,"

6. through Thy Child Jesus Christ our Lord, through Whom to Thee be glory, might and praise, to the Father and to the Son with the Holy Spirit now and ever and world without end. Amen.

We can distinguish three elements in the ordination of a bishop as described by Hippolytus: the choice of the candidate, the laying-on of hands, and the prayer for the Holy Spirit.

We see, first of all, that the whole local church is involved in the choice of the man to be ordained bishop: he is chosen, proposed, and found acceptable by all. But the local church is not self-sufficient to ordain its bishop; it must call upon the bishops of other churches, and they must approve the choice as well.

Secondly, we see that all the bishops who are present, and only the bishops, lay hands upon the man being ordained. Here we have a practical recognition of the collegial nature of the episcopate. The ordination of a bishop involves his aggregation to an episcopal body of men sharing a common ministry in the church. It is only those who are already members of this body who are qualified to introduce others into it, and thus share with them the mandate they themselves have received. Their laying-on of hands is a sign of their willingness to accept this man into their body, and to share their episcopal ministry with him.

Thirdly, we see that all present, but in different ways, take part in the prayer for the outpouring of the Holy Spirit on the candidate. At a first moment, while the bishops are laying their hands, everyone is to pray in silence for the coming of the Spirit. Subsequently, one of the bishops, "at the request of all," is to pray aloud, while he alone lays hands on the one being ordained. It is possible that one of the reasons why only one bishop would pray aloud was to give him freedom to improvise his prayer. It is not likely that the prayer which Hippolytus presents here was a fixed formula from which the ordaining bishop could not deviate. However, we can assume that this is a good example of the prayers of ordination in use at Rome in Hippolytus' day. Gregory Dix assures us: "We may safely take it that in outline and essentials the rites and customs to which the *Apostolic Tradition* bears witness were those practised in the Roman Church in his day, and in his own youth c. A.D. 180."[148]

The prayer for the ordination of a bishop which Hippolytus gives us, then, is a precious source of light on the understanding which the second-century church had of the nature and source of the episcopal ministry. First of all, the prayer attributes to God the Father the "giving of ordinances to his church," and the provident care of his sanctuary so that it will not lack ministers of his own choosing. This is a clear profession of faith in the divine origin of the ministry to which the candidate is being ordained.

Secondly, the prayer expresses confidence that the man "chosen by all the people" and "found acceptable by all" is the one whom the Father himself has chosen: "Father, who knowest the hearts of

all, grant upon this thy servant whom thou has chosen for the episcopate . . . "

Thirdly, the prayer is essentially an *epiclesis*, a prayer for the
sending of the Holy Spirit upon the ordinand, to equip him with
the power and gifts for episcopal ministry. The prayer (which, in
this part, is preserved in the original Greek) uses two adjectives of
the Spirit invoked for the bishop: *hegemonikou*, which Dix renders
"princely," and *archieratikô*, "high-priestly." A comparison with the
prayers for the ordination of a presbyter and of a deacon shows that
in each case the words that qualify the Spirit that is to be given are
appropriate to the kind of ministry the man will have. Thus, for the
presbyter, the bishop prays that the Father would impart "the Spirit
of grace and counsel," while for the deacon he asks "the Spirit of
grace and earnestness and diligence." The two adjectives used of the
Spirit in the prayer for the bishop, then, likewise correspond to the
kind of ministry he will have. The first adjective, *hegemonikou*, is
translated in the lexicon of Arndt and Gingrich as "guiding" and
"leading." A cognate word, *hegoumenoi*, is used in the letter to the
Hebrews, first of the "leaders" from whom the addressees of the letter first heard the word of God, men who have already died (Heb
13:7), and then of their present "leaders," whom the faithful are
urged to obey (13:17) and whom they are asked to greet, with all the
saints (13:24). It would not seem incorrect, then, to translate the
term *tou hegemonikou pneumatos* as "the Spirit of leadership." It must
also be noted that what the Father is asked to pour out is "the power
that comes from him" of this Spirit. It is significant that the prayers
for the ordination of presbyters and deacons do not speak of "power"
in connection with the Spirit they are to receive.

The second adjective describing the Spirit that is invoked upon
the bishop is *archieratikô*, "high-priestly." The ministry of the
bishop is also described with the verb *archierateuein*: "to serve as high
priest." The prayer goes on to spell out the various ministries which
the bishop will exercise in virtue of the powers that are conferred on
him by the Spirit of leadership and the Spirit of high-priesthood.
We have already noted the use of the word "power" (*dunamin*); we
should also note the word *exousia* (authority, or power), which occurs twice: of authority to forgive sins and to loose every bond.

We come now to the point we are particularly concerned with:

namely, the elements in the prayer which manifest the church's consciousness of the apostolicity of episcopal ministry. First, we note that the Father is asked to pour out the power of the Spirit which he first gave to Jesus, and which Jesus in turn bestowed *on the apostles who established the church*. Secondly, in virtue of the Spirit he has received, the bishop will be able to "loose every bond *according to the authority given to the apostles*." It can hardly be doubted that this prayer expresses the conviction that the mandate which Jesus gave to his apostles, and the authority which he gave them to carry it out, continued to exist in the church, maintained from generation to generation in the body of men ordained to the episcopate.

It is true that the gift of the Spirit had to be implored anew each time a man was ordained to share this ministry. Jesus, who received the Spirit from the Father, was able to bestow it on his apostles, but there is no suggestion that the ordaining bishop actually gave the Spirit to the ordinand. The Spirit, each time, was given in answer to prayer: first the prayer of the whole community, and then the prayer of the ordaining bishop.

However, from the fact that it was only the bishops present who laid hands on the candidate, and that the solemn prayer was pronounced only by a bishop "at the request of all," we can conclude that it was understood by the second-century church that it was only those who already belonged to the episcopal order who could aggregate others to it, and so share their collegial mandate with them. It was only in this way that the new bishop's authority would be derived from the authority which Jesus had given to his apostles.

Conceivably, a local Christian church could choose someone qualified to be its bishop, and could pray for the Spirit to descend on him. However, the local church was not self-sufficient to ordain its own bishop. It had to call upon the bishops of other churches to come and approve the choice, lay their hands on the man chosen, and pronounce the prayer of the church over him. In this requirement, we can see two ways in which the church's apostolicity was being safeguarded.

First, apostolicity of faith. When the local church chose a man to be its bishop, it no doubt tested his faith, and found it satisfactory. However, one could not exclude the possibility that a particular local church might go astray in its faith, and so not recognize the faulty nature of the faith of the man chosen for its bishop. The requirement that the choice be approved by bishops of other churches provided a guarantee of the apostolicity of the faith of the man to be ordained bishop.

Secondly, apostolicity of ministry. In order for the new bishop to be able to "loose every bond by the authority which Jesus gave to his apostles," he had to share in the mandate which Jesus had given to the twelve. The requirement that bishops of other churches had to come and lay their hands on the candidate shows the conviction that in order for a man to have part in the apostolic mandate, he had to be accepted into the living body of men by whom that mandate had been exercised and handed down from the apostles. The necessary participation of those who were themselves members of that body provided the assurance that the new bishop would really possess the authority to "loose and bind" which Jesus had given to the apostles.

To sum up: in the ordination of a bishop as described in *The Apostolic Tradition*, we can distinguish three factors: the ecclesiological, the christological, and the pneumatological. By the ecclesiological I mean the part played by the church of which the man was to be the bishop. We have seen that he had to be a man "in all things without fault," "chosen by all the people," and "found acceptable by all." While Hippolytus does not specify all the things in which he had to be found without fault, we can be sure that a primary consideration would have been the soundness of his faith, known to the church he lived in. Further, we see that the ordination takes place in the presence of the whole community, that all take part in the prayer for the descent of the Holy Spirit, and that it is "at the request of all" that one of the bishops will pronounce the prayer of ordination. Finally, it is obvious that the ordination is with a view to this man's ministry as bishop for this particular church. Immediately after being ordained, he was joined by the presbyters of his church in celebrating the Eucharist for the first time as its bishop.[149] It was because his ordination would make him become the bishop of *this* church that his church had an indispensable part to play in the ordination itself.

The christological factor consists in the link which ordination established between the new bishop and Christ: namely, that by his incorporation into the episcopal college, he began to share in the mandate which Christ gave to his apostles. The prayer of ordination called down upon him that "Spirit of leadership" which Jesus received from the Father, and which Jesus in turn bestowed on his apostles. The laying-on of the hands of the several bishops present symbolized the sharing of the mandate which linked the new bishop to Christ as the ultimate source of the authority he would now have to forgive sins and to "loose every bond" in the Lord's name.

The pneumatological factor consists in the gift of the Holy Spirit for which first the whole church and then one of the bishops prayed. As we have seen, this prayer is an *epiclesis*. The ordaining bishop did not confer the Spirit; he had to pray that it be given, but with confidence that God had chosen the man who had been proposed and found acceptable to all. The specific gifts of the Spirit that are mentioned in the prayer are those that will equip the new bishop for the ministry he will have. They include power and authority: gifts that are not mentioned in the prayers for the ordination of a presbyter or a deacon. The Spirit that is called down upon the bishop is a "Spirit of leadership" and a "Spirit of high-priesthood." The various ministries that are mentioned in the prayer correspond to these two aspects of the bishop's role in his church. The prayer of ordination clearly expresses the mind of the second-century church that it is only a man upon whom the Spirit has come in power who can fulfill the ministry of a bishop. At the same time, the attitude is one of serene confidence that the Spirit will be given in answer to the church's prayer. In the language of a subsequent development of Christian theology, we can say that we find here a sense of what will be termed the sacramental efficacy of the prayer of ordination when this is pronounced over a suitable candidate by a bishop with the laying-on of hands.

We conclude this section on the apostolicity of the post-New Testament church by recalling the two aspects of apostolicity which our sources have, in different ways, illuminated for us, and by reflecting on how these two aspects of apostolicity are related to each other.

The first aspect of apostolicity, and the one that is clearly most basic, is apostolicity of faith. The essential conviction of the second-century church was that its faith was soundly based on the revelation that Jesus had entrusted to his apostles, and that this revelation had been preserved and transmitted faithfully in the churches that the apostles had founded. Two arguments were used to demonstrate the apostolicity of the faith that was then being taught in the Christian churches: one from the past and one from the present. Looking back, one appealed to the unbroken succession of bishops from the time of the apostles, who had handed on the faith that they themselves had received. Looking to the present, one appealed to the agreement of all the Christian churches in the profession of the same faith, as proof that they must have derived their faith from the common apostolic source.

The other aspect of apostolicity that we have seen in these sources is that of the church's ministry. Recognizing, on the one hand, the uniqueness of the role which the apostles had played in the foundation of the church, our second-century sources nonetheless saw the bishops of their day as true successors of the apostles in their pastoral ministry. As we have seen, Irenaeus and Tertullian stressed their succession in that they had followed one another in the episcopal chair: the symbol of their teaching authority. Hippolytus gives us precious information about the ordination of a bishop, where the laying-on of hands by bishops of other churches, and the prayer for the coming of the Holy Spirit, testify to the understanding that ordination meant incorporation into an episcopal body in which the same mandate that Christ had given to his apostles was maintained and handed on.

We can also see how apostolicity of faith and apostolicity of ministry were interrelated. Apostolicity of faith, of course, was a quality of the whole church, and all the faithful had their part in preserving and handing on the faith they had received. But the transmission of the apostolic deposit was especially the responsibility of those who had the official ministry of teaching in the churches. Hence, their credentials as successors to the apostles in their ministry provided an assurance of fidelity to the apostolic teaching which unofficial teachers would not have had. On the other hand, when a man was being considered as a candidate for the episcopate, the soundness of his faith was a primary consideration. In choosing a man to be their bishop, the faithful of that community judged his faith in the light of the faith which they had received from his predecessors. Likewise, the candidate's faith had to be approved by the bishops of other churches who would come to ordain him. Thus, there was a futher assurance that the one ordained to apostolic ministry would be a man of apostolic faith, who would in turn hand on this faith to the next generation.

Are Bishops Successors to the Apostles by Divine Institution?

We have put off this question to the end of this chapter, because we are convinced that it cannot be answered from the New Testament alone, but must be seen in the light of the texts we have seen from Clement, Irenaeus, Tertullian and Hippolytus. There can be no doubt about the fact that toward the end of the second century, orthodox Christians recognized their bishops as the successors to the apostles, with a special responsibility and authority for maintaining the apostolic tradition of faith. But, as we mentioned briefly at the end of the first part of this chapter, we do not find in the New Testament a clear distinction between *episkopoi* and *presbuteroi*, nor do we find any indication that the apostles left one "bishop" in charge of each local church. The second century saw a transition from the earlier collegial ministry in local churches to the threefold structure of ministry, in which one bishop presided over the presbyters and deacons, as well as over the congregation. Hardly anyone seriously questions the assertion that the emergence of the historical episcopate was a post-New Testament development of church organization. The question, then, is: can the result of such historical development be understood as of "divine institution"?[150] The crucial nature of this question for ecumenical dialogue will become evident in the next chapter, where we will see to what extent the difference between a "catholic" and a "protestant" understanding of apostolicity depends on whether a positive or a negative answer is given to this question.

It hardly needs to be said that the Catholic Church's answer to this question is in the affirmative. Vatican II expressed the Catholic position—one shared by the Orthodox and others of the "Catholic" tradition—when it said: "Therefore, this sacred Synod teaches that by divine institution bishops have succeeded to the place of the apostles as shepherds of the Church, and that he who hears them, hears Christ, while he who rejects them, rejects Christ and him who sent Christ (cf. Lk 10:16)."[151]

What remains to be clarified, however, is the sense in which the concept of "divine institution" is applicable to such elements of church structure as the historical episcopate. Hardly any Catholic theologian nowadays takes this to mean that Christ explicitly determined the episcopal structure of the local churches. Christ did not leave a "blueprint" for his disciples to follow in the organization of the church.[152] It is apparent, rather, that the apostles made decisions about church structures as the need arose (as, for instance, in the appointment of the "seven" at Jerusalem), and that they felt guided by the Spirit in making such decisions (cf. Acts 6:1–6). It is quite consistent with what we see taking place in the New Testament, that in the post-New Testament period such development of church structure continued, as the need became more urgently felt of a focal point of unity in each local church. If, while the founding apostle or apostolic co-worker was still alive, there was not the felt need of a single pastoral leader in each church, it is reasonable to surmise that such a need was felt afterward, when the apostle was no longer there to maintain unity. In any case, the fact is that within a century or so after the death of the apostles, each church was being led by a single bishop, and these bishops were being recognized as the legitimate successors to the apostles in their role of pastoral leadership.

Can we then speak of "divine institution" in this case? Obviously not in a simplistic sense. But Catholics believe we can, in the sense that we have good reason to believe that this development, which is consistent with what was already taking place in the New Testament church, was guided by the Holy Spirit, and was part of God's design for his church.

In support of the claim that this development was consistent with what was already taking place in the New Testament church, we can appeal to the following factors. First, the church clearly understood that the pastoral charge given to the apostles of "making disciples, baptizing, teaching people to observe all that Jesus had taught them" (cf. Mt. 28:19–20), was to continue to the end of the age. This is the obvious sense of the last words of Matthew's gospel. Therefore, while in many respects the original apostles could have no successors, for in many ways their role was unique and intransmissible, their pastoral ministry was to continue, and that meant that others had to succeed them, and therefore their mandate, and the authority to carry it out, had to be transmitted to others. Secondly, within the New Testament, we have seen provision being made for the carrying on of the apostles' ministry by those who would succeed them.

What reason, then, do we have for believing that the post-New Testament development of the historical episcopate was "guided by the Holy Spirit" and was "part of God's design for his church"? It seems to me that the most convincing reason we have for believing this is the fact that the Christian church came to recognize its bishops as the legitimate successors of the apostles, with the consequence that the church accepted the *teaching* of these bishops as *normative for its faith*. Now it is surely a basic article of Christian faith that the Holy Spirit maintains the church in the true faith.[153] This is a consequence of Christ's definitive victory, and of his promise that the Spirit of truth would lead his church into all truth (cf. Jn 16:13). Now a church that is divinely maintained in the true faith could hardly have been mistaken when it determined the norms of its faith. If, then, our confidence that the Holy Spirit must have guided the second and third century church in its discernment of the writings that were going to be normative for its faith justifies our acceptance of the New Testament as inspired scripture, we have equal reason for confidence that the Holy Spirit must have guided the same second and third century church in the universal recognition of its bishops as the authoritative teachers whose decisions about matters of doctrine would be normative for its faith. But if it was the Holy Spirit who guided the church in its acceptance of bishops as the rightful successors of the apostles, than I believe we have also good reason to believe that the development of the episcopate itself was also guided by the Holy Spirit, was part of God's design for his church, and in that sense "of divine institution."

9 || Apostolicity in Ecumenical Dialogue

Of the four properties which most Christians profess the church to have when they recite their creed, apostolicity is the one that involves the questions on which Christians are the most deeply divided. We have seen that the early church understood itself to be apostolic in its faith and its ministry. These continue to be the basic elements of the apostolicity which Christian churches attribute to themselves today. One can hardly imagine a Christian church that does not claim that its faith and its ministry are apostolic.

The deeply divisive questions arise when each church sets out to explain how it substantiates its claim to profess apostolic faith and to continue apostolic ministry. For instance, some will insist that the sole norm of apostolicity in faith is had in the written record of their teaching which the apostles left to the church in the New Testament. For these churches, only what is explicitly set down in these apostolic writings has any claim to be normative for the apostolicity of Christian faith. Other churches, while recognizing the primary importance of the New Testament, will also insist on the normative role of tradition as a vehicle by which the church has handed on its understanding and its practice of the apostolic faith. These churches will see the apostolicity of their faith also shown in their adherence to the teaching of the Fathers of the church, and to the doctrinal decisions of the great ecumenical councils.

Likewise, churches will employ different criteria as the basis of their claim to apostolicity of ministry. For some, the apostolic mandate was transmitted to the whole post-apostolic church, so that each Christian congregation holds the fullness of apostolic ministry, and imparts a share in its apostolic mandate to the person whom it chooses as its minister. For some, the role of the community is simply to recognize and confirm the charismatic gifts by which the Holy Spirit designates certain persons for ministry. Others see in the New Testament a distinction between purely charismatic ministry, and the more stable pattern of ministry which the apostles and their co-workers established by choosing qualified men in each community and ordaining them by the laying-on of hands with prayer. Some churches hold that only those so ordained can in turn ordain others, but since the New Testament does not clearly distinguish between men called "presbyters" and those called "*episkopoi*" they maintain that presbyters have the fullness of apostolic ministry and can share this by ordaining others. There are churches, however, which consider bishops to be successors to the apostles in the ministry of pastoral leadership and authoritative teaching, in a sense that is not true of presbyters. These churches take as permanently normative the ancient tradition that limits to bishops the power to share the apostolic mandate by ordination. Finally, the Catholic Church alone believes the local church of Rome to have a special title to apostolicity, such that communion with the bishop of this church is an element of the full apostolicity of all other bishops and their churches.

It is not difficult to see the correlation between the various understandings of apostolicity in faith, on the one hand, and the various patterns of ministry, on the other. Those churches which insist that the New Testament writings constitute the sole criterion of apostolicity in faith will find in the New Testament the basis of the apostolicity of their pattern of ministry, whether it be charismatic, congregational or presbyterian. The churches which recognize the normative character of apostolic tradition, along with scripture, are the ones that insist that apostolicity of ministry requires ordination by bishops who share the apostolic mandate through their own membership in the episcopal college.

These two ways of understanding the church's apostolicity in faith and ministry justify the common practice of dividing the Christian churches into two broad categories: those with a "protestant" view of apostolicity, and those with a "catholic" view. Among the latter are listed the Anglican, Old Catholic, Orthodox and other

Eastern churches, and the Roman Catholic, while the first category would include all other churches.

For centuries the separation between these two groups of churches had seemed an impassible chasm. However, the ecumenical movement of the twentieth century has given reason to hope that it can be bridged, and that one day unity can be restored. The first indication of this was the fact that churches of the "catholic" category, like the Anglican and some of the Orthodox churches, became full participants in the World Council of Churches, where the majority of member churches are of the "protestant" type. This gave rise to genuine dialogue about matters that had previously seemed altogether intractable. Then, with the Second Vatican Council, the Catholic Church became a full participant in the ecumenical movement (though not in the World Council of Churches), and has since then entered into ecumenical dialogue with the major churches of the "protestant" tradition.

I have entitled this chapter "Apostolicity in Ecumenical Dialogue" because I am convinced that the best way to understand what Christians mean when they claim that their churches, their faith and their ministry are "apostolic" is to listen to what they say when they explain their beliefs to other Christians in ecumenical dialogue. Furthermore, when participants in dialogue really listen to one another and seriously try to understand the other's point of view, it not infrequently happens that they mutually agree that their views are not so profoundly incompatible as they had previously thought them to be. Indeed, in some cases they find themselves able to agree on a common statement that manifests the extent to which they recognize one another to share a common faith.

There are three respects in which progress has been made on the question of apostolicity through ecumenical dialogue.

First, it has resulted, on both sides, in a more comprehensive notion of apostolicity. Whereas previously those of the "protestant" tradition had tended to identify apostolicity with fidelity to apostolic doctrine, and "catholics" had tended to identify it with apostolic succession in ministry, the concept of apostolicity that is being expressed in ecumenical statements today is generally a well-balanced one that includes all its major components. We shall present some such statements in this chapter.

Secondly, it is a fruit of dialogue that the participants are obliged to clarify their position for those who do not share their point of view. This helps each side to know exactly what the other means, thus helping to eliminate the false impressions and misunderstandings that have often made differences seem greater than they really were. At the same time, unjustified optimism that expects long-standing differences to be easily and quickly resolved is also chastened, when both sides explain frankly where they stand, and for what reasons they find the other's position unacceptable. There is a real advantage in knowing exactly what the other really holds, and how it differs from one's own point of view. The ecumenical dialogues provide this advantage, and we shall present some statements that will help us the better to know just how apostolicity is understood in the various Christian churches today.

Finally, when both sides in a dialogue have come fully to understand the other's point of view, it is sometimes possible for them to recognize that their positions are not so far apart as they had thought them to be. With regard to apostolicity, for instance, those of the "protestant" side might come to recognize the sense in which tradition can also be seen as a criterion of apostolicity, and those of the "catholic" side might come to recognize the sense in which ministry in a church that has not maintained apostolic succession through episcopal ordination can still be apostolic. We shall see some examples of such positive assessments of the other side's position also in the course of this chapter.

What we propose to do in the rest of this chapter is to substantiate, from statements issued as the fruit of ecumenical dialogues, our assertion about progress having been made in three respects toward an ecumenical understanding of the church's apostolicity. To begin, we must say something about the dialogues that provide us with the material we shall be presenting. A glance at the *Bibliography of Interchurch and Interconfessional Dialogues* published by the Centro pro Unione in Rome[154] suffices to show that there is an astonishing number and variety of such dialogues going on among churches today. A great many of these are between churches within a particular country or region, and some are unofficial in character. For our present purpose we are going to consider those dialogues that are officially sponsored by the churches or confessional bodies involved, and are worldwide in their participation. Almost all of these are bilateral: between two churches or confessional bodies. But we shall also be making use of two documents that are the fruit of the work of the Faith and Order Commission of the World Council of Churches, and which have involved the participation of Roman Catholics along with representatives of the many churches that are members of the WCC. Almost all the documents we are going to use have been very conveniently gathered and edited in one volume by Harding Meyer and Lukas Vischer, under the title: *Growth in Agreement.*[155]

A More Comprehensive Notion of Apostolicity

We shall begin with the document that is the earliest of the series to have been issued, and is actually of a different nature from the rest we shall consider. This is the "Study Document" prepared by the Joint Theological Commission on "Catholicity and Apostolicity," which was formed in 1967 at the request of the Joint Working Group between the WCC and the Catholic Church.[156] This Joint Working Group was established in 1965 as an immediate fruit of the Catholic Church's opening to the ecumenical movement accomplished by Vatican II. In its first report, the Joint Working Group proposed the setting up of a joint theological commission to study the fundamental issues that arise in dialogue between the Catholic Church and member churches of the WCC. This has since led to the full participation of the Catholic Church in the work of the Faith and Order Commission of the WCC (something that does not require membership in the WCC itself).

The Joint Theological Commission on "Catholicity and Apostolicity" held three meetings during 1967 and 1968, and in 1970 published what it insisted was a "Study Document," that is, "not a joint statement nor a doctrinal consensus, but essentially a tool in the service of joint research."[157] Obviously, we have to take this document for what it intends to be. However, there is a passage in it that does speak of "significant agreements" among presently divided Christians, precisely on the question we are concerned with. We offer this as our first sample of what we mean by the "more comprehensive notion of apostolicity" that is taking the place of the more one-sided views that were typical of controversy in the past.

There has been a great diversity of forms in the ministries accomplished in the Spirit and made effective by his power, and Christians are far from being agreed in the way they evaluate them. But they believe that the Church is apostolic because it continues faithfully, by the grace of God, the mission, the preaching and the ministry which it has received from the apostles. For many Churches, this is the fundamental significance of the apostolic succession. Thus, from this fidelity, there results a much broader view of the apostolic succession than that which confines itself to legal categories. New possibilities here take shape in the direction of a consensus between the Churches.

It is in fact in respect of various conceptions of the ministry that the contemporary Churches discover some of their most serious divisions. However, even in this domain, significant agreements can be found. Three examples of this are:

a) The conviction that, in the life of the Church, the apostolic preaching transmitted by Scripture and Tradition, the apostolic ministry, and life in accordance with the Gospel are inseparable. All three are essential to its apostolicity.

b) The conviction that in spite of many changes in the course of history in the conceptions and functions of ministry, these changes are not all necessarily prejudicial to the continuity of the Church with its apostolic origins. It must constantly affirm its responsibility in the continuation of the original mission of the apostles, within the unfolding design of God and in changing situations. It is by a greater fidelity to this mission that it will eventually be able to renew in a spirit of penitence its conception of its ministry.

c) The conviction that one of the principal objects of the ministry is the accomplishment of the missionary vocation of the Church in submission to the Holy Spirit and in the expectation of the Lord.[158]

In view of the fact that this Joint Theological Commission included theologians of both "protestant" and "catholic" traditions, it is surely encouraging that they could witness to a significant agreement about the three elements which they described as being all essential to apostolicity.

We shall now see that a similarly comprehensive notion of apostolicity has been set forth in common statements that have resulted from bilateral dialogues between churches of these two traditions. We begin with the "Pullach Report" of the Anglican-Lutheran Conversation, issued in 1972.[159] This is the part of their common statement that sets out their understanding of apostolicity and apostolic succession.

> The apostolicity of the church is God's gift in Christ to the church through the apostles' preaching, their celebration of the gospel sacraments, and their fellowship and oversight. It is also God's sending of the church into all the world to make disciples of all nations in and through the apostolic gospel. Thus apostolicity pertains first to the gospel and then to the ministry of Word and sacraments, all given by the risen Lord to the apostles and through them to the church. Apostolicity requires obedience to the original and fundamental apostolic witness by reinterpretation to meet the needs of each new situation.
>
> The succession of apostolicity through time is guarded and given contemporary expresion in and through a wide variety of means, activities and institutions: the canon of Scriptures, creeds, confessional writings, liturgies, the activities of preaching, teaching, celebrating the sacraments and ordaining and using a ministry of Word and Sacrament, the exercising of pastoral care and oversight, the common life of the church, and the engagement in mission to and for the world.[160]

One of the most productive of the international bilateral dialogues has been that between Lutherans and Catholics, which has been conducted since 1967 by a Joint Commission appointed by the Executive Committee of the Lutheran World Federation and the Vatican Secretariat for Promoting Christian Unity. In 1972 this commission published its "Malta Report" on "The Gospel and the Church,"[161] in which we find the following paragraph under the heading "The Understanding of Apostolic Succession":

> The basic intention of the doctrine of apostolic succession is to indicate that, throughout all historical changes in its proclamation and structures, the church is at all times referred back to its apostolic origin. The details of this doctrine seem to us today to be more complicated than before. In the New Testament and the early fathers, the emphasis was obviously placed more on the substance of apostolicity, i.e., on succession in apostolic teaching. In this sense the entire church as the *ecclesia apostolica* stands

in the apostolic succession. Within this general sense of succession, there is a more specific meaning: the succession of the uninterrupted line of the transmission of office. In the early church, primarily in connection with defence against heresies, it was a sign of the unimpaired transmission of the gospel and a sign of unity in the faith. It is in these terms that Catholics today are trying once again to develop a deeper understanding of apostolic succession in the ministerial office. Lutherans on their side can grant the importance of a special succession if the preeminence of succession in teaching is recognized and if the uninterrupted line of transmission of office is not viewed as an *ipso facto* certain guarantee of the continuity of the right proclamation of the gospel.[162]

Nine years after the publication of the "Malta Report," the Lutheran-Catholic Joint Commission returned to the question of apostolicity in its document entitled "The Ministry in the Church."[163] Building upon what had been said in 1972, the new statement expresses greater confidence that agreement is developing between the two churches on this fundamental issue. Here is the pertinent section of the 1981 statement:

The most important question regarding the theology of the episcopal office and regarding the mutual recognition of ministries is the problem of the apostolic succession. This is normally taken to mean the unbroken ministerial succession of bishops in a church. But apostolic succession is also often understood to refer in the substantive sense to the apostolicity of the church in faith.

The starting point must be the apostolicity of the church in the substantive sense. "The basic intention of the doctrine of apostolic succession is to indicate that, throughout all historical changes in its proclamation and structures, the church is at all times referred back to its apostolic origin."[164] In the New Testament and in the period of the early fathers, the emphasis was placed more on the substantive understanding of the apostolic succession in faith and life. The Lutheran tradition speaks in this connection of a *successio verbi*. In present-day Catholic theology, more and more often the view is adopted that the substantive understanding of apostolicity is primary. Far-reaching agreement on this understanding of apostolic succession is therefore developing.

As regards the succession of the ministers, the joint starting point for both Catholics and Lutherans is that there is an integral relation between the witness of the gospel and witnesses to the gospel. The witness to the gospel has been entrusted to the church as a whole. Therefore, the whole church as the *ecclesia apostolica* stands in the apostolic succession. Succession in the sense of the succession of ministers must be seen within the succession of the whole church in the apostolic faith.[165]

It seems obvious that one of the reasons why "agreement is developing" here is that the ecumenical dialogue process is resulting in a more comprehensive notion of apostolicity than either side would have been likely to enunciate in a climate of confessional controversy.

This would seem to hold true also of the brief statement which the participants in the Methodist-Roman Catholic Conversations made in their "Dublin Report, 1976" with reference to apostolicity.[166] They said: "We all agree that the church's apostolicity involves continuous faithfulness in doctrine, ministry, sacrament and life to the teaching of the New Testament. In considering the ordained ministry of another church we use this faithfulness as our criterion, but we differ in the account we give of apostolic succession."[167]

With regard to this statement, we would observe that while the notion of apostolicity as involving "faithfulness in doctrine, ministry, sacrament and life" shows the comprehensiveness we have been finding in other reports, the source of the difference in regard to apostolic succession is suggested by the fact that this statement mentions only "faithfulness to the teaching of the New Testament." Differences with regard to apostolic succession will no doubt arise when one asks to what extent the teaching and practice of the early, post-New Testament church should be accepted as a reliable interpretation and application of what is said in the New Testament, and whether such teaching and practice can be normative for the church of subsequent ages.

One of the major world-level dialogues between Protestants and Catholics has been that between the World Alliance of Reformed Churches and the Vatican Secretariat for Promoting Christian Unity, which, after five annual meetings, published its final report in 1977, entitled "The Presence of Christ in Church and

World."[168] In the last part of this report, on the topic of ministry, we find the following statement concerning apostolicity and apostolic succession, on which the participants were in agreement (with only one reference to an area of disagreement). A significant aspect of this statement is the emphasis which it puts on the pneumatological and ecclesiological elements in a comprehensive notion of apostolicity.

> The whole Church is apostolic. To be an apostle means to be sent, to have a particular mission. The notion of mission is essential for understanding the ministry of the Church. As Christ is sent by the Father, so the Church is sent by Christ. But this mission of the Church has not simply a Christological reference. The sending of Christ and the equipment of the Church in his service are also works of the Holy Spirit. The mission of the Holy Spirit belongs to the constitution of the Church and her ministry, not merely to their effective functioning. . . .
>
> The Church is apostolic because it lives the faith of the original apostles, continues the mission given by Christ to them, and remains in the service and way of life testified to by those apostles. The canonical scriptures are the normative expression of this apostolicity. It is within the normative expression of this apostolicity contained in the New Testament that a witness is given to the special ministry given by Christ to the Twelve, and to Peter within that circle of Twelve. . . .
>
> Within apostolicity in general there is a special ministry to which the administration of Word and Sacrament is entrusted. That special ministry is one of the charismata for the exercise of particular services within the whole body. Ordination, or setting apart for the exercise of those special services, takes place within the context of the believing community. . . .
>
> There are several senses of "apostolic succession"; but when it is taken in its usual meaning to refer to the continuity of the special ministry, clearly it occurs within the apostolicity which belongs to the whole church. Reformed and Roman Catholic both believe that there is an apostolic succession essential to the life of the Church, though we locate that succession differently. We agree that no one assumes a special ministry solely on personal initiative, but enters into the continuous special ministry of Word and Sacrament through the calling of the community and the act of ordination by other ministers.

Apostolic succession consists at least in continuity of apostolic doctrine; but this is not in opposition to succession through continuity of ordained ministry. The continuity of right doctrine is guarded by the application of Holy Scripture and transmitted by the continuity of the teaching function of the special ministry. As with all aspects of the Church's ministry, so with the particular case of apostolic succession: it requires at once a historical continuity with the original apostles and a contemporary and graciously renewed action of the Holy Spirit. The Church lives by the continuity of the free gift of the Spirit according to Christ's promises, and this excludes a ritualistic conception of succession, the conception of mechanical continuity, a succession divorced from the historical continuity.[169]

In the following section of their report the Reformed and Catholic participants speak of the "different emphases between the two traditions" with regard to succession in ministry, explaining how they "locate that succession differently."[170] For now it is enough to have seen how much they were able to say together about the elements that enter into a comprehensive notion of apostolicity.

Our final witness to the "more comprehensive notion of apostolicity" which we see as the first fruit of ecumenical dialogue on this topic is the document "Baptism, Eucharist and Ministry" which the Faith and Order Commission of the WCC prepared over a number of years, and published as its "Lima Report" in 1982.[171] This is an extraordinary document in a number of respects. The members of the Commission who participated actively in its preparation represented virtually every confessional tradition, including the Roman Catholic. While the document does not present itself as a "consensus statement," in the sense that every member of the Commission would subscribe to everything said in it, nevertheless the Preface was able to assert that "this Lima text represents the significant theological convergence which Faith and Order has discerned and formulated." It goes on to say: "That theologians of such widely different traditions should be able to speak so harmoniously about baptism, eucharist and ministry is unprecedented in the modern ecumenical movement."[172]

A distinctive feature of the Lima document is the fact that many of the paragraphs of the text are accompanied by a commentary. The Preface explains the intention of the Commission with regard to this feature of the document by saying: "The main text demonstrates the major areas of theological convergence; the added commentaries either indicate historical differences that have been overcome or identify disputed issues still in need of further research and reconciliation."[173]

Chapter 4 of the Lima text on ministry has the title: "Succession in the Apostolic Tradition," and its first paragraph (n. 34) has the sub-title: "Apostolic Tradition in the Church." Here is the text of this paragraph, which, being part of the main text, is to be taken as an expression of theological convergence.

> In the Creed, the Church confesses itself to be apostolic. The Church lives in continuity with the apostles and their proclamation. The same Lord who sent the apostles continues to be present in the Church. The Spirit keeps the Church in the apostolic tradition until the fulfilment of history in the Kingdom of God. Apostolic tradition in the Church means continuity in the permanent characteristics of the Church of the apostles: witness to the apostolic faith, proclamation and fresh interpretation of the Gospel, celebration of baptism and the eucharist, the transmission of ministerial responsibilities, communion in prayer, love, joy and suffering, service to the sick and the needy, unity among the local churches and sharing the gifts which the Lord has given to each.[174]

On this paragraph of the main text there is also a commentary, which its contents show to be one of those which "indicate historical differences that have been overcome." The commentary is as follows.

> The apostles, as witnesses of the life and resurrection of Christ and sent by him, are the original transmitters of the Gospel, of the tradition of the saving words and acts of Jesus Christ which constitute the life of the Church. This apostolic tradition continues through history and links the Church to its origins in Christ and in the college of the apostles. Within this apostolic tradition is an apostolic succession of the ministry, which serves the continuity of the Church in its life in Christ and its faithfulness to the words and acts of Jesus transmitted by the apostles. The ministers appointed by the apostles, and then the *episkopoi* of the churches, were the first guardians of this transmission of the ap-

ostolic tradition; they testified to the apostolic succession of the ministry which was continued through the bishops of the early Church in collegial communion with the presbyters and deacons within the Christian community. A distinction should be made, therefore, between the apostolic tradition of the whole Church and the succession of the apostolic ministry.[175]

Perhaps one will have noticed that the term "apostolicity" does not occur either in the text or the commentary. The Commission evidently preferred the more concrete term "apostolic tradition." However, I suggest that there would be hardly any difference in meaning if one were to substitute the word "apostolicity" in some instances where the text reads "apostolic tradition." This is particularly the case in the long sentence which makes up the second half of the paragraph of the main text. I believe that one could just as well have said: "The apostolicity of the Church means its continuity in the permanent characteristics of the Church of the apostles: witness to the apostolic faith . . . " etc. If this is granted, I would offer this sentence as a good example of the "more comprehensive notion of apostolicity" which is the fruit of ecumenical dialogue.

Along the same line, I would point to the way that the commentary first identifies "the gospel" with "the tradition of the saving words and acts of Jesus Christ which constitute the life of the Church," and then inserts apostolic succession in the ministry *within this apostolic tradition*. Here again I submit that we find a comprehensive presentation of the essential elements of the Church's apostolicity (even without the use of the term).

The Frank Expression of Differences That Remain

We have suggested that a second fruit of ecumenical dialogue is the fact that the participants are obliged to clarify their respective positions for those who do not share their points of view. The same documents that have shown the development of a convergence on the notion of apostolicity have also provided some clear expressions of the divergences that remain to be overcome. As could have been foreseen, the most obvious divergence concerns the question whether the apostolicity of ministry requires ordination by bishops in unbroken apostolic succession. But divergence on this question is invariably linked with divergence on the question of the relative weight to be given to post-New Testament tradition, as compared with the text of the New Testament itself.

On these questions there is substantial agreement among the various churches of the "catholic" tradition, except, of course, if one includes the special claim to apostolicity on the part of the bishop of Rome, as successor to St. Peter and heir to his primacy. But this question would take us far beyond the limits we have set for ourselves in this book, and we shall prescind from it.

What we plan to do, then, is to see how the representatives of some of the churches of the "protestant" tradition have expressed their divergence from the "catholic" position in these dialogues. We begin with the "Report of Theological Conversations Sponsored by the World Alliance of Reformed Churches and the Baptist World Alliance" published in 1977.[176] The section of this report entitled "The Ministry of the Church of Jesus Christ and the Ministries in the Church" brings out the extent to which the Baptist and the Reformed Churches are in agreement, and in what respects they differ from one another. At the same time, it brings out, perhaps even more clearly, their common difference from the "catholic" point of view, as the following portion of their report will show.

>   According to biblical interpretation today, no one structure of the ministry of the church can claim to be the one New Testament pattern of ministry. But from the New Testament the general principles may be derived for the ordering of the life of the people of God according to the gospel for the furthering of the service of the Christian community in the world.
>
>   Both Baptists and Reformed are averse to the sacramental concept of a ministerial priesthood and rather put the emphasis on the functional nature of the pastoral office and of the particular ministries. Together they reject the doctrine that a particular understanding of spiritual office and succession in office, bound with the historic form of the episcopate, belongs to the being of the church and is therefore essential to it.
>
>   In both Reformed and Baptist traditions the preaching of the Word and the administration of the sacraments belong usually to the ministry of the pastor. Neither family of churches however ties these acts of service exclusively to the ordained ministry. . . .

Among Baptists and Congregationalists what is required is delegation by the local congregation since the congregation has and exercises in principle responsibility for all ministries. Usually it entrusts its pastor with the discharge of these particular tasks, but they are also frequently entrusted to lay people.

The function of presiding over the affairs of the congregation is in Reformed churches usually linked with the office of the pastor. Among Baptists it may be entrusted to the pastor, and there are places where this system is customary. But in principle among both Reformed and Baptists the various ministries on which responsibility rests for the building up of the congregation are so distinct that they can be entrusted to different persons, according to the gifts of the Spirit. . . .

While the doctrine concerning episcopal succession is rejected by Reformed and Baptists, there exists among both Baptists and Reformed in particular areas a type of ministry which superintends a number of individual congregations; among Baptists this ministry is never designated by the title "bishop," nor does it have juridical authority. For both Reformed and Baptists, encounter with episcopally ordered churches can usefully raise the question as to the beneficial role of the "pastor pastorum" (pastor of the pastors) in the life of the church for the encouragement of the ministry.[177]

Looking back over this rather long quotation, one can see that the first paragraph provides the key to what follows. For Baptists and Reformed, only the New Testament can lay down norms for Christian ministry, and what one finds there are some general principles, but no one pattern or structure of ministry that all churches would be obliged to follow. Therefore Baptists are free to adopt a congregational pattern of ministry, and Reformed a presbyterian structure, because each denomination finds sufficient warrant in the New Testament for its system of ministry. On the other hand, since neither finds in the New Testament sufficient basis for a sacramental concept of ministerial priesthood, or for the idea that episcopal succession is something essential to the nature of the church, they both feel free to reject these and to structure their churches without them.

It hardly needs to be said that there remains a wide gap to be narrowed before one could speak of a convergence on these questions between the Baptist and Reformed, on the one hand, and churches of the "catholic" tradition on the other. One conclusion that suggests itself is that one can hardly expect to make much progress on the question of apostolicity of ministry until progress is made on the question of the normative role of apostolic tradition. Most Catholics engaged in ecumenical dialogue would agree that the New Testament by itself does not provide a sufficient basis for their church's position on what is essential for the apostolicity of ministry. Any future development of a convergence on the question of apostolic ministry is going to depend on progress in the area of basic questions about scripture and tradition.

Much the same reflections are suggested by the section on Ministry in the "Dublin Report" of the dialogue between Methodists and Roman Catholics. We have already quoted the two sentences in which they expressed their agreement about a generic notion of apostolicity, but their disagreement on the question of apostolic succession. In the following paragraphs each side then explained how its respective church understands the apostolicity of its ministry.

> For Roman Catholics the graded three-fold ministry is derived from the teaching of the New Testament through the living tradition of the church. True succession in ministry is guaranteed only by episcopal laying-on of hands in historical succession and authentic transmission of the faith within the apostolic college.
>
> Methodists hold that the New Testament does not lay down any one form of ministry as binding for all times and places, and therefore the single form of ministry which British Methodists and other non-episcopal churches have is at least as consonant with the presbyter-bishops of the New Testament as the three-fold ministry is. Methodists have no difficulty in accepting as true ministries those which emerged at the Reformation and in the eighteenth century, so long as they are faithful to New Testament ministry. They accept, however, the appropriateness of the three-fold ministry of other churches or for a united church. . . .
>
> Moreover Methodists, both British and American, preserve a form of ministerial succession in practice and can regard a succession of ordination from the earliest times as a valuable *symbol* of the church's continuity with the church of the New Testament, though they would not use it as a *criterion*.[178]

Here again we see that differences between Catholics and Protestants on questions of ministry can be traced back to the difference between those who derive their ministry from the New Testament "through the living tradition of the church," and those who look only to the New Testament, where they do not find any one form of ministry as binding for all time.

The idea expressed in the last sentence of our quotation from this dialogue report, namely, that succession of ordination from the earliest times can be recognized as a *symbol*, though not a *criterion*, of apostolicity, is one that we will find also being expressed by Lutherans in these dialogues. We must now see how Lutherans have explained what is distinctive of their church's understanding of the apostolicity of its ministry. While they spoke briefly on this issue in their dialogue with Anglicans, the most satisfactory exposition of their point of view is found in the 1981 report of the Lutheran-Catholic international dialogue, "Ministry in the Church." Here is their presentation of their church's position on "the problem of apostolic succession."

> For the Lutheran tradition also the apostolic succession is necessary and constitutive for both the church and for its ministry. Its confessional writings claim to stand in the authentic Catholic tradition, and emphasize the historical continuity of the church which has never ceased to exist.
>
> For the Lutherans in the sixteenth century, the authenticity of apostolic succession in the form of historic succession in the episcopal office was called in question because it failed to witness to agreement in the proclamation of the gospel, and because the episcopate refused fellowship with them, especially by denying them the service of ordaining their preachers, and thus deprived them of the historic succession in office. For them, therefore, apostolic succession came to focus on the right preaching of the gospel, which always included the ministry, and on faith and the testimony of a Christian life. Yet they were convinced that the gospel had been given to the church as a whole and that, with the right preaching of the Word and the celebration of the sacraments according to the gospel, apostolic succession in the substantive sense continued within the congregation. Based on this, the ordination of ministers by ministers continued to be performed in the Lutheran church. This ordination remained oriented towards the entire church and towards recognition by its ministers.

Thus despite diverse historical developments, the Lutheran Reformation affirmed and intended to preserve the historical continuity of church order as an expression of the unity of the apostolic church among all peoples and throughout all centuries, presupposing, of course, that the gospel is rightly proclaimed. This intention must be maintained even in the face of contrary historical developments for the sake of the faith that the church abides. This point is expressly stressed in the fundamental articles of the Augsburg Confession, and also by the references made in the confessional writings to church teachers of all times.

These considerations provide the basis for a Lutheran evaluation of the historic succession as a sign of such unity. The Lutheran conviction is that acceptance of communion with the episcopal office in the historic succession is meaningful not as an isolated act, but only as it contributes to the unity of the church in faith and witnesses to the universality of the gospel of reconciliation.[179]

The reader will surely have recognized a far more positive attitude toward historic succession in the episcopate in this Lutheran statement than we found expressed by the Baptists, Reformed and Methodists in their dialogues. It is evident that for the Lutherans at the time of the Reformation it was not a question of renouncing the historic episcopate in order to return to a pattern of ministry found explicitly in the New Testament. At that time they felt that the break with the episcopate was forced upon them by their fidelity to the gospel. Another section of the same dialogue report brings this out even more clearly, and it seems best to see how they put this in their own words.

The *Lutheran Confessions* wanted to retain the episcopal polity of the church and with it the differentiation of the ministerial office on the condition that the bishops grant freedom and opportunity for the right proclamation of the gospel and the right administration of the sacraments and not prevent these by the formal requirement of obedience. The fact that it was impossible at this time to arrive at an agreement in doctrine and to persuade the bishops to ordain Reformation ministers led perforce to forsaking continuity with previous order. In this emergency situation the installation of ministers by non-episcopal ministers or even by the congregation appeared legitimate provided it took place *rite*, i.e. publicly and in the name of the whole church. . . .

In view of the emergency situation, the Lutheran Confessions avoided prescribing any specific form of *episcopé* in the sense of regional church leadership. Episcopacy, to be sure, was normal at least for the Confessio Augustana. The loss of this office in its historic character has nevertheless had certain consequences for the Lutheran understanding of the church's ministerial structure. The Lutheran office of pastor, comparable to that of presbyter, has really taken over the spiritual functions of the bishop's office, and was even at times theologically interpreted as identical with it. This was seen as a return to an earlier ministerial structure in church history in which the bishop's office was a local one. Within this context the function of *episcopé* was retained as necessary for the church; but its concrete ordering was taken to be a human and historical matter. The holders of this superordinated office are at present given a variety of titles: bishop, church president, superintendent. In some Lutheran areas, where this was possible, the historical continuity of the episcopal office has been maintained.[180]

With reference to this final sentence, it should be noted that the Lutheran churches of Sweden and Finland, which have maintained the historical continuity of the episcopal office, consider equally valid the ministry in Lutheran churches which have not maintained episcopal succession or the episcopal ordination of their pastors. This is in keeping with what comes through as the fundamental Lutheran position: that while church ministry, including some form of *episcopé*, is necessary and can even be described as of divine institution, its concrete ordering is seen as an historical and human matter. At the same time one cannot fail to sense the respect which Lutherans have for Christian tradition, and their regret that at the time of the Reformation it was not possible, in most of Europe, for their forebears to maintain continuity with the ancient church in the unbroken succession of episcopal ordination. They clearly recognize the positive value of such continuity as a sign and expression of the unity of the church throughout the ages. In the final part of this chapter we shall have occasion to see how far the Lutheran participants in dialogue are willing to have their churches go in order to make episcopal succession a more effective sign of unity among the Christian churches today. But this remark leads us to what we see as the third fruit of ecumenical dialogue about apostolicity.

Positive Assessments of the Other's Point of View

For this part of our chapter we are going to focus our attention on two reports which are among the most significant, as well as the most recently published, results of ecumenical discussion at the international level: the 1982 "Lima Report" of the Faith and Order Commission, and the 1985 Report "Facing Unity" of the Roman Catholic-Lutheran Joint Commission.[181] The reader will recall that a unique feature of the "Lima Report" is the fact that the commission that prepared it and approved its distribution to the churches for comment included representatives of virtually all the Christian traditions. It is all the more significant, then, that this report, while admittedly not a statement of the full consensus of all its signers, could manifest such a degree of mutual respect with which churches of very different traditions now look upon one another's ministry. Here are some passages of the report that manifest this new climate of understanding that is beginning to prevail.

36. Under the particular historical circumstances of the growing Church in the early centuries, the succession of bishops became one of the ways, together with the transmission of the Gospel and the life of the community, in which the apostolic tradition of the Church was expressed. This succession was understood as serving, symbolizing and guarding the continuity of the apostolic faith and communion.

37. In churches which practise the succession through the episcopate, it is increasingly recognized that a continuity in apostolic faith, worship and mission has been preserved in churches which have not retained the form of historic episcopate. This recognition finds additional support in the fact that the reality and function of the episcopal ministry have been preserved in many of these churches, with or without the title "bishop". Ordination, for example, is always done in them by persons in whom the Church recognizes the authority to transmit the ministerial commission.

38. These considerations do not diminish the importance of the episcopal ministry. On the contrary, they enable churches which have not retained the episcopate to appreciate the episcopal succession as a sign, though not a guarantee, of the continuity and unity of the Church. Today churches, including those engaged in union negotiations, are expressing willingness to accept episcopal succession as a sign of the apostolicity of the life of the whole Church. Yet, at the same time, they cannot accept any suggestion that the ministry exercised in their own tradition should be invalid until the moment that it enters into an existing line of episcopal succession. Their acceptance of the episcopal succession will best further the unity of the whole Church if it is part of a wider process by which the episcopal churches themselves also regain their lost unity.[182]

51. In order to advance towards the mutual recognition of ministries, deliberate efforts are required. All churches need to examine the forms of ordained ministry and the degree to which the churches are faithful to its original intentions. Churches must be prepared to renew their understanding and their practice of the ordained ministry.

52. Among the issues that need to be worked on as churches move towards mutual recognition of ministries, that of apostolic succession is of particular importance. Churches in ecumenical conversations can recognize their respective ordained ministries if they are mutually assured of their intention to transmit the ministry of Word and sacrament in continuity with apostolic times. The act of transmission should be performed in accordance with the apostolic tradition, which includes the invocation of the Spirit and the laying on of hands.

53. In order to achieve mutual recognition, different steps are required of different churches. For example:

    a) Churches which have preserved the episcopal succession are asked to recognize both the apostolic content of the ordained ministry which exists in churches which have not maintained such succession and also the existence in these churches of a ministry of *episkopé* in various forms.

    b) Churches without the episcopal succession, and living in faithful continuity with the apostolic faith and mission, have a ministry of Word and sacrament, as is evident from the belief, practice and life of those churches. These churches are asked to realize that the continuity with the Church of the apostles finds profound expression in the successive laying on of hands by bishops and that, though they may not lack the continuity of the apostolic tradition, this sign will strengthen and deepen that continuity. They may need to recover the sign of the episcopal succession.[183]

Looking back over these sections of the Lima Report, we can distinguish between the affirmation of a growing consensus, between churches of the "protestant" and the "catholic" traditions, on the question of apostolic succession in ministry, and the exhortation addressed to these churches about further steps to be taken toward the mutual recognition of ministries. The elements of consensus include: on the "catholic" side, the recognition that "a continuity in apostolic faith, worship and mission has been preserved in churches that have not retained the form of historic episcopate," and on the "protestant" side, the recognition of episcopal succession as a sign of the apostolicity of the church.

Such a consensus, it must be noted, does not mean that Catholics are ready to admit that non-episcopal orders are fully valid, nor that Protestants are ready to admit that their ministry has been invalid. Moreover, the exhortation to take the next steps toward the mutual recognition of ministry does not require that either side should renounce its stand on these points. Catholics are asked merely to recognize "the apostolic content" of Protestant ministry; Protestants are asked to recognize that episcopal ordination is a sign of apostolicity, and to be open to recovering this sign for their churches. But it is clear that this should not be interpreted as a recognition that their ministry, lacking this particular sign, has lacked validity.

The members of the Faith and Order Commission who elaborated this report show great sensitivity to the convictions of both sides, and their awareness of the limits of what their respective churches could be expected to accept, at least at this stage of the ecumenical process. At the same time, they showed a good deal of courage, as well as a spirit of ecumenical hope, in making the concrete proposals about the steps to be taken, on both sides, toward the mutual recognition of ministries.

Three years after the publication of the Lima Report, the Roman Catholic-Lutheran Joint Commission published the latest fruit of its ongoing dialogue in a lengthy report entitled "Facing Unity. Models, Forms and Phases of Catholic-Lutheran Fellowship."[104] Building on the doctrinal consensus that had been ascertained in the previous dialogues: "The Gospel and the Church" (1972), "The Eucharist" (1978), "All Under One Christ" (on the *Confessio Augustana*, 1980), and "The Ministry in the Church" (1981), the Joint Commission now presents a common statement which first seeks to clarify the kind of unity that is sought, and then to outline step by step how such unity could be achieved. The unity is described as "complete fellowship in word, sacrament and ministry," which of course does not mean absorption or uniformity but "unity in reconciled diversity." The process of arriving at such unity is set out in four phases, to be undertaken successively: 1) preliminary forms of a joint exercise of pastoral leadership (*episcopé*); 2) an initial act of mutual recognition, whereby each church would formally recognize that the church of Christ is realized in the other, and would declare its will to live in fellowship with it; 3) the collegial exercise of *episcopé*, whereby the Catholic bishop and the Lutheran pastor with episcopal responsibility in each area would exercise their ministry conjointly, including the ministry of ordaining candidates to the ministry; and 4) transition to a common ordained ministry, as the eventual result of the joint exercise of the ministry of ordaining.[185]

One can see how far this detailed proposal goes beyond the suggestions given in the Lima Report. It presupposes the considerable degree of consensus between Lutherans and Catholics already affirmed in the previous reports of this international dialogue (as well as in the reports of other Lutheran-Catholic dialogues, especially the one going on in the United States). It is not my intention here to offer a detailed description or analysis of this report. For the present purpose, it suffices to point out how this proposal involves the positive assessment by each church of the apostolicity of the other's faith and ministry, while at the same time it indicates positive steps to be taken in order to eliminate the problem caused by the fact that the Catholic Church does not recognize the full apostolicity of Lutheran ministry. The following paragraphs of "Facing Unity" spell out the problem and its possible solution.

95. (1) While according to the Lutheran understanding of church, the existence of ministry in the Catholic Church is not to be called into question, Catholics cannot yet fully recognize the ordained ministry in Lutheran churches because, according to their view, these churches lack the fullness of the ordained ministry since they "lack of the sacrament of orders."[186] This would only be possible through a process of "acceptance of full church communion",[187] of which fellowship in the historical episcopacy is an essential part.

96. (2) Catholics and Lutherans share the conviction that the ordained ministry of the church which, because it is "instituted by Jesus Christ" "stands over against the community as well as within the community", is "essential" for the church.[188] Nevertheless it is *possible* for Lutherans, and in this they differ from Catholics, to give a theological description of the church without making explicit mention of the ministry, because it is either "presupposed" or implied by the proclamation of the word and the administration of the sacraments.

97. Lutherans, like Catholics, can recognize as "the action of the Spirit"[189] the historical differentiation of the one apostolic ministry into more local ministry and more regional forms, and they can consider "the function of *episcopé* . . . as necessary for the church."[190] Likewise, Lutherans feel free "to face up to the call for communion with the historic episcopal office,"[191] i.e., the historically evolved pattern of episcopal ministry in the form of the office of bishop standing in apostolic succession. Nevertheless, Lutherans and Catholics place different accents on the significance of that historic episcopal office for the church.

98. The two problems are closely related: The "lack of the sacrament of orders" that the Catholic side claims to be inherent in the ministry of the Lutheran churches cannot, because of its very nature, be annulled solely by theological insights and agreements or by ecclesiastical or canonical declarations and decisions, as, for example, by the theological and canonical act of recognizing these ministries. What is needed, rather, is acceptance of the fellowship in ecclesial ministry, and this, ultimately, means acceptance of the fellowship in episcopal ministry which stands in apostolic succession. Lutherans are fundamentally free and open to accept such fellowship in the episcopal office. Yet within this understanding of the importance or significance of the episcopal office for the cath-

olicity, apostolicity and unity of the church, Lutherans are inclined to place the accent differently from Catholics.

99. The problems mentioned here need not block the road to fellowship in the church ministry and therefore to a fully structured ecclesial fellowship. But it does call for renewal and deepening of the understanding of the ordained ministry, particularly the ministry serving the unity and governance (*episcopé*) of the church.[192]

With this positive and forward-looking report coming from the Roman Catholic-Lutheran Joint Commission, we conclude our chapter on "apostolicity in ecumenical dialogue." We believe that the ecumenical statements we have surveyed show that differences concerning apostolicity still raise formidable obstacles in the way to church unity, especially with regard to the necessity of episcopal ordination in apostolic succession for the validity of orders and ministry. On the other hand, we have seen a growing recognition, on the part of Catholics, of the apostolic character of the faith, life and ministry of Protestant churches, and a growing appreciation, on the part of Protestants, of the importance of episcopal ordination as a sign of the apostolicity of ministry.

We can only hope that the deepening of the understanding of the ordained ministry, particularly that of *episcopé*, which "Facing Unity" calls for, and the kind of sensitive step-by-step procedure this document proposes, will prove effective in lessening, and eventually removing, the obstacles that remain in the way to the restoration of full communion among all the presently separated Christian churches.

10 || One, Holy, Catholic and Apostolic

I would not be surprised if some readers who have persisted to this point might remark that they had not expected to be led down the many avenues that we have explored in our discussion of the four properties that the creed attributes to the church. I can only hope that now, having followed me down those avenues, they can agree that they have a better idea of what is involved when they say they believe in the one, holy, catholic and apostolic church.

At the same time, I am aware that in discussing separately each of these four properties, as we have done, we run the risk of losing sight of what they have in common. In this concluding chapter, then, what we propose to do is to look at all four properties of the church together. This approach will have the advantage, we hope, of pulling together what might have seemed rather disparate strands of thought, and thus help the reader to end with a more unified grasp of the meaning of what the creed tells us about the church.

The Four Properties As Matters of Faith

The first thing the four properties have in common is that they are all objects of the faith that we profess when we recite the creed. In our first chapter we have explained the sense in which the church is something we believe in—not that we believe in the church in the same way that we believe in God—but that the church is a mystery that we can grasp only by faith. The reason for this is that the church is an integral part of the divinely revealed plan of salvation that will always surpass our efforts fully to understand it.

What we wish to recall here is that this "mystery" concerning which we profess our faith in the creed is the church precisely as "one, holy, catholic and apostolic." Each of these attributes is a matter of faith for the believing Christian. We cannot say "we believe in the church" without believing in its oneness, holiness, catholicity and apostolicity. Furthermore, each of these properties is part of the divinely revealed mystery; we cannot expect fully to understand how the church is one, holy, catholic or apostolic, or why it must always be so. Our treatment of these properties has to be an exercise of "faith seeking understanding," without expecting fully to grasp the mystery. However, as Vatican I tells us, human reason aided by grace is capable of achieving some understanding of the mysteries of our faith.[193] This is what we have been trying to accomplish in this book.

Are We Dealing with a "Dogma of Faith"?

At this point we shall raise a question that may seem somewhat technical, but that we believe important enough to warrant consideration. The question is whether the proposition that the church is and must always be one, holy, catholic and apostolic is a "dogma of faith," and, if so, whether it is a "solemnly defined" dogma. Before answering, we must first explain how these terms are commonly understood by Catholic theologians.

What we mean by a "dogma of faith" is a truth that is contained in the deposit of revelation (whether in scripture or in apostolic tradition) and has been declared by the church to have been divinely revealed and thus to be believed with the "obedience of faith." In this case, our act of faith is directed not to the church, but to God as the one who has revealed this truth to us, although it is the church that gives us absolute assurance that this particular truth is really part of God's word.

Now there are two kinds of dogmas of faith: those that have been solemnly defined, and those that have not. This distinction is brought out in the following statement of the First Vatican Council: "All those things are to be believed with divine and catholic faith which are contained in the Word of God, whether written or handed down, and are proposed by the church, whether by a solemn judgment or by the ordinary and universal magisterium, as matters that have been revealed by God and are to be believed as such."[194] What this statement refers to as a "solemn judgment" is the act whereby either an ecumenical council, or a Pope speaking *ex cathedra*, "defines" a doctrine: that is, pronounces a judgment that is clearly intended to be definitive, calling for the absolute assent of all the faithful to a truth that is now an element of the normative faith of the church. It is important to realize that in the course of history, the church has pronounced such solemn definitions only with regard to those elements of its faith that were in danger of being obscured or distorted by heresies, or concerning which other circumstances made it seem opportune to pronounce such a definitive judgment. The consequence is that there are a good many "undefined dogmas," that is, truths that the church has never had reason to define, but which its official teachers (popes and bishops) have consistently and universally proposed, in the "ordinary" exercise of their teaching function, as part of the total object of Christian faith.

The question, then, is whether the ecumenical council (Constantinople I, in 381), which included the statement of belief in the church as one, holy, catholic and apostolic in its creed, can be said to have solemnly defined this as a dogma of faith. To this question I believe the answer should be negative, on the grounds that there is no evidence that this council had any intention to pronounce a solemn judgment on a question concerning the church. The problem before the council of 381 had to do with the Holy Spirit as a truly divine Person, and this explains why the third article of its creed is more fully developed than was that of the Council of Nicea. But there is no reason to think that Constantinople I intended to define any of the other doctrines that are mentioned in its third article. And it is a basic principle of conciliar exegesis that a council should be understood to have defined only what it clearly intended to define. This principle is even a matter of church law; canon 749,3 of the new Code of Canon Law reads: "No doctrine is understood to be infallibly defined unless this is manifestly demonstrated."

The second question, then, is whether the proposition that the church is one, holy, catholic and apostolic, is an "undefined dogma," that is, whether it has been consistently and universally proposed by the ordinary magisterium as a matter of normative Christian faith. To this question I believe an affirmative answer should be given. Some reflections on the history of this creed will explain the reasons for this.

While the acts of the First Council of Constantinople have not come down to us, there is sufficient information from other sources to show that the controversy which this council intended to settle had to do with the divinity of the Holy Spirit. To refute those who denied this, the bishops at this council saw no need to compose a new creed; they simply confronted the heretics with a baptismal creed already in current use, which clearly affirmed the church's doctrine about the Holy Spirit. The baptismal creed which they adopted for this purpose was substantially the one which we know was already being used in the churches of Cyprus, since it is found in a work of Epiphanius, bishop of Salamis, that was written seven years before the council.[195] It is important to realize that the creed formulated by the Council of Nicea in 325, whose third article said merely "And in the Holy Spirit," was not being used in that form as a baptismal creed. The churches already had baptismal creeds with a more fully developed third article, and accepting the creed of Nicea did not mean omitting anything that was already part of their baptismal creed. What the churches did after Nicea was to incorporate into their baptismal creeds the essential dogma defined at Nicea about the divinity of Christ. Any creed that did this was recognized as "Nicene," even though its third article said much more than the conciliar formula had contained.

It was such a baptismal creed that the council of 381 ratified as expressing orthodox faith about the Holy Spirit, and as a sufficient refutation of the heresy they wished to condemn. However, it was only about a century later, after the Council of Chalcedon (451) had confirmed the creed of the Council of Constantinople as thoroughly "Nicene," that this became the common baptismal creed of the churches of the east. For several centuries it even supplanted the "Apostles' Creed" as the baptismal creed at Rome and in other churches of the west. Then, from about the sixth century, it became customary to recite the "Nicene" creed of 381 at the eucharistic liturgy: a custom that spread from the eastern churches to the western, and was eventually accepted at Rome, about the same time that the "Apostles' Creed" was restored as the baptismal creed of the Latin church.[196]

What conclusions can we draw, from this history, about the

dogmatic status of our profession of faith in the church as "one, holy, catholic and apostolic"? I believe that this history justifies our claim that we have here an example of an "undefined dogma of faith," that is, a truth that has consistently and universally been taught, though not defined, as an element of normative Christian faith. While there is no evidence that either Constantinople or Chalcedon intended specifically to define any doctrine concerning the church, both of these ecumenical councils ratified as orthodox a profession of faith in the church as one, holy, catholic and apostolic. Subsequently, it was this creed that was universally received in the east as the common baptismal creed, and which came to be prescribed in the churches of both east and west as the creed with which the faithful would profess their faith during the eucharistic liturgy. I do not know what better proof could be offered than this, in support of the claim that a doctrine has been proposed as a matter of obligatory faith by the "ordinary and universal magisterium."

We shall now consider some of the implications of the fact that when we speak of the church as one, holy, catholic and apostolic we are enunciating a dogma of faith. The first consequence is that since this is a statement of faith, it must always remain true, and therefore the church can never cease to be one, holy, catholic and apostolic. In other words, each of these properties, like the church itself, has a divine guarantee of indefectibility.

Indefectibly One, Holy, Catholic and Apostolic

First we shall recall some statements made by the Second Vatican Council which show that this is indeed the Catholic Church's understanding of our profession of faith about the church.

With regard to unity, the council declared in its Decree on Ecumenism: "We believe that the unity which Christ bestowed on his church from the beginning subsists in the Catholic Church as something she can never lose, and we hope that it will continue to increase until the end of time" (UR 4). In this context, it is certain that the words "we believe" are an expression of faith, and not merely of opinion.

The council likewise described the indefectible holiness of the church as something to be accepted on faith, when it stated: "The church, whose mystery is set forth by this sacred council, is held, as a matter of faith, to be unfailingly (*indefectibiliter*) holy" (LG 39).

Confidence that the church can never cease to be catholic or universal is implied in the following statements of Vatican II: "All men are called to belong to the new people of God. Wherefore this people, while remaining one and unique, is to be spread throughout the whole world and must exist in all ages, so that the purpose of God's will may be fulfilled. . . . This characteristic of universality which adorns the people of God is a gift from the Lord himself. By reason of it the Catholic Church strives energetically and constantly to bring all humanity with all its riches under Christ as its Head in the unity of the Spirit" (LG 13).

Finally, we can see expressions of faith that the church can never cease to be apostolic in the following passages of the conciliar documents. "That divine mission entrusted by Christ to the apostles will last until the end of the world (Mt 28:20), since the gospel which was to be handed down by them is for all time the source of life for the church" (LG 20). "In his gracious goodness God has seen to it that what He had revealed for the salvation of all nations would abide perpetually in its full integrity and be handed on to all generations" (DV 7). "And so the apostolic preaching, which is expressed in a special way in the inspired books, was to be preserved by a continuous succession of preachers until the end of time" (DV 8).

Why the Church Cannot Fail To Be
One, Holy, Catholic and Apostolic

Although, in considering each of these properties separately in the course of this book, we have already spoken of the reasons we have for believing that the church cannot fail to be one, holy, catholic and apostolic, it seems useful now to gather these various reasons together, so as to show how these properties are inseparable from one another as well as from the church. Our approach here will be to suggest how these four properties are rooted in the very nature of the church as people of God and body of Christ animated by the Holy Spirit.

People of God

The basic reason why the people of God must be one is the oneness of God whose people it is. Having described the "mystery of the unity of the church," the Decree on Ecumenism states: "The supreme exemplar and source of this mystery is the unity, in the Trinity of Persons, of one God, the Father and the Son in the Holy Spirit" (UR 2). The reason for Jesus' death, and consequently for the establishment of his church, was "to gather into one the children of God who are scattered abroad" (Jn 11:52). *Lumen gentium* uses this scriptural text effectively in showing why the people of God must be one and only one:

> In the beginning God made human nature one. After His children were scattered, He decreed that they should at length be unified again (cf. Jn 11:52). It was for this reason that God sent His Son, whom He appointed heir of all things (Heb 1:2), that He might be Teacher, King and Priest of all, the Head of the new and universal people of the sons of God. . . . It follows that among all the nations of the earth there is but one people of God . . . " (LG 13).

The holiness of God is likewise the ultimate reason why his people must be holy. The first letter of Peter applies to the church what God had said through his prophet to the people of the old covenant: "You shall be holy, for I am holy" (1 Pet 1:15, cf. Lev 11:44–45). Being "a chosen race, a royal priesthood, God's own people," the church must also be a "holy nation" (1 Pet 2:9).

The people of God must also be a catholic, or universal people, because God's salvific will embraces all of humanity: "God our Savior desires all men to be saved and to come to the knowledge of the truth" (1 Tim 2:3–4). It is because "all men are called to salvation by the grace of God" that all are likewise "called to be part of the catholic unity of the people of God" (LG 13).

The apostolicity of the church is also rooted in her nature as People of God, since the apostolic mission of the church comes ultimately from God the Father. As the Decree on the Missionary Activity of the Church puts it: "The pilgrim church is missionary by her very nature. For it is from the mission of the Son and the mission of the Holy Spirit that she takes her origin, in accordance with the decree of God the Father. This decree flows from 'that fountain of love' or charity within God the Father" (AG 2). St. Paul was confident that his call to be an apostle of Christ came from God the Father: "Paul, an apostle not from men nor through man, but through Jesus Christ and God the Father who raised him from the dead" (Gal 1:1). He likewise knew that it was God the Father who had set him apart before he was born and called him through his grace, and was pleased to reveal his Son to him, in order that he might preach him among the Gentiles (cf. Gal 1:15–16). As Jesus was the "apostle" sent by the Father, (cf. Heb 3:1), so he could say to his apostles: "As the Father sent me, so I send you" (Jn 20:21).

Body of Christ

It hardly seems necessary to dwell on the point that the church, as the body of Christ, must be and ever remain one. This is one of the key themes of Paul's teaching on the nature of the church as Christ's body. "For just as the body is one, and has many members, and all the members of the body, though many, are one body—so it is with Christ" (1 Cor 12:12). "For as in one body we have many members, and all the members do not have the same function, so we, though many, are one body in Christ, and individually members of one another" (Rom 12:4–5). "For there is one body and one Spirit, just as you were called to the one hope that belongs to your call, one Lord, one faith, one baptism, one God and Father of us all" (Eph 4:4–6).

That the body of Christ must be holy is equally evident. Being his body, she is also his bride. "Christ is the head of the church, his body, and is himself its Savior. . . . Husbands, love your wives, as Christ loved the church, and gave himself up for her, that he might sanctify her, having cleansed her by the washing of water with the word, that he might present the church to himself in splendor, without spot or wrinkle or any such thing, that she might be holy and without blemish" (Eph 5:23–27).

The catholicity of the church as the body of Christ is a corollary of the role of her Head as the one mediator of salvation for all of humanity. "For there is one God, and there is one mediator between God and men, the man Christ Jesus, who gave himself as a ransom for all" (1 Tim 2:5). As St. Peter declared before the Sanhedrin: "There is salvation in no one else, for there is no other name given among men by which we must be saved" (Acts 4:12). The Father's plan is to bring all things, whether in heaven or on earth, under Christ as the one Head (cf. Eph 1:10). For "he has put all things under his feet, and made him the head over all things for the church, which is his body, the fullness of him who fills all in all" (Eph 1:22–23).

Finally, as Christ's body, the church can never cease to be apostolic, since the apostles are the church's link with Christ. It is only by fidelity to the apostles' teaching, their mission and their ministry, that the church can be assured of inheriting the promise that Christ made to them, and through them to his church: "Behold, I am with you all days, even to the end of the world" (Mt 28:20).

Animated By the Holy Spirit

Thus far we have seen why the church, precisely because it is the people of God and the body of Christ, must always be one, holy, catholic and apostolic. What we wish to point out now is that it is the Holy Spirit who effectively brings about and maintains the church's unity, holiness, catholicity and apostolicity.

First of all, it is the Spirit who makes the church one: "For by one Spirit we were all baptized into one body—Jews or Greeks, slaves or free—and all were made to drink of one Spirit" (1 Cor 12:13). While the Spirit is the source of the variety of gifts, the body is one, because "all these are inspired by one and the same Spirit" (1 Cor 12:11). The Spirit, "existing as one and same being in the head and in the members, vivifies, unifies and moves the whole body, in such a way that His work could be compared by the holy Fathers with the function which the soul fulfills in the human body" (LG 7). "It is the Holy Spirit, dwelling in those who believe, pervading and ruling over the entire church, who brings about that marvelous communion of the faithful and joins them together so intimately in Christ that He is the principle of the church's unity" (UR 2).

The Christian conviction that it is the Holy Spirit who makes the church holy is manifested by the inseparable connection between "Holy Spirit" and "holy church" in the very earliest baptis-

mal creeds that have come down to us. It is the indwelling Holy
Spirit that makes God's temple holy (cf. 1 Cor 3:16–17; Eph 2:21–
22). Enumerating the gifts that make the people of God a holy people. "love, joy, peace, patience, kindness, goodness, faithfulness,
gentleness, self-control"—St. Paul sums them all up as "the fruit of
the Spirit" (Gal 5:23). *Lumen gentium* names "sanctifying the church"
as the primary work the Spirit was sent to do: "When the work
which the Father had given the Son to do on earth was accomplished, the Holy Spirit was sent on the day of Pentecost in order
that he might forever sanctify the church" (LG 4). The holiness of
the earthly church calls for perpetual self-renewal and purification;
this also is the work of the Holy Spirit. "Moving forward through
trial and tribulation, the church is strengthened by the power of
God's grace promised to her by the Lord, so that in the weakness of
the flesh she may not waver from perfect fidelity, but remain a bride
worthy of her Lord; that moved by the Holy Spirit she may never
cease to renew herself, until through the cross she arrives at the light
which knows no setting" (LG 9).

Vatican II describes the church's catholicity as "a gift from the
Lord by which the church strives energetically and constantly to
bring all humanity under Christ as its head in the unity of the Spirit"
(LG 13). The "energy" and "constancy" with which the church
strives to realize its catholicity can only be understood as the work
of the Spirit. This is evident from the final words of Jesus to his
disciples before his ascension: "You shall receive power when the
Holy Spirit has come upon you; and you shall be my witnesses in
Jerusalem and in all Judea and Samaria and to the end of the earth"
(Acts 1:8). What was true of the apostles will be true of the church
until the end of time: it is from the Spirit that it must continue to
receive the power to witness to Christ, and thus spread the message
of the gospel to the furthest corners of the world. The Spirit is also
the source of the intensive, or qualitative, catholicity of the church:
of that unity in diversity that is so prominent an aspect of St. Paul's
notion of the church as Christ's body. After enumerating various
gifts that equip people for different roles in the body, Paul insists:
"All these are inspired by one and same Spirit, who apportions to
each one individually as he wills" (1 Cor 12:11). The Spirit is the
source of the rich variety of gifts, both hierarchical and charismatic,
with which the church is endowed (cf. LG 4), but it is the same

Spirit who maintains the essential unity in diversity that is the mark of the church's catholicity. It is the Spirit "who, on behalf of the whole church and each and every one of those who believe, is the principle of their coming together and remaining together in the teaching of the apostles and in fellowship, in the breaking of bread and in prayers" (LG 13; cf. Acts 2:42).

Finally, it is the abiding gift of the Spirit that maintains the church in fidelity to the faith, mission and ministry that it has received from Christ through the apostles. As the apostles themselves could not begin their task until they had received the empowering gift of the Spirit (cf. Lk 24:48–49; Acts 1:4–8), so the church can remain faithful to its apostolic mandate only by the continuing presence and working of the Spirit. The Spirit keeps the church faithful to the apostolic teaching, both by sustaining the sense of faith by which the whole people of God is maintained in the truth (cf. LG 12), and by the charisms with which the successors of the apostles are endowed (cf. LG 25). The liturgical prayer of episcopal ordination is an invocation of the Holy Spirit, who alone can equip the new bishop with the gifts and graces that will enable him to carry on the apostolic mission and ministry. Thus it is by virtue of the abiding and at the same time ever-newly-given gift of the Holy Spirit that the church remains unfailingly apostolic.

"Indefectibly" Does Not Mean "Perfectly"

To say that the church is indefectibly, or unfailingly, one, holy, catholic and apostolic means that it can never lack these four properties; it can never cease to be one, holy, etc. From what we have been just saying, it is obvious that our certitude about this is not based on any merely human considerations; it is matter of our faith in the fidelity of God to his promises, and in the abiding presence of the Holy Spirit in the church.

What we wish to recall here is the fact that Vatican II, while professing its faith that the church is and must always be one, holy and catholic, at the same time explicitly acknowledged the fact that the church in its earthly pilgrimage is by no means perfectly one, perfectly holy, or perfectly catholic.

We have seen in Chapter 2 of this book that one of the crucial changes made at Vatican II was to recognize that the church of

Christ cannot be simply and exclusively identified with the Roman Catholic Church. This led to the understanding that while the unity which Christ gave to his church is a gift she cannot lose—indeed, it "subsists" in the Catholic Church (cf. UR 4)—nevertheless the imperfect communion which at present binds the various Christian churches and ecclesial communities together is not the kind of unity that Christ wishes his church to have. The recognition that the Catholic Church is not the whole church of Christ, and that as long as the Christian churches remain divided from one another the church of Christ itself will be very imperfectly one, opened the way to full participation of the Catholic Church in the ecumenical movement.

At the same time, Catholics have no reason to be complacent about the unity that "subsists" in their church, especially in view of the teaching of Vatican II that only those Catholics are "fully incorporated in the society of the church" who are living in the state of sanctifying grace (cf. LG 14). This means that full communion within the church depends on the holiness of its members, since those lacking charity diminish not only the holiness of the church but also its unity. Until they repent of grave sin and are reconciled with God and the church, they are excluded from sharing in the Eucharist, which is an essential element of full ecclesial communion. One must also take account of the great number of people baptized as Catholics who rarely participate in the celebration of the Eucharist, and of the many others who have simply abandoned the practice of their faith. Furthermore, there are many indications that the "union of minds and hearts" among Catholics today is hardly such as to justify a claim that the Catholic Church offers to other churches or to the world a model of perfect communion. With good reason, then, in the same sentence in which the bishops at the council professed their faith that unity is a gift which the Catholic Church can never lose, they also expressed their hope that this unity would continue to increase (UR 4); indeed, it is far from perfect today.

In our chapter on the holiness of the church we have already quoted several texts from the documents of Vatican II which acknowledge the fact that during its earthly pilgrimage the church "is marked with a genuine though imperfect holiness" (LG 48). The council's recognition of the fact that the church itself is in need of purification (LG 8), and of continual reform (UR 6), is a consequence of its identification of the church with the people of God. This excludes any real separation between a "holy church" and a "sinful people." If the church really is the people of God, then since this people is both holy and sinful, the church itself must be both holy and sinful. In Chapter 4 we have explained in what sense this is true, and why our experience of the church's sinfulness does not diminish our faith in her indefectible holiness.

The council has described the catholicity of the church as the gift by which she "strives energetically and constantly to unite all of humanity under Christ as its one head in the unity of the Spirit" (cf. LG 13). In this description we can see at least two reasons why the church must be recognized as being imperfectly catholic. First, because the perfection of its catholicity will depend on *how* "energetically and constantly" it strives to unite all humanity under Christ. In other words, the church's catholicity is in proportion to the zeal with which it pursues its missionary task. It would be a very lenient judge who would be able to give the church an "A" for missionary effort in every period of its history. But it must also be judged on achievement, if catholicity has to mean actual, and not merely potential, universality. In this respect, one need think only of the vast continent of Asia where Christians are still a tiny minority, to arrive at a rather sober judgment. Furthermore, one would have to reckon with the extent to which the spread of the gospel has been hampered not only by external factors, but also by mistakes made by the church and her own missionaries, as, for instance, in the failure, for so long, to recognize the need of a genuine inculturation of Christianity among non-European peoples.

A major obstacle to the spread of Christianity in the non-Christian world is the scandal of the divisions that separate the Christian churches from one another and prevent them from preaching the gospel with one voice. The Decree on Ecumenism points out how this prevents the church from fully realizing its catholicity.

> Nevertheless, the divisions among Christians prevent the Church from effecting the fullness of catholicity proper to her in those of her sons who, though joined to her by baptism, are yet separated from full communion with her. Furthermore, the Church herself finds it more difficult to express in actual life her full catholicity in all its aspects. (UR 4).

Properties of the Pilgrim People of God

We can sum up what we have been saying about the properties of the church as "indefectibly given" but "imperfectly realized" by observing that they are properties of the pilgrim people of God. On the one hand, it is because the church is truly God's own people, the people to whom the Father has said a definitive "yes" through the resurrection of his Son Jesus, that the church has an absolute assurance of entering into God's ultimate kingdom with all the gifts that he has given her. Christ has won a definitive, "eschatological" victory over all the forces of evil, and he shares the fruits of his victory with his bride. She can never be snatched away from him, nor can any of the gifts he has won for her be taken from her.

On the other hand, as a people on pilgrimage to its final home, the church has to struggle against the forces of evil from without and against her own weakness from within. The time of earthly pilgrimage is a time when the ultimate victory has been won by Christ and is guaranteed to the church, but when there is no assurance of victory in every skirmish that must still take place along the way. The gifts that Christ has bestowed on his church cannot be lost, but they can be obscured, diminished, imperfectly realized. There is need of constant effort to maintain them, foster them, renew them.

Hence, each of the church's properties is a gift definitively given, but also a task to be achieved. Because the church is indefectibly one, it must work to overcome divisions and to achieve full communion. Because the church is indefectibly holy, it can never give up the struggle against its own sinfulness, or give up the practice of penance and purification. Because the church is indefectibly catholic, it must strive to become present in every place where the gospel is still unknown. Because the church is indefectibly apostolic, it has to examine itself constantly to see whether it is being wholly faithful to the message and the mission it has inherited from the apostles.

It follows that during its earthly pilgrimage, each of the church's properties is both an object for our faith and a test of our faith. While we believe that the church is one, we see how divided it is, and how slow is the progress being made toward reunion. While we believe the church is holy, we experience the sinfulness of God's people in ourselves and in what the sins of others cause us to suffer within the church. While we believe the church is catholic, statistics tell us that Christians are a diminishing minority of the world's people today and will be for the foreseeable future. While we believe the church is apostolic, we cannot help remarking on the contrast between the church today and the church that the New Testament describes for us.

How then can we reconcile the church of our profession of faith and the church of our experience? Surely not by imagining that there are two churches: one the ideal church of the creed, the other the real church of everyday life. Nor can we settle for the idea that it is only when the church has arrived at the ultimate kingdom of God that it will really be one, holy, catholic and apostolic. True enough, it is only then that it will have any of these qualities in their absolute perfection, But to deny them to the church during its earthly pilgrimage would mean that the church would be free to give up the effort here and now to be more one, more holy, more catholic, more apostolic.

What we say about the church in the creed is indeed an expression of Christian hope, grounded in the promises of the Lord, that the church will enter the kingdom as the one, holy, universal people of God. But what we say is also a profession of faith about the church as it is now, during its pilgrimage on earth. And, finally, it is a call to action, to take our part in the unceasing task laid upon the church, to strive to be ever more fully the one, holy, catholic and apostolic church we believe her already to be.

Notes

1. For further information about this council and the sources of its creed, see Chapter 10.

2. The reason why this creed is called "Nicene" is explained in Chapter 10.

3. Cf. G. Thils, *Les notes d l'Eglise dans l'apologétique catholique depuis la réforme,* Gembloux, 1937.

4. The Latin creed says: "Credo *in* unum Deum . . . et *in* unum Dominum Icsum Christum . . . et *in* Spiritum sanctum" but not *in* Ecclesiam: "Et unam sanctam catholicam et apostolicam Ecclesiam."

5. Cf. St Thomas Aquinas, *Summa Theologiae* IIa IIae, q.1, a.9, ad 5; q.2, a.2.

6. Hippolytus, *The Apostolic Tradition*, 21; tr. Gregory Dix, London, 1937, p. 37. See also J.N.D. Kelly, *Early Christian Creeds*,[3] New York, 1972, p. 91 and 114.

7. What wc know as the "Apostles' Creed" is the more developed form of the early baptismal creed of the church of Rome. The popular attribution of this creed to the twelve apostles is without historical foundation.

8. *Early Christian Creeds*, p. 159–160.

9. *Adversus haereses* III, 24, 1; PG 7, 966; Harvey II, 131.

10. AS III/1, 170. Our reference here is to the report (*relatio*) given to the bishops at the council by the theological commission responsible for the text. These reports, which are all published in the *Acta Synodalia*, provide valuable help for interpreting the conciliar documents.

11. *Enarr. in Ps.* 138, 2; CCL 40, 1991.

12. *De oratione dominica* 23, PL 4, 553.

13. Mansi 51, 751–763.

14. AAS 35 (1943) 199.

15. AAS 35 (1943) 202; D-S 3802.

16. AAS 42 (1950) 571.

17. AS III/1, 176.

18. AS III/1, 180.

19. AAS 20 (1928) 15.

20. AS I/4, 15.

21. Thus: Card. Liénart, AS I/4, 126–7; Bishop De Smedt, AS I/4 142–4; Card. Bea, AS I/4, 228.

22. AS II/1, 219–220.

23. AS III/1, 177.

24. G. Philips, *L'Eglise et Son Mystère au IIe Concile du Vatican,* vol. I, p. 119; C. Butler, *The Theology of Vatican II,* London, 1967, p. 61; Y. Congar, "Le développement de l'évaluation ecclésiologique des Eglises non catholiques," *Rev. Droit can.* 25 (1975) 215–16; J. Feiner, in *Commentary on the Documents of Vatican II,* Herder, Vol. II, p. 69; A. Grillmeier, in *Commentary on the Documents of Vatican II,* vol. I, p. 150; E. Fischer, *Kirche und Kirchen nach dem Vatikanum II,* München, 1967, pp. 79–80; H. Fries, "Church and Churches" in *Problems and Perspectives in Fundamental Theology,* ed. R. Latourelle and G. O'Collins, New York/Ramsey, 1982, p. 317; A. Dulles, "The Church, the Churches and the Catholic Church," *Theol. Stud.* 33 (1972) 211; A. De Halleux, "Les principes catholiques de l'oecuménisme," *Rev. Th. Louv.* 16 (1985) 320–322.

25. G. Dejaifve, "La Magna Charta de Vatican II: La Constitution *'Lumen gentium,'* " *NRT* 87 (1965) 8; J. Willebrands, "The Ecumenical Movement, Its Problems and Driving Force," *One in Christ* 11 (1975) 218.

26. AAS 56 (1964) 1012–13.

27. AS III/1, 176.

28. Thus, G. Baum interprets *subsistit in* to mean that the church of Christ is "realized and embodied in the Catholic Church;" it is the "realization of the Church of Christ on earth," in "The Ecclesial Reality of the Other Churches," *Concilium* 4/1 (1965) 38.

29. See, in this sense, F. Ricken, "Ecclesia . . . universale salutis sacramentum," *Scholastik* 40 (1965) 373.

30. The standard German translations are: "ist verwirklicht in" or "hat ihre konkrete Existenzform in." See the critique of these translations by W. Dietzfelbinger in "Die Grenzen der Kirche nach der dogmatischen Konstitution 'De Ecclesia,' " *Kerygma und Dogma* 11 (1965) 169, and by E. Fischer in *Kirche und Kirchen nach dem Vatikanum II*, p. 78.

31. A particularly authoritative rejection of such an interpretation is given by J. Willebrands in "The Ecumenical Movement," *One in Christ* 11 (1975) 219. Others who reject it are A. Dulles, "The Church, the Churches and the Catholic Church," *TS* 33 (1972) 211; M.J. LeGuillou, "Church," *Sacr. Mundi* I, 324; P.W. Scheele, "Das Kirchensein der Getrennten," *Catholica* 22 (1968) 30.

32. Leonardo Boff, *Church, Charism and Power*, New York, Crossroad, 1985.

33. AAS 71 (1985) 758–59, my translation. The official Italian text reads as follows: "Il Concilio aveva invece scelto la parola 'subsistit' proprio per chiarire che esiste una sola 'sussistenza' della vera Chiesa, mentre fuori della sua compagine visibile esistono solo 'elementa Ecclesiae' che—essendo elementi della stessa Chiesa—tendono e conducono verso la Chiesa cattolica (*LG* 8). Il Decreto sull'ecumenismo esprime la stessa dottrina (*UR* 3–4), la quale fu di nuovo precisato nella Dichiarazione *Mysterium Ecclesiae*, n. 1 (*AAS* LXV, 1973, pp. 396 398)."

34. AS III/1, 204.

35. AS III/7, 36.

36. See UR 14–18, and the *Relatio* which replies to an objection to such use of the term "churches." The objection was: "There is only one Church, namely the Catholic Church, and non-catholic communities cannot be called Churches in the proper sense." The response was: "The two-fold expression 'Churches and ecclesial communities' has been approved by the Council, and is used in a completely legitimate way. There is indeed only one universal Church, but there are many local and particular churches. It is the custom in Catholic tradition to call the separated eastern communities Churches—local or particular ones to be sure—and in the proper sense of the term. It is not the business of the council to investigate and decide which of the other communities ought to be called Churches in the theological sense" (AS III/7, 35, my translation).

37. It is highly significant that in UR 22 the council did not use the term "Churches and ecclesial communities," but only "ecclesial communities," as the subject of the sentence in which it denied the presence of the "genuine and total reality of the Eucharistic mystery" by reason of the "lack of the sacrament of orders." That such was the mind of the theological commission in making this distinction is also indicated in its *relatio* (AS III/2, 335), where it recognized the propriety of speaking of the Orthodox and Old Catholic "Churches," precisely because they had preserved valid orders and the full reality of the Eucharist.

38. AS III/2, 335.

39. Chicago, Loyola Univ. Press, 1972.

40. *Communio*, tr. Wicks, p. 16.

41. See E. Lanne, "Eglises-soeurs. Implications ecclésiologiques du *Tomos Agapis*," *Istina* 20 (1975) 47–74.

42. AS III/2, 335.

43. AAS 62 (1970) 753: "There will be no seeking to lessen the legitimate prestige and the worthy patrimony of piety and usage proper to the Anglican Church when the Roman Catholic Church—this humble 'Servant of the Servants of God'—is able to embrace her ever beloved Sister in the one authentic communion of the family of Christ: a communion of origin and of faith, a communion of priesthood and of rule, a communion of the Saints in the freedom and love of the Spirit of Jesus."

44. AS III/2, 335.

45. *Summa* III, q.64, a.2, ad 3; *IV Sent.* d.17, q.3, a.1, sol.5.

46. This expression is used in the following key statements of Vatican II regarding the episcopal office: "Hence, one is constituted a member of the episcopal body by virtue of sacramental consecration and by hierarchical communion with the head and members of the body" (LG 22). "Episcopal consecration, together with the office of sanctifying, also confers the offices of teaching and of governing. These, however, of their very nature, can be exercised only in hierarchical communion with the head and members of the college" (LG 21). For a full discussion of the concept, one might consult G. Ghirlanda, *Communio hierarchica*, Roma, Pont. Univ. Gregoriana, 1980.

47. See above, pp. 51–52.

48. OE 26–29.

49. Louis Bouyer, *L'Eglise de Dieu, Corps du Christ et Temple de L'Esprit*, Paris, Cerf, 1970, p. 629.

50. Paul VI, Letter *Anno ineunte*, AAS 59 (1967) 852–854.

51. Yves Congar, *Diversités et Communion*, Paris, Cerf, 1982, pp. 109 and 132f.

52. AAS 65 (1973) 398.

53. AS I/4, 15.

54. The Latin text has "indefectibiliter sancta creditur." The Abbott edition translates: "in a way which can never fail"; Flannery has "unfailingly."

55. *Summa* III, q.64, a.2, ad 3.

56. *Summa* IIa IIae, q.1, a.9, ad 3.

57. See the propositions of John Hus, condemned by the Council of Constance, and by Pope Martin V in 1418: D-S 1201, 1205, 1206.

58. See the theses of Paschase Quesnel that were condemned by Pope Clement XI in 1713: D-S 2472–2478.

59. *Retractationum Liber Secundus* 18, PL 32, 637f.

60. D-S 229, 1537, 1573.

61. *Letter to the Smyrnaeans* 8,2; ed. K. Lake, *The Apostolic Fathers*, Cambridge, 1965, vol. I, pp. 260–261.

62. For this opinion I am following the recent study of A. de Halleux, "L'Eglise catholique dans la lettre ignacienne aux Smyrniotes," *ETL* 58 (1982) 5–24.

63. *The Martyrdom of Polycarp*, Salutation, ed. Lake, *The Apostolic Fathers*, vol. 2, pp. 312–313.

64. 8,1; Lake, pp. 322–323.

65. 19,2; Lake, pp. 338–339.

66. " 'Catholic' and 'Apostolic' in the Early Centuries," *One in Christ* 6 (1970) 277.

67. *Martyrdom of Polycarp* 16,2; Lake, pp. 334–335.

68. " 'Catholic' and 'Apostolic'," p. 278.

69. Catechesis 18, 23; PG 33, 1044; tr. L.P. McCauley and A.A. Stephenson, *The Works of St. Cyril of Jerusalem*, Washington, 1970, vol. 2, p. 132.

70. J. Jeremias, *Jesus' Promise to the Nations*, Naperville, 1958.

71. "Unity of the faith and theological pluralism," *Tablet* 227 (1973) 647.

72. See the following articles in *Theological Investigations:*

"Anonymous Christians," vol. 6, pp. 390–398; "Anonymous Christians and the Missionary Task of the Church," 12, pp. 161–178; "Observations on the Problem of the 'Anonymous Christian'," 14, pp. 280–294; "Anonymous and Explicit Faith," 16, pp. 52–59.

73. "The One Christ and the Universality of Salvation," *Th. Inv.* 16, pp. 199–224.

74. Philip J. Hefner, *The Church*, in *Christian Dogmatics*, ed. Carl E. Braaten and Robert W. Jenson, Philadelphia, Fortress, vol. 2, p. 198.

75. *Ibid.* In support of this statement, Hefner quotes one of the leading systematic Lutheran theologians of the seventeenth century, Johann Gerhard, who, in his work *Confessio Catholica*, declared: "We do not affirm that there are two churches, the one true and internal, and the other nominal and external; but we say that the Church is one and the same, viz., the entire assembly of the called considered in a twofold manner, namely, from within and from without. . . . In the former manner and respect we grant that even hypocrites and those who are not saints belong to the Church; but in the latter manner and respect we contend that only true believers and saints belong to it." The Eng. tr. of this text is taken from H. Schmid, *The Doctrinal Theology of the Evangelical Lutheran Church*, tr. C.A. Hay and H.E. Jacobs, Minneapolis, Augsburg, 1961, p. 592.

76. A.D. Sertillanges, *L'Eglise*, Paris, 1917, vol. 2, p. 130, distinguished between the visible church and the church that he described as "the universal society of souls united to God through Christ under the influence of grace." The latter church would obviously be invisible. In a similar vein, see P. Lippert, *Die Kirche Christi*[3], Freiburg, Herder, 1956, pp. 258–273, and O. Karrer, *Religions of Mankind*, tr. E.I. Watkin, London, 1936, pp. 250–278.

77. For Bellarmine's distinction between "soul" and "body" of the church, see his *De Controversiis Liber III*, *De Ecclesia Militante*, cap. 2, ed. J. Giuliano, Naples, 1857, vol. 2, p. 75. On his recognition that one could be saved by being of the church "by desire," see *De Ecclesia Militante*, cap 3, ed. Giuliano, p. 76.

78. See, for instance, the explanation of this distinction given by A. Castelein: "We have to grasp the distinction between the soul of the Church, which consists in the invisible society of all the souls that are actually in the state of grace and have a right to salvation, and the body of the Church, which consists in the visible society of

Christians under the authority of the Pope," in his work: *La rigorisme, le nombre des élus, et la doctrine du salut*, Brussels, 1898, p. 212. For E.I. Watkin the "soul of the Church" is "the invisible Church-body of all souls who share in the supernatural life," *"The Church as the Mystical Body of Christ"* in *God and the Supernatural*, London, 1920, p. 178. P. Lippert identifies the "soul of the church" with "all those who are called and really are children of God" in *Die Kirche Christi*[3], p. 262.

79. This is a prominent feature of the ecclesiology of Charles Journet. See his *L'Eglise du Verbe Incarné*, vol. II, Paris, 1951, pp. 604–705.

80. Emile Mersch, *The Theology of the Mystical Body*, tr. C. Vollert, St. Louis, Herder, 1951, pp. 479–480.

81. It should be noted that Mersch's final redaction of this part of his book was lost; the editors used a prior redaction dating from about the year 1935.

82. See above, pp. 15ff.

83. See above, pp. 24f.

84. Cyprian, *De Ecclesiae Catholicae Unitate*, nn. 6 and 14; ed. M. Bévenot, Oxford, 1971, p. 66, 79. Augustine, *Ep.* 141,5, PL 33, 579; *Ep.* 185, 42, PL 33, 811; *Ep.* 185,50, PL 33, 815.

85. Cyprian, *Ep.* 70, Ed. Bévenot, p. 258–262; Augustine, *De Baptismo contra Donatistas* III, 15; PL 43, 144.

86. *Ep.* 43,1; PL 33, 160.

87. *De Fide, ad Petrum*, 38, 79; PL 65, 704.

88. D-S 802.

89. D-S 870, 875.

90. D-S 1351.

91. D-S 2429. See also D-S 2305, 2308, 2311.

92. *De Controversiis Liber III, De Ecclesia Militante*, cap. 3, ed. Giuliano, vol. 2, p. 76.

93. *Summa* III, q.69, a.4, ad 2.

94. *De Fide theologica*, Disp. XII, 4, 22, ed. Vives, vol. 12, p. 359.

95. AAS 35 (1943) 242–43; D-S 3821.

96. Letter *Suprema haec sacra* of Aug. 8, 1949, published with English translation three years later in *Amer. Eccl. Rev.* 127 (1952) 308–315; cf. D-S 3866–3873.

97. AAS 35 (1943) 213.

98. For a positive answer to this question, see K. Rahner, "Church, Churches and Religions," *Th. Inv.* 10, 30–49, and "On the Importance of the Non-Christian Religions for Salvation," *Th. Inv.* 18, 288–295.

99. Official Latin text in AAS 63 (1971) 401–441. I am using the English version as given in Joseph Gremillion, *The Gospel of Peace and Justice, Catholic Social Teaching Since Pope John*, Maryknoll, 1976, pp. 485–512.

100. N. 48, Gremillion, pp. 509–510.

101. N. 6, p. 488.

102. English version in Gremillion, pp. 513–529. The paragraph numbers are those given by Gremillion.

103. Philip Land, SJ, *An Overview;* Pedro Arrupe, SJ, *Witnessing to Justice;* Juan Alfaro, SJ, *Theology of Justice in the World;* Mary Linscott, SND, *Education and Justice;* Barbara Ward, *A New Creation?—Environmental Issues;* all published in Vatican City, 1972.

104. N. 2, Gremillion, p. 514.

105. N.5, p. 514.

106. N.6, p. 514.

107. N.6, p. 514. For a discussion of the interpretations that have been given of this text since the synod, see Charles M. Murphy, "Action for Justice as Constitutive of the Preaching of the Gospel. What Did the 1971 Synod Mean?" TS 44 (1983) 298–311.

108. The theologian principally responsible for the drafting of this part of the text, Juan Alfaro, SJ, explored the relationship between salvation and liberation more fully in the final chapter of his work *Christian Hope and the Liberation of Man*, Rome and Sydney, 1978 (English translation of the original Spanish, published in 1972), and in the brochure mentioned in note 103.

109. N. 34, p. 520.

110. Nn. 35–36, p. 521.

111. The English version distributed by the Vatican Press Office is given by Gremillion, pp. 593–598. I am using the version by Austin Flannery, OP, published in *Doctrine and Life* 25 (1975) 53–58. An account of the preparation and approval of this text is given by G. Caprile in *Il Sinodo dei Vescovi, Terza Assemblea Generale*, Roma, 1975, pp. 727–734; 751–52, 760–61.

112. Flannery, p. 56; Gremillion, p. 597.

113. Flannery, p. 57; Gremillion, p. 597.

114. N. 6, Gremillion, p. 514.

115. Latin text in AAS 68 (1976) 5–76. I am using the English version released by the Vatican, as published in booklet form by the Catholic Truth Society, London, 1976.

116. N. 38, p. 47.

117. N. 9, p. 15.

118. N. 27, p. 38.

119. N. 29–31, pp. 40–42.

120. N. 35, p. 45.

121. N. 38, p. 48.

122. N. 38, p. 47.

123. I am using the English version as published in *The Tablet*, 14 December 1985, pp. 1324–1329.

124. II, D, 3; *Tablet* p. 1328.

125. II, D, 6–7; *Tablet* p. 1329.

126. Text in *Origins* 14 (1984–85) 193–204.

127. Text in *Origins* 15 (1985–86) 713–728.

128. N. 63, p. 722.

129. N. 64, p. 722.

130. N. 80, p. 725.

131. N. 96, p. 726.

132. N. 99, p. 727.

133. *Catechesis* 18, PG 33, 1043–1050; D-S 41.

134. *Ancoratus*, c. 119, PG 43, 232; D-S 42.

135. In the salutation of this letter, Ignatius greets the church of the Trallians "in apostolic fashion": *The Apostolic Fathers*, ed. K. Lake, vol. I, p. 212–213.

136. *The Martyrdom of St. Polycarp*, n. 16: *The Apostolic Fathers*, ed. K. Lake, vol. II, p. 334–335.

137. Eusebius, *Historia Ecclesiastica*, IV, 23, PG 20, 388.

138. *The Apostolic Fathers*, ed. K. Lake, vol. I, pp. 78–81, 82–85.

139. *Adversus haereses* III, 3, 1; PG 7, 848. Eng. tr. in *The Ante-Nicene Fathers*, vol. I, p. 415.

140. *Adversus haereses* III, 3, 3; PG 7, 851; *Ante-Nicene Fathers* I, 416.

141. *Adversus haereses* III, 4, 1; PG 7, 855; *A-N F.* I, 416.

142. *De praescriptione haereticorum* 20, PL 2, 32; *A-N F.* III, 252.

143. *De Praescr. haer.* 21, PL 2, 33; *A-N F.* III, 252.

144. *De Praescr. haer.* 32, PL 2, 45; *A-N F.* III, 258.

145. Edited, with an English translation, by Gregory Dix, London, SPCK, 1937; and with a French translation, by Bernard Botte, *Sources Chrétiennes* 11 bis, Paris, Cerf, 2nd ed., 1968.

146. Dix, pp. xliii–xliv.

147. Dix, pp. 2–6.

148. Dix, pp. xxxix–xl.

149. *The Apostolic Tradition* IV,2; Dix, p. 6.

150. Hans Küng gives a negative answer to this question in his book *Infallible? An Inquiry*, tr. E. Quinn, Garden City, 1971, p. 82.

151. LG 20. The Decree *Christus Dominus* says: "The apostolic office of bishops was instituted by Christ the Lord" (CD 20).

152. Raymond Brown offers a critique of "blueprint ecclesiology" in his book *Biblical Reflections on Crises Facing the Church*, New York, 1975, pp. 52–55.

153. See my book *Magisterium. Teaching Authority in the Catholic Church*, New York/Dublin, 1983, pp. 4–6.

154. Compiled and edited by J.F. Puglisi and S.J. Voicu, Rome, 1984. An annual supplement is published in the *Bulletin* of the Centro pro Unione.

155. *Growth in Agreement. Reports and Agreed Statements of Ecumenical Conversations at World Level*, edited by Harding Meyer and Lukas Vischer (Ecumenical Documents II), New York/Ramsey and Geneva, 1984; hereafter GiA.

156. This *Study Document* was published in *One in Christ* 6 (1970) 452–483. The same issue of *One in Christ* also contains the papers which were presented to the Commission in the course of its work by eight of its members.

157. *One in Christ* 6 (1970) 453.

158. *Ibid.*, pp. 460–461.

159. GiA, p. 14–34.

160. Nos. 73–74, GiA, pp. 23–24.

161. GiA, pp. 168–189.

162. No. 57, GiA, pp. 181–182.

163. GiA, pp. 248–275.

164. "Malta Report", no. 57, GiA, p. 181.

165. Nos. 59–61, GiA, pp. 266–267.

166. GiA, pp. 340–366.

167. No. 84, GiA, pp. 357–358.

168. GiA, pp. 433–463.

169. Nos. 94–101, GiA, pp. 457–458.

170. Nos. 103–107, GiA, pp. 459–460.

171. *Faith and Order Paper no. 111*, published by WCC, Geneva, 1982. It is also in GiA, pp. 466–503.

172. WCC ed. p. ix, GiA, p. 468.

173. *Ibid.*

174. WCC ed., p. 28; GiA, pp. 490–491.

175. WCC ed., p. 28, GiA, p. 502.

176. GiA, pp. 131–151.

177. Nos. 31–34; GiA, pp. 148–149.

178. Nos. 85–87, GiA, p. 358.

179. Nos. 63–66, GiA, p. 268.

180. Nos. 42–43, GiA, pp. 262–263.

181. The latter of these has been published by the Secretariat for Promoting Christian Unity in its *Information Service* No. 59 (1985, III–IV), pp. 44–72. The text of the Report is followed by "Excursus on the Practice of Ordination in the Early Church" by Hervé Legrand, OP (72–73) and by "Observations on 'Facing Unity,' " by Jared Wicks, SJ (74–78).

182. WCC ed., p. 29–30; GiA, pp. 491–492.

183. WCC ed., p. 32; GiA, pp. 494–495.

184. SPCU *Information Service*, No. 59 (1985, III–IV) 44–72.

185. No. 118, p. 63.

186. "The Ministry in the Church," Nos. 75–78, GiA, pp. 271–272; cf. Vatican II, UR 22c.

187. "The Ministry in the Church," No. 82, GiA, p. 273.

188. *Ibid.*, Nos. 20, 23, 17; GiA, pp. 254, 255, 253.

189. *Ibid.*, No. 45, GiA, p. 263.

190. *Ibid.*, No. 43, GiA p. 263.

191. *Ibid.*, No. 80, GiA, p. 273.

192. SPCU *Information Service*, n. 59 (1985) 60.

193. Constitution "Dei Filius," chap. 4, D-S 3016.

194. *Ibid.*, chap. 3, D-S 3011.

195. *Ancoratus*, PG 43, 232; D-S 42.

196. For this historical account I have followed J.N.D. Kelly's work: *Early Christian Creeds*, 3rd. ed., London, 1972, pp. 332–357.

Index of Names

Alfaro, Juan, 232nn.103, 108
Athenagoras, Patriarch, 63
Augustine, St., 9f., 17, 79f.,
  111f., 113, 114, 120, 231n84

Baum, Gregory, 226n28
Bellarmine, St. Robert, 106,
  116, 230n77
Bévenot, Maurice, 231nn.84,
  85
Boff, Leonardo, 29, 227n32
Boniface VIII, Pope, 115, 117
Botte, B., 234n145
Bouyer, L., 63, 229n49
Brown, Raymond, 234n152
Butler, C., 226n24

Callistus, Pope, 173
Caprile, G., 232n111
Castelein, A., 230n78
Chrysostom, St. John, 114
Clement I, Pope, 168f., 182
Clement XI, Pope, 229n58
Clements, Teresa, D.M.J., 1
Congar, Yves, 63, 226n24,
  229n51

Cushing, Richard Cardinal,
  117f.
Cyprian, St., 12, 111f., 120,
  231n84f.
Cyril of Jerusalem, St., 86,
  152, 229n69

Dejaifve, G., 226n25
Dietzfelbinger, W., 227n30
Dionysius of Corinth, 168
Dix, Gregory, 173f., 176f.,
  225n6, 234n145
Donatists, 79
Dulles, Avery, 226n24, 227n31

Epiphanius, St., 152, 213
Eusebius of Caesarea, 233n137

Feeney, Leonard, 117f.
Feiner, J., 226n24
Fischer, E., 226n24, 227n30
Flannery, A., 232n111
Fries, H., 226n24
Fulgentius of Ruspe, St., 114f.,
  120

236

Gerhard, J., 230n75
Ghirlanda, G., 228n46
Gregorian University, 1
Gremillion, J., 232n99
Grillmeier, A., 226n24

Halleux, A. de, 226n24,
 229n62
Hefner, P.J., 230n74f.
Hertling, L., 46, 48
Hippolytus, St., 7, 173ff.,
 225n6
Hus, John, 229n57

Ignatius of Antioch, 85, 152,
 233n135
Irenaeus, St., 7, 170f., 181f.

Jeremias, J., 90, 229n70
John XXIII, Pope, 23
Journet, C., 231n79

Karrer, O., 230n76
Kelly, J.N.D., 7, 85, 225n6,
 235n196
Küng, H., 234n150

Lake, K., 229nn.61, 63ff.
Land, P., 139, 232n103
Lanne, E., 228n41
Latourelle, R., 226n24
Legrand, H., 235n181
Le Guillou, M.J., 227n31
Leo XIII, Pope, 53
Linscott, Mary, 232n103
Lippert, P., 230nn.76, 231,
 78
Luther, Martin, 105

Martin V., Pope, 229n57
McCauley, L.P., 229n69
Mersch, F., 107f., 231n80f.
Meyer, H., 189, 234n155
Murphy, C., 232n107

O'Collins, G., 1, 226n24
O'Donnell, Christopher, 1
Ottaviani, A., 23

Paul VI, Pope, 25, 29, 52, 63,
 137ff., 142ff., 229n50
Philips, G., 226n24
Pius XI, Pope, 23
Pius XII, Pope, 16, 23, 107f.,
 117f., 126
Polycarp, St., 85, 152,
 229nn.63, 67
Pontian, Pope, 173
Puglisi, J.F., 234n154

Quesnel, Paschase, 229n58

Rahner, Karl, 104, 106, 232n
 98
Ricken, F., 226n29

Scheele, P.W., 227n31
Schmid, H., 230n75
Sertillanges, A.D., 230n76
Stephenson, A., 229n69
Suarez, F., 116f.

Tertullian, 171f., 181f.
Thils, G., 225n3
Thomas Aquinas, St., 56, 70,
 76f., 116, 225n5
Tromp, S., 23

Vischer, Lukas, 189, 234n
    155
Voicu, S.J., 234n154

Ward, Barbara, 232n103
Wicks, Jared, 46, 228n40,
    235n181
Willebrands, J., Cardinal,
    226n25, 227n31

Index of Topics

Anglicans, 27f., 53, 99, 186f.
Anonymous Christians, 104, 106, 229n72
Apostles, 153–164
Augsburg Confession, 202f., 207

Baptism, 14, 61, 64, 98f., 100
Baptists, 198f., 202
Blessed Virgin Mary, 80
Buddhism, 101, 130

Centro pro Unione, 188
Charism, 18, 36
Charismatic renewal, 94
Code of Canon Law, 212
Commission on Justice and Peace, 137ff.
Communion, 38ff., 55ff.; full, 61f., 64, 221f.; hierarchical, 59; imperfect, 64f., 221; juridical, 57, 58f., 60, 98f.; spiritual, 104f., 110; theological, 56f., 59f., 98ff.

Congregation for the Doctrine of the Faith (Holy Office), 29ff., 64f., 117f., 148f.
Congregationalists, 199
Councils, ecumenical: Nicea, 212f.; Constantinople I, 3, 7, 152, 212ff.; Chalcedon, 213f.; Constance, 229n57; Lateran IV, 115; Florence, 115, 117, 119f.; Vatican I, 15, 211; Vatican II, *passim*
Creeds: baptismal, 6f., 152, 213, 218f.; "Apostles'," 7, 152, 213, 225n7; Nicene, 3, 5, 213; of the Council of Constantinople, 3, 5, 212f.

Dialogues: Anglican-Lutheran, 191; Lutheran-Catholic, 191f., 192f., 201ff., 207ff.; Methodist-Catholic, 193, 200; Reformed-Catholic, 193f.; Reformed-Baptist, 198f.
Diocese, 49f.
Dogma, 211–214

Eastern Catholic Churches, 50,
    59
Eastern separated Churches,
    50ff., 59ff., 95
Ecclesial communities, 53ff.,
    60ff., 63ff.
Epiclesis, 177, 180
Eucharist, 14, 61, 62, 98, 127f.,
    132, 221
Eucharistic ecclesiology, 32
Evangelization, 131, 141–146,
    148

Faith and Order Commission,
    189, 195ff., 204ff., 207

Gnostics, 7, 170

Heretics, 111f., 119
Hinduism, 101, 130
Holy Spirit, 12, 14, 17ff., 21,
    27, 58, 70, 74ff., 78f., 92,
    104, 112, 124ff., 194f., 212f.,
    218ff.

Inculturation, 93, 96, 222
Infallibility, 18
International Theological
    Commission, 96
Invisible church, 105f.
Islam, 129

Jansenists, 116f.
Jesuits, 116
Jewish people, 82, 88ff., 101f.,
    113ff., 117, 119ff., 129

Kingdom of God, 11f., 79f.,
    89, 93, 103, 135, 137, 149,
    223f.

Liberation, 140–146, 148f.
Lima Report, 195ff., 204ff.,
    207
Lutherans, 105, 201f., 207ff.
Lutheran World Federation,
    191

Magisterium, 1
Membership by desire (in voto),
    100, 116ff.
Methodists, 200, 202
Moslems, 101, 113, 115
Mystery of faith, 6ff., 8, 66
Mystical Body, 13ff., 23f.,
    107f., 117, 217f.

No salvation outside the
    church, 110–121
Non-Christians, 100ff., 113ff.,
    128; non-Christian religions,
    129ff.
Notes of church, 4

Old Catholics, 53, 186
Orthodox, 3, 98, 99, 186f.

Pagans, 114f., 119ff.
Parish, 49
Particular churches, 50ff., 59,
    62, 94
Pelagians, 114
People of God, 100, 216f.
Petrine ministry, 52, 98
Pilgrim church, 66, 79ff., 216,
    220f., 223f.
Pluralism, 95f.
Priesthood of faithful, 126ff.

Reformed, 198f., 202

Sacrament (church as), 8ff., 70, 109ff., 122ff.
Schismatics, 111f., 119f.
Secretariat for Promoting Christian Unity, 191, 193
Sinful church, 79ff., 222
Sister churches, 52

Soul of church, 106f.
Synod of bishops: of 1971, 138ff.; of 1974, 141ff.; of 1985, 146ff.

Trinity, 11, 19

Women in ministry, 165f.
World Council of Churches, 187, 189